THE GENOCIDAL MIND

*SELECTED PAPERS FROM THE 32ND
ANNUAL SCHOLARS' CONFERENCE ON THE
HOLOCAUST AND THE CHURCHES*

*Kean University
Union, New Jersey
March 2–5, 2002*

Edited by

Dennis B. Klein
Richard Libowitz
Marcia Sachs Littell
Sharon Steeley

OTHER PARAGON HOUSE BOOKS ON
GENOCIDE AND THE HOLOCAUST

Against All Hope: Resistance in the Nazi Concentration Camps, 1938-1945
    Hermann Langbein

Courage to Remember: Interviews on the Holocaust
    Kinue Tokudome, Foreword by Richard L. Rubenstein

Different Voices: Women and the Holocaust
    Carol Rittner and John K. Roth, eds.

Ethics After the Holocaust: Perspectives, Critiques, and Responses
    John K. Roth, ed.

Genocide in Rwanda: Complicity of the Churches?
    Carol Rittner, John K. Roth and Wendy Whitworth, eds.

Holocaust: Religious and Philosophical Implications
    John K. Roth and Michael Berenbaum, eds.

Righteous Gentiles of the Holocaust
    David P. Gushee

Narrow Escapes: A Boy's Holocaust Memories and their Legacy
    Samuel Oliner

Job: The Story of a Holocaust Survivor
    Joseph Freeman

The Road to Hell: Recollections of the Nazi Death March
    Joseph Freeman

Will Genocide Ever End?
    Carol Rittner, John K. Roth and James M. Smith, eds.

THE GENOCIDAL MIND

First Edition 2005

Published in the United States by
Paragon House
2285 University Avenue West
St. Paul, MN 55114

Copyright © 2005
by The Annual Scholar's Conference on the Holocaust and the Churches

The Annual Scholars' Conference on the Holocaust and the Churches was founded in 1970 by Franklin H. Littell and Hubert G. Locke as an interfaith, interdisciplinary, and international organization. Throughout the decades, the Conference has been devoted to remembering, learning, and teaching the lessons of the Holocaust in tandem with educators clergy and community leaders examining the issues raised by the "Final Solution." Website: http://www.sju.edu/events/scholars_conference/

All rights reserved. No part of this book may be reproduced, stored in a retrieval system, or transmitted in any form or by any means, electronic, mechanical or otherwise, without the prior written consent of the publishers, unless by a reviewer who wishes to quote brief passages.

Library of Congress Cataloging-in-Publication Data

Scholar's Conference on the Holocaust and the Churches (32nd : 2002 : Kean University, Union, N.J.)
  The genocidal mind: selected papers from the 32nd annual scholars' conference on the Holocaust and the churches / edited by Dennis B. Klein ... [et al.].-- 1st ed.
    p. cm.
  Papers pesented at conference held at Kean Univ., Union, N.J. March 2-5, 2002.
  Includes bibliographical references.
  ISBN 1-55778-853-7 (pbk. : alk. paper) 1. Holocaust, Jewish (1939-1945)--Moral and ethical aspects--Congresses. 2. Holocaust, Jewish (1939-1945)--Psychological aspects--Congresses. 3. Genocide--Moral and ethical aspects--Congresses. 4. Genocide--Psychological aspects--Congresses. 5. Genocide--Social aspects--Congresses. 6. National socialism and religion--Congresses. I. Klein, Dennis B. II. Title.

D804.3.S35 2002
940.53'18'019--dc22
                                   2005001554

Manufactured in the United States of America
10 9 8 7 6 5 4 3 2 1

The paper used in this publication meets the minimum requirements of American National Standard for Information Sciences—Permanence of Paper for Printed Library Materials, ANSIZ39.48-1984.

For current information about all releases from Paragon House,
visit the web site at http://www.paragonhouse.com

This volume was made possible by a grant from

THE SHARON GUTMAN—CHARLES LIGHTNER
PUBLICATION FUND

with the cooperation of

THE PHILADELPHIA CENTER ON THE HOLOCAUST, GENOCIDE
AND HUMAN RIGHTS

In Memory of

Judith Doneson

1946–2002

We miss you, dear friend.

Contents

xiii   Introduction

GENOCIDE AND OUR TIMES

1   **CHAPTER 1**
Mass Murder and the Holocaust in the Twentieth Century
Steven T. Katz

39   **CHAPTER 2**
The Genocidal Mind:
In Search of a Definition
Paul Vincent

61   **CHAPTER 3**
Early Warning: Perverting the Lessons of the Holocaust—The Protocols of the World Conference Against Racism
Shimon Samuels

69   **CHAPTER 4**
Canada Attempts to Curb Hate Mail:
The Lessons of the Zündel Case
Frederick M. Schweitzer

81   **CHAPTER 5**
The Nazification of the German Legal System: Some Lessons for Modern Constitutionalism
Alan S. Rosenbaum

105   **CHAPTER 6**
The Complicity of Modern Philosophy in the Extermination of the Jews
David Patterson

125 **CHAPTER 7**
Adorno and Lifton: Subjectivity and the Psychology of Genocide
Gary A. Mullen

GENOCIDE AND RELIGION

139 **CHAPTER 8**
Elite Catholic Isolationism in the United States: Impediment or Failure in the Fight Against Nazi Genocide?
Patrick J. Hayes

157 **CHAPTER 9**
Christian Hope as a Factor in How Protestants Followed Hitler
Drew A. Parsons

175 **CHAPTER 10**
Jewish-Christian Dialogue in Light of Dietrich Bonhoeffer's Understanding of Jews and Judaism
Renate Wind

185 **CHAPTER 11**
Resisting or Defending the Faith? Clerical Responses to the National Socialist State
Kevin Spicer

GENOCIDE AND CULTURE

199 **CHAPTER 12**
Re-Reading Bernhard Schlink's *The Reader* as a Mirror of Germany's Holocaust Memory
Karin Doerr

225 **CHAPTER 13**
Literary Representations of the 1915 Genocide of Armenians: An Important Topical Genre Continuing in the New Millennium
Rubina Peroomian

245 **CHAPTER 14**
Testimony from the Ashes: Final Words from
Auschwitz-Birkenau Sonderkommado
Susan L. Pentlin

263 **CHAPTER 15**
Imre Kormos: Unknown Hero of the Hungarian Jewish
Rescue and Resistance
George S. Pick

277 **CHAPTER 16**
The German Resistance to Hitler and he Jews: The
Case of Carl Goerdeler
Peter Hoffmann

Reflections

293 **CHAPTER 17**
Lessons of the Holocaust: The Early Warning System
Franklin H. Littell

301 **CHAPTER 18**
Reflections on the Consideration of the Holocaust in
American Life
Michael Berenbaum

321 **Contributors**

Introduction

In Nazi Germany and in Stalinist Russia, wrote critic George Steiner, "the cry of the murdered sounded in earshot of the universities; the sadism went on a street away from the theaters and museums." These words suggest something intimate and quite unexpected about the relationship, if not complicity, between literate civilization and mass murder. The Nazi era set the tone: The Final Solution's top leaders—Goebbels, Hess, Speer and Himmler—were university trained. So too were the SD leaders who commanded *Einsatzgruppen* squads and the medical establishment that supported the Nazi quest for "racial purity."

Other modern regimes exhibited a similar paradox: Newspapermen, missionaries, and educators were committed to plundering and destroying indigenous peoples in North America; the Young Turks trained its technocrats and professional bureaucracy against Armenians; highly educated leaders of the Khmer Rouge orchestrated a systematic assault against the Cambodian middle classes; the U.S. political and educated elite advocated or participated in turn-of-the-century forced sterilization of the poor and maladjusted; high culture was implicated in genocide in Bangladesh, Nigeria, Rwanda and Paraguay.

The Shoah was not the first act of genocide in the 20th century, nor did it prove to be the last. In a post 9/11 age, in which the uncertainties and fear of terrorism have transcended oceans and continents, the need to understand the human propensity for violence and mass destruction continues to grow. Education's modern legacy is deeply ambiguous. Answers vaporize in response to Steiner's disquieting question, "How to explain those who sing Schubert in the evening and torture in the morning?" Whatever the answers, however, they do not include the possibility of certain moral defect in the trained and cultivated mind. Heartening stories are legion about rescuers and resisters who transcended an era's constituent ideologies and mass movements to honor the preciousness of sovereign human life.

The organizers of the 32nd Annual Scholars' Conference on the Holocaust and the Churches planned the 2002 meetings with a specific theme, "The Genocidal Mind," as its central focus. With more than thirty years of conferences and many hundreds of papers "in the bank," we have learned a great deal about what happened before, during and after the Holocaust, both in Europe and abroad. The stories of the victims have been retold; the actions of perpetrators, bystanders and rescuers have been probed. Many facts pertaining to the "how" of the Shoah have also been uncovered, analyzed and presented. Novelists, poets, playwrights, film makers, painters, sculptors, composers, and dancers have used their artistic abilities to tell facets of the story and, like philosophers and theologians, wrestle with the most difficult of the Shoah's questions: Why? The contents of this volume represent a selected set of papers presented at Kean University in March 2002, dealing with the "hows, whats and whys" of the Shoah and other acts of genocide.

These investigations begin with Steven Katz discussing mass murder and the Holocaust in the 20th century. Paul Vincent offers a search for definitions of the genocidal mind. Shimon Samuels then confirms the continuing strength of anti-Semitism in his report on the World Conference against Racism and Frederick Schweitzer reviews one particular case, that of Ernst Zundel. Turning to specific aspects of the genocidal process, Alan Rosenbaum discusses the Nazification of the German legal system, David Patterson looks at the complicity of modern philosophy in the Shoah and Gary Mullen analyzes the psychology of genocide as viewed by Theodore Adorno and Robert J. Lifton.

Four independent yet interweaving studies explore aspects of the Church struggle. Patrick Hayes examines "Elite Catholic Isolationism" in the United States during the period of the Third Reich, while Drew Parsons discusses "Christian hope" as a factor in support of Hitler by German Protestants. Renate Wind reviews Dietrich Bonhoeffer's understanding of Jews and Judaism, a study which offers sharp contrasts to Kevin Spicer's report on clerical responses to the National Socialist state.

Literary responses to genocide compose the next section of the text. Karen Doerr reviews Berhard Schlick's novel *The Reader* as a mirror of Germany's Holocaust memory; Rubina Peroomian looks at literary representations of the Armenian Genocide of 1915, and Susan Pentlin discusses the literary legacies of several Auschwitz-Birkenau Sonderkommandos.

George Pick and Peter Hoffmann offer studies of rescuers; Pick reports on Imre Kormos, a nearly unknown hero of Hungarian Jewish rescue and resistance, while Hoffmann's discussion of resistance in Germany focuses upon Carl Goerdeler.

In the final section, Conference co-founder Franklin Littell reports on the "Early Warning System" against genocide, which he has developed over decades of research and reflection, and Michael Berenbaum discusses the consideration of the Holocaust in American life.

No conference (or book, for that matter) can be produced without the help of a great many people. The number of women and men who contributed to the success of the 32nd Annual Scholars' Conference was so great that, in noting the efforts of specific individuals, we run the risk of inadvertently omitting others, equally deserving of recognition. With that caveat in mind, sincere appreciation for the work of Ronald Applbaum (then Kean University President), Conference Chair Jeffrey Glanz, Program co-Chairmen Dennis Klein and Bernard Weinstein, Associate Dean George Sisko, Conference Coordinator Melissa Bahleda and Sister Rose Thering. Sharon Heesh served again as typesetter for this volume; best wishes to her, upon her relocation across the country. We are grateful to Molly Voorheis, Stockton College graduate student who helped with the editing. Sharon Steeley, Associate Executive Director of the Annual Scholars' Conference and co-editor of this volume, whose dedication made it all happen. Kathleen Curran of Stockton College whose diplomacy and hard work are consistent and brought us through the Conference.

No Conference can take place without financial support. Bob Warren, of the Warren Family Foundation not only gave his intellectual commitment but also his financial support. Felix Zandman has supported our work these many years beginning with the First Conference. Sharon Gutman and Charles Lightner are true partners in the work. Their encouragement sustains us intellectually as well as financially.

Finally, thanks to all of the participants in the 32nd Annual Scholars' Conference, presenters, listeners, professional staff and volunteers. Without you, there is no Conference; with you, we continue to go from strength to strength.

The Editors

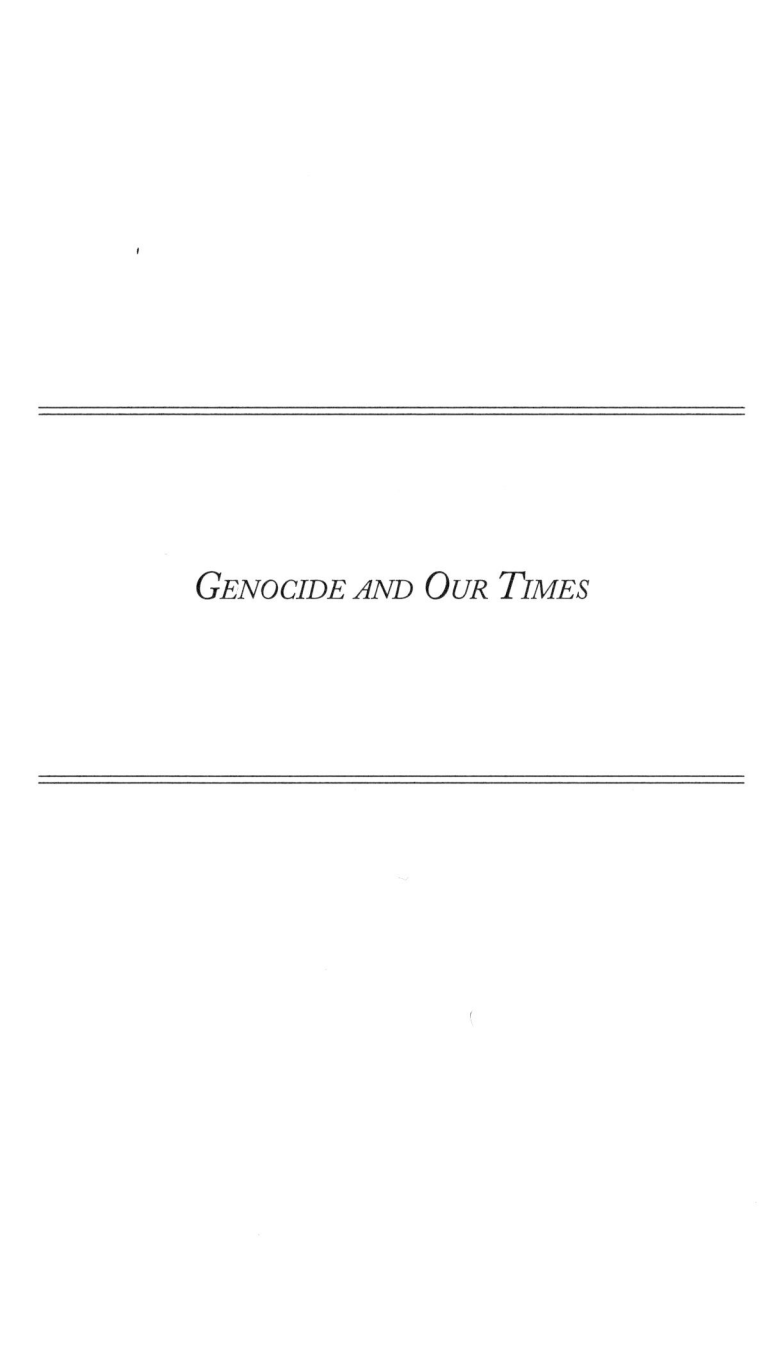

Genocide and Our Times

CHAPTER 1

Mass Murder and the Holocaust in the Twentieth Century

Steven T. Katz

I

Introduction

To begin I need to make three preliminary remarks.[1]

1. I do not want to spend the brief time I have today arguing over the definition of "genocide," though this is not an irrelevant matter. Instead I will suggest that for the purposes of this talk I will grant any of the normally accepted definitions of the term, in particular the most important and widely used, that of the *United Nations Treaty on Genocide,* and then add that if one works with this definition one needs to say that the Holocaust is this plus X. That is, the definition of the *Holocaust* needs to be, in some fundamental way, different from that of genocide. Why this is so I hope will become clear as I proceed.

2. When making historical comparisons of the kind I will make I am not making *moral* comparisons. To say X suffered a greater numerical loss than Y is not to say that what happened to X is more immoral than what happened to Y, or even that X suffered more than Y. Numerical findings are not simply translatable into moral conclusions. Nor again, in defending the uniqueness of the Holocaust, am I simultaneously endorsing the injudicious claim that the Holocaust is *more evil* than alternative occurrences of extensive and systematic

persecution, organized violence, mass death. The character of the uniqueness that I am prepared to champion is not tied to a scale or hierarchy of evil (of event X being more or less malevolent than another event Y, or previous events E1 to En).

3. When I talk of comparisons and of uniqueness, I am referring strictly to what I call phenomenological characteristics, especially the property of intentionality and the issue of mediation. What I mean by both will, I think, become clear as I begin to decipher the cases chosen for analysis.

Given the need at this learned gathering for substantive discussion of historical and ideological particulars I will limit my comments, as requested by the Conference organizers, to major events in the twentieth century vis à vis comparisons to the Holocaust. In particular, I will address only seven major cases, given the limits of time. However, the primary methodological claim I want to advance relative to what I call "mediation" can be applied to all the major cases usually considered in the discussion of modern (and I would add pre-modern) mass-murder and "genocide."

The seven cases I will comment on are:

1. Native Americans in the United States
2. South American Indians in their generality
3. Stalin's persecution:
   (3a) as manifest if the phenomenon of the Gulag as a whole
   (3b) of the Kulaks
   (3c) of the deported nationalities
   (3d) and the Ukrainian famine
4. The Armenian Tragedy during World War I

II

I will begin my detailed discussion with the case of the Native Americans of the United States because though part of the greatest tragedy in history—the decline of the Native Peoples of the New World—it is the least relevant. But why it is not relevant is relevant to our overall understanding of the issue of comparative study.

In considering the situation of the Native Americans in America in the twentieth century, I need to begin with the Dawes Severalty Act of 1887. This Act and the amendments thereto—the main federal initiative on the Indian front between 1880 and 1928 (the year of the publication of the Meriam Report) intended, on the one hand, to force Indian cultural assimilation through a strategy of individual land allotments, and on the other, to open tribal, now primarily reservation, lands to non-Indian settlement. Its key provisions aimed to undermine the collective identity of the Indian and the ideology of tribal collectivism by extinguishing tribal title to common lands substituting in its place individual land titles in severalty. According to the provisions of the allotment each Indian family resident on the reservation to be dismembered was to receive one hundred and sixty acres of land. Individuals over eighteen were to receive eighty acres and individuals below the age of eighteen, forty acres. In an amendment passed by Congress in 1891, the size of these allotments was cut in half. Between 1887 and 1921, 118,660 individual allotments were made involving the disposition of 17,585,00 acres and additional preparations were made for the allotting of a total of 73,000,000 acres to 300,000 Indians in place. At the same time, between 1887 and 1900 28,500,000 acres of Indian land were ceded to the government and between 1900 and 1910 another 18,000,000 acres were ceded. Altogether, between 1887 and the 1930s, when the Dawes program was finally rejected, Indian land holdings declined from 139 million to 48 million acres. One, therefore, does not err in judging the Dawes Act a collective atrocity perpetrated against the Indian—though Dawes and other "friends" of the Indian genuinely intended it to benefit them by decisively resolving their problematic, deeply tragic, circumstance once and for all through their transformation into responsible individual farmers who might reasonably come to belong to the American mainstream.

At the same time, however odious one judges the Dawes Act, no one familiar with its logic could legitimately decipher its instigation, the very mixed motives of those who supported it, or its consequences in terms of genocide. The citizenship provisions of the Dawes Act—in 1890 members of the so-called Five Civilized Tribes became eligible for citizenship, in a first step towards the universal inclusion of the Indian in the American polity. In 1901 all Native Americans in the Indian territories became citizens—the education of Native American children supported by the Federal government, the existence and expansion of Indian courts and police agencies, the extension of agricultural education for Indians, the more than 118,000 allotments totaling nearly 18 million acres, with plans for the allotment of an additional 73 million acres—in the event the Federal government actually allotted over 40 million acres by 1934—and even the creation of new reservations in response to particular crises, e.g., that of the Papago that was resolved by President Wilson's executive orders of January 1, 1916 and February 1, 1917 establishing a territory of 3,700,000 acres for them, all support this contra-genocidal argument. So, too, do the millions of acres of land on the over on hundred reservations. And so also do the fiscal reparations, though inequitable, that were built into even the most one-sided and iniquitously administered land cessions after 1880. By 1926 the Federal government was spending $48.5 million from all sources on Indian programs. For example, already by the 1890's the federal government was maintaining more than twenty off reservation schools and nearly two hundred on reservation schools, and supplying in excess of two million dollars per annum—a sum that would grow to just under five million dollars by 1920—for Indian education on and off the reservations. This, of course, is not to recommend these schools, or the behavior and attitudes of those who oversaw them; for whatever their geographical setting, they suffered from a multitude of irreducible problems, not least their *a priori* antagonism towards native culture. But, for all their manifest flaws, their continual existence over decades, as the continued existence and growth of the indigenous community they served, contradicts any assertion of a national annihilatory design. Rather, what now transpired, what now became the blueprint for national action was a dramatic broadening of the older program of ethnocidal assimilation, pursued in inseparable conjunction with the Severalty Act. The 1895 Federal Commission survey of Indian lands, the 1896 Act of Congress creating the Indian citizenship roll, the Curtis Act of June 28, 1898, and the Burke Act of May 8, 1906, were all part of this overall national effort aimed at the quick and final abolition of corporate Indian identity and the simultaneous metamorphosis of the Indian into an "American."

In 1924 all Indians resident in the United States were made citizens (many had already been made citizens prior to this date) for a variety of reasons. In the late 1920's the federal authorities also backed away from the unrealized goal of full assimilation in response to the valid criticisms of this ambition- including a long list of documented economic crimes—made by the so-called Meriam Report that was published in 1928 under the official title of *The Problems of Indian Administration*. Above all else, this report provided conclusive evidence that the contemporary condition of the Native American community nearly a half century after the Dawes Act was abominable: Indians had twice the national infant mortality rate, seven times the national death rate from tuberculosis, and suffered disproportionately from mass unemployment, economic exploitation, illiteracy, drunkenness and disease. Yet even under these prevailing conditions their population was growing. Given this horrific, if paradoxical, set of circumstances, a change in national policy was urgently required.

Accordingly, in place of the discredited ideology of acculturation through farming allotment—the Dawes approach—the Federal government, at the urging of the Meriam Report, substituted the policy of continued Indian severalty under various forms of governmental guardianship. In so doing it once again unintentionally created opportunities for land and mineral exploitation, and failed altogether to consider future Indian population growth. Moreover, the fledgling program also had the objectionable effect of placing unwarranted limitations on Indian civil and legal rights as citizens. However, these undesirable iatrogenic consequences not withstanding, the immediate ambition of the federal authorities, was laudable, i.e., ameliorative, and the energizing inspiration behind the changes that took place was, for the most part, paternalistic and protective. State governmental behavior, bowing to local constituencies, was more intractable and continued to be more discriminatory than federal actions, but even on this level no state or local government in the twentieth century, and certainly no state since the late 1920s, has actively pursued a policy whose consequences were demographically devastating. Even if one is highly critical of the 1950s efforts under Eisenhower at termination—including the legal settlement of Indian tribal land claims, and the transfer of civil and criminal jurisdiction over Indian reservations to the state governments-as well as of the overall assimilationist ideology that inspired it, there is no comparability in any significant sense between this integrationist approach to the "Indianfrage" and the realities of the *Endlösung*. And the same judgment can be confidently made regarding federal and state actions in the 1960s, 70s, 80s and 90s. However problematic the movement toward self-determination and economic development on the reservations in the last twenty-five years, has been there is nothing remotely connected to it that is relevant to a consideration o0f the issue of comparative mass murder. Moreover, the past four decades have witnessed an unprecedented national concern for the nation's poor and racially disadvantaged including America's Indian population, at the same time that we have witnessed the recovery of tribal lands through legal challenges and court settlements. We are here worlds away from Auschwitz and Treblinka. Most simply put, this is demonstrated by the relevant demographic statistics. Indian population in the United States reached its nadir in the 1870s and 1880s at around 250,000-300,000; in the twentieth century it grew to over two million.

But beyond the numbers, what is particularly consequential in the comparative analysis of the destruction of the Native American and the Holocaust is the disparate morphologies that define each case. When taken as *gestalts*, as prescriptive and empirical wholes, these two substantive instances of despoliation, subjugation and mass death are disjunctive, in terms of their elemental structural form. In the conquest and settlement of America, where the lust for wealth and possession of the land was the dominant motive, and the "problem," the "crime" of the Indian was literally being in the way, the operative norm that governed the emerging continental reality involved a series of *mediated* historical and normative circumstances. These included: dispossession and financial corruption accompanied by insufficient, yet real, exchanges of goods and financial annuities in return for land taken; the assignment by the conquerors of millions of acres of land, however poor and arid, to native reservations on which Indian life was allowed to continue; unending, continual, however culturally chauvinistic, efforts at missionizing; the creation of medical services and hospitals, however understaffed or poorly maintained; the establishment and maintenance of, however mismanaged and impoverished, Indian schools and colleges; the encouragement, however misguided, of Indian agriculture; and a whole host of plans, usually misconceived, to domesticate, miscegenate, amalgamate, acculturate, civilize and assimilate the Indian. And most significant: the great majority of deaths (death on a scale unparalleled in human history) occurred as the undesired consequence of disease. In contrast, the Holocaust is defined by the absence of mediating programmatic and ideological phenomena. Thus, Jewish reservations—called by their traditional name, ghettos—in however small a space, were ultimately unacceptable, even though at the very high rate that Jews were dying in the ghettos created by the Third Reich, the entire Jewish people would have been extinguished in twenty-five and a half years. There were no governmental annuities, however meager and miserly, for land and property taken, instead there were absolutely unlimited financial and human expropriations—in the end including gold teeth and women's hair. There was no religious mission, however patronizing, indeed even Jewish converts to Christianity had to die. There were no state supported or endorsed schools or colleges, however limited, however bare, for Jewish children; and no programs, however misconceived, to make Jews over into productive citizen farmers. There were no efforts to domesticate, miscegenate, amalgamate, acculturate, civilize, and assimilate the Jews. Indeed all of these transformational and survivalist strategies were criminal actions, and involved "degenerate" values, according to the principles that reigned supreme in the Nazi racial state. In place of inclusionary tactics the Third Reich purposely created *Einsatzgruppen* and death camps that unfailingly served the iron law that all Jews must be murdered.

III

Throughout Central and South America, through calculated acts of dispossession, Indian territories have been pulled into the growing national and international capitalist economy, with its increasing concern with exports and its foreign hegemony. At the same time, as an intended consequence of the ruling economic dialectic, the native community was remade into an exploitable, mass, proletariat,—capitalist expansion required and requires workers not corpses—and in this way complemented its already existing roles as these roles had been created through debt peonage, and other forms of labor exploitation on the haciendas and in agriculture. In and through this previously non-existent class identity the Indians were integrated into the burgeoning capitalist order, if at its absolute bottom. In their reconstituted socioeconomic guise, their near absolute dependency assured by their lack of material possessions, the labor of the Indian could be functionally adapted, however brutally, to contemporary productive requirements. In effect, as peons in the rural environment and as an expanded underclass in the cities the indigenous peoples were reconquered by the expansive, unprecedented, material and political realities that came to dominate Central and South American life in the nineteenth and twentieth centuries.

And why does this matter to us? Because this entire structural transformation of Central and South American social and economic life, necessarily including the mutated role of the Indian within this refashioned context, is altogether at variance with what happened to the Jew during the Third Reich. Hitler's grand objective was to totally disgorge—finally through an enacted program of physical genocide—the Jew from the national and international socio-economic order, even from occupying the very lowest rung of that order. In contrast, economic, political, demographic, religious and moral considerations all conspired together in Latin America to create a non-genocidal policy of *ethnocidal socio-cultural re-absorption* whereby the indigene would continue to exist, if on inequitable terms dictated by the ruling non-Indian community. There were local variations, modal alterations, on this common theme as it was empirically incarnated, but the ruling imperative, the socio-political aspiration, throughout the region—for all the pervasive, civilizational violence that continually threatened and coerced the indigene—was ethnocidal re-absorption of the indigenous population not its extermination. In consequence, myriad forms of conscious and unconscious social, cultural, religious, demographic, political and commercial mediation have been fashioned so as to allow, to encourage, if not without great pain and enormous dislocation, the integration and acculturation of the massive indigenous population that, even after 1880, remained the human (biological) cornerstone of Latin society.

Miscegenation and ethnocide, the two key issues here, have succeeded in facilitating, however imperfectly, the integration of most Indians into the composite fabric of Latin life as a whole. (I note explicitly that the logic, the phenomenological form, of both miscegenation and ethnocide assume the common, shared, humanity of the Indian.) Alternatively, Nazism stringently rejected just such workable, functional, forms of mediation in respect of the Jew. The uncompromising metaphysics of Nazi racial theory denied, *a priori*, any and all modes of Jewish ethnocide, absolutely opposed sexual relations between Aryans and Jews, and ruled out every form of Jewish ethnic, religious, cultural and economic transmutation and re-absorption. The *only* "solution to the Jewish Problem" that Nazism was willing to countenance, given the racial metaphysical nature of this "problem" as Nazism defined it, was extermination.

Given the historic and economic contexts that created modern Latin America that were mediated by a variety of material and ideological factors, and the present racial ethnic composition of the population it does not make sense to speak of physical genocide relative to the Indian population. Indeed the relevant contemporary demographic statistics that relate to the Native American segment of Central and South America are unexpected, even remarkable, in light of the widely held, though highly erroneous, view that the aboriginal inhabitants of Central and South America were the victims of a premeditated program of extermination. The relevant statistics on the current number of persons of Indian descent in this geographical region, excluding Brazil and Mexico, are as follows:

Guyana	35,000 to 45,000
Paraguay	50,000 to 100,000
Colombia	3 million (of whom the majority live assimilated lives)
Ecuador	4.5 million
Peru	8.5 million (1983 figure)
Panama	80,000 to 140,000
Bolivia	4 to 5 million
Costa Rica	20,000
Guatemala	up to 5 1/2 million (the official government estimate of 2.7-3 million is too low)
Nicaragua	178,000 to 200,000
Argentina	1 million
Belize	15,000
Honduras	500,000
El Salvador	500,000 to 960,000
Venezuela	150,000 (Almost certainly an underestimate given the many Indians who have "passed" into the more general national community.)
French Guyana	4,500
Chile	2.5 to 3.1 million (this includes 1.5 to 2.5 million persons who have "passed" into the larger social order. Indigene, who retain more traditional markers of ethnic identity, number about 600,000 to 700,000)
Surinam	8,000

Approximate Total: 30,540,500 to 32,742,500

This total of the present indigene population outside of Brazil—Brazil's Indian peoples numbers between three and eleven million today—and excluding the Native American inhabitants of Mexico who were estimated at six, 411,972 in 1990, and today are in excess of eight million, is approximately thirty million. With the Indian populations of Brazil and Mexico included the current total indigenous population of Central and South America comes to well over forty million persons—and possibly more than forty-five million persons—drawn from hundreds of ethnic groups. And this tally of thirty million does not fully count those individuals of full Indian descent who have passed completely into the general population as *mestizos* (or something else) and who are now identified under different census (and social) rubrics. Moreover, this aggregate is, in fact, larger than the total number of Indians projected to have populated this geographical expanse (south of Mexico) before the arrival of the European on most respected estimates of what the pre-Columbian Native American population was. Indeed my minimal total of 30.5 million approximates almost exactly the much discussed 1992 regional demographic estimate of 47,114,000 by William M. Denevan, that includes 17,174,000 for Mexico. Despite the myriad, profoundly indecent, forms of exploitation, despoliation, expropriation, proselytization, forced deculturation, slavery, debt peonage, rape, miscegenation, and murder that the native peoples of Latin America have been subjected to, they have still, as a biological entity, been allowed to avoid extinction.

Focusing our attention more narrowly, it is to be noted that a study published by the Minority Rights Group (of London) in 1987 put the total number of South America's indigene at 18,492,000, and gave the following figures for that segment of the aboriginal population of the region that still resides in the continent's rainforests.

Country	*Rainforest*
Venezuela	100,000
Colombia	100,000
Ecuador	65,000

Peru	100,000
Bolivia	150,000
Argentina	100,000
Paraguay	50,000
Brazil	100,000
Guyana	45,000
Surinam	8,000
Fr. Guiana	4,500
Total	822,500

It is these special communities that are the most threatened by an ever-encroaching, often rapidly invading, non-Indian civilization and populace. Representing between two and three percent of the total Native American inhabitants of Latin America it is these relatively small collectivities, rather than the Indian peoples as such, that are authentically at risk of complete eradication. No one can be optimistic about their long-term future or about their fate, either individual or collective. The unceasing forces of modernization and the uncompromising aggressiveness of the world capitalist economic order do not provide grounds for reasoned hope that these last remnants of aboriginal civilization will be able to preserve themselves in meaningful ways. Reservations and other forms of political and socio-economic compromise are, even with the sincerest goodwill, at best, temporary buffers between the majority civilization and these groups.

But, at the same time, the historical experience of the native peoples over five hundred years, and the dialectic of domination and inclusion that has defined the development of Central and South America for the past half millennia, lead one to conjecture that the eventual eradication of the rainforest peoples and their cultures will come about through old-new forms of religious conversion, social reconstruction, linguistic adaptation, economic negotiation, cultural amalgamation and marginal political integration rather than as a consequence of campaigns of physical annihilation. This has been the unwavering, unstoppable, pattern since Columbus' heirs arrived to conquer and control Latin America and there is no good reason to think that it will be substantially otherwise in the future. The character of human nature and the force of economic and political imperatives promise to conspire together to make the future, at least in this regard, like the past. This is certainly not a "consummation devoutly to be wished," but it is an end consistent with the compulsions of western civilization as this civilization has taken shape in its characteristic, sometimes paradoxical, New World incarnation(s).

To sum up, Indians since contact have been continually forced to relinquish their tribal lands, to abandon their cultural and religions traditions, to become Christian, to sell their individual property, to enserf themselves, to be slaves, to prostitute their women, to mortgage their labor, to contract the labor of their children, if not to sell them, and after all of this, to become acculturated peasants poorly integrated into the emerging, modernizing, capitalist matrix in a functional way. To comprehend the history of the New World since the arrival of Columbus is to confront this horrendous pattern of domination and exploitation. Yet, for all the constant, incarnate evil, these humanly distorted relationships, meant to enrich the oppressors and to insure an uninterrupted supply of cheap labor for the growing national economy, were, as enacted, the antithesis of a program of extermination. And this because empires depend on dominated masses who can be controlled and taxed, missionaries desire proselytes, hacienda owners require farm laborers, rubber barons must have rainforest tappers, ranchers are in need of cowboys, and capitalists cannot do without workers. All of these roles and occupations can only be filled by the living. Accordingly, to attempt to deconstruct the lived reality of the native peoples in the republican era by analogy with the largely unmediated relationship that existed at, say, Buna, or even less appropriately, with the uncompromising, wholly unmediated, circumstances that existed at Treblinka or Sobibor, is not to understand it at all. Plainly put, the synergistic consequences of colonization and (imperfect) proletarian-ization, along with the integrally related phenomena of conversion, migration, urbanization and *mestizage*, are not the equivalent of an unceasing, unrestrained program of total annihilation.

While advancing this carefully arrived at conclusion I do not want to be misunderstood. The more than five centuries-long mistreatment of the South American Indian by "white" society is one of the great collective crimes in human history—perhaps even its very greatest—but nothing is gained by misdescribing it, especially through the use of erroneous analogies, and nothing is lost by respecting its particularity. We owe it not least to the native peoples whose tragedy we here reflect on to comprehend their concrete situation as it is and as it has been. Their determinate tragedy should not, and must not, be treated as just another indistinct instance of man's inhumanity to man, as another ill-defined case in which the actual details and structural configuration do not matter. Instead, any truthful decipherment of the dark experience of the native American peoples, as well as any sound comparative judgment about the plight of the Indian relative to the fate of Jews during the *Shoah*, must rest on the recognition of fundamental systemic contrasts, irreducible structural disjunctions, and radically alternative ideological foundations rather than on overly neat, finally superficial, commensurabilities. To insist on this is not to lose sight of the nightmarish quality of native history since the arrival of Columbus and his heirs; nor, more narrowly, of the complicated, often ghastly, experience since circa 1800. But it is to treat these empirical events in Latin America as real spatio-temporal happenings rather than as instances of some archetypal, a-temporal pattern of good and evil. Indeed, only such a historically informed and deliberately nuanced approach—that is respectful of difference(s)—can allow the exceptional tale of Iberoamerica its own incommensurability. And hence allow it to validate its own experiential and ethical claims to our attention and our concern.

IV

As to the Stalinist repression and the Gulag, let the following suffice by way of an introduction to its dissimilarity with Auschwitz. The Gulag has roots in two familiar sociological categories—penal detention and slavery. Penal institutions, including the use of special incarceration centers for political "dissidents," are an all too common, easily comprehended, historical phenomenon that require no extended analysis here. The structural relationship between Stalin's Gulag and the normative modalities of slavery is more complex. Yet for all its complexity, at the most basic level, both the Gulag and slavery are defined by their ruthless exploitation of unfree human labor. The Gulag, like slavery, is grounded in and maintained by specific economic and social needs that are believed to be best met, even in only specific loci, by unfree labor.

Stalin held that the forced acceleration of industrialization had to be "aided" by reducing a significant percentage of Russia's population into, effectively, "slaves," if by another name. They would provide the crucial cheap labor for a variety of projects, ranging from the mining of raw materials to the building of transportation networks that were seen to be essential to the larger national goal of socialist modernization. Representing, at its peak, on some accounts, more than one-sixteenth of the adult male population, this "enslaved" group comprised the largest single industrial working class in Russia.

This captive class could be set tasks that: (a) were necessary to the economy as a whole, yet which were situated in geographical locations where labor on the free market would have been very costly to procure; and (b) which could be accomplished by the calculated substitution of a large work force in place of expensive technology and machinery that could only be procured through foreign currency that the Soviet Union did not have.

Hitler, or more precisely Himmler and Speer, would also create, during the war, a slave empire comprised of captured prisoners of war, conquered Slavic peoples, citizens of occupied countries in Western Europe—and Jews. However, Jewish slave labor was utilized differently than any other (even in German camps or in the Gulag). The overriding German intent with regard to the Jewish workers was not, à la the Gulag, to foster economic efficiency or substantive production gains. Instead, it sought to establish a disutilitarian equation, consistent with the racial imperatives of Nazism, that balanced labor utilization with guarantees that Jewish workers were to be worked to death in a very specific, highly rigid period of time.

Stalin's system, in significant contrast—theoretically at least, and more often than not in practice—was predicated on a fixed period of forced labor. The dominant, unwavering concern of the regime was the unobstructed realization of the labor quotas. Thus, for example, workers were fed in relationship to their productivity, i.e., good workers were fed more so that they would remain productive. If inmates could survive under the prevailing execrable conditions—well and good—but their individual fate was not primary, aside from the bearing this had on productivity. Human beings were invariably reduced in this strange ecology to "things," but as "things" they were permitted to endure. Good workers were fed more. In the organization of the Gulag, there was certainly much malice, a great deal of sadism, and a good deal of murder. Brutality was normal, and the norm was brutal. What was absent, however, was a national policy of mass murder. Gulag workers did not, of necessity, generate ontic or normative outrage at their *being*, and therefore they did not have to die.

Despite the high death toll in the Gulag—with the partial and still disjunctive exception of that exceptional year 1938—the vast majority of those who died were not murdered. They died as a direct result of the unyielding and immoral system; but the system did not wish, did not intend, their death, it did not require their annihilation. Indeed, many would eventually be reprieved. Recently revealed official sources indicate that between 1941 and 1944, no fewer than 3.4 million prisoners (out of 4.85 million) were freed from Gulag detention. In March 1953, following Stalin's death, Beria pardoned 1,181,264 (out of 2,526,402) inmates.

The operative ideological superstructure of Stalinism did not define the death of inmates of the Gulag as a desired goal, as a dogmatic ambition. Their death lacked all ritual density—it had no cathartic, liberating or transformative power; it was, indeed, meaningless. Thus, between 1934 and 1947, the average mortality rate in the Gulag was 70 to 1,000 per annum. This statistic indicates, in Robert Conquest's balanced summary of the Gulag phenomenon as a whole, that:

Previous years (pre-1938) had seen, on occasion, massive casualties. But these had been due to inefficiencies in supply, attempts to carry out assignments in impossible conditions, and in fact—if in exaggerated form—the normal incompetence and brutality of Soviet life. When the difficulties could be overcome, conditions, as we have seen, were tolerable. But above all, prisoners were not subjected to lethal conditions on purpose.[2]

Moreover, the Gulag killed people distributively, i.e., it took its lethal toll on all groups, singling out none for "special treatment." (And I say this with full awareness of the fate of the Kulaks and the deported national minorities, on which more below.)

The Gulag also allowed for compromise. The powerful streak of pitiless realism in Stalin's perception of reality caused him to acknowledge the need to balance prudential economic requirements over or against the primitive desire to "punish" real or imagined enemies. Compared to a total of forty thousand shootings in the Kolyma in 1938, Kolyma's most terrible year, ten thousand Jews a day were gassed in Auschwitz on some days in 1944. Treblinka consumed 870,000 victims in less than a year; the *Einsatzgruppen* and police units efficiently murdered about 1.5 to 2 million Jews.

In addition, the mediations that existed in the Gulag—food parcels from home, family visits, the abundance of sexual relations, the relatively better treatment of women and children, the camp hospitals, the limited sentences, and the release of prisoners, among other things, decisively distinguish it from the Nazi death camps.

V

Now let us consider the crucial matter of the Kulaks. To begin, I would argue that for all the conceptual, mythic, logical, bureaucratic and murderous similarities that exist between Nazism and Stalinism, which are both post-Hegelian historicized forms of manicheanism, the *defining difference* between them must also be recognized. That is to say, Nazism and Stalinism ultimately understand their manichean-Social Darwinian manifestos, their energizing first principles, in radically disparate ways. Given the dialectical material premises of Marxist-Leninism, the imperative is to annihilate an oppressive class regime, the real opponent being an exploitative labor system. The class enemy is an enemy by virtue of the place he occupies in the deformed, extant, socio-economic arrangement. "Our policy is a class policy," Stalin prosaically reminded the Central Committee. "He who thinks that one can conduct in the countryside a policy that will please everybody, the rich as well as the poor, is not a Marxist but an idiot...."[3] Accordingly, the visionary ambition is to alter the reigning immoral organization of society which, in turn, will eliminate the regressive economic superstructure, and transform the offending *status* of one's class enemy. Theoretically at least, such far reaching social renovation dissolves the very notion of class or, put differently, creates a social order with only one class, the proletariat—and hence necessarily eliminates the notion of the class enemy. Such fundamental socio-economic reconstruction might require terror on a grand scale, as evidenced, for example, in the protracted and deadly war against the Kulaks, for the bourgeoisie and their class allies will not give up their privilege easily or willingly, but the intent of such official violence, according to official party doctrine, is not to destroy the Kulak *qua* being, i.e., to physically extirpate all Kulaks, but, rather, to transform the defining power structure that makes the Kulak an antagonist. Ideologically, even for Stalin, socio-economic reconstruction and *re-education* rather than physical extermination is the consummate goal. Bolshevism declares an uncompromising war against the class enemy *qua* class enemy, i.e., against his class status; it does not declare an unlimited, annihilatory war against his person *qua* person. In this Bolshevism articulates a conversionary doctrine and militant zeal somewhat analogous to that previously displayed by the Catholic church in its approach to Jews, or perhaps closer still to that manifest by Islam towards Pagans. Re-educated, the former bourgeoisie can take their rightful place in the "workers paradise," just as a converted Jew can become a fully equal member of Christian society, even a "Prince of the Church," and a pagan convert can become a respected Muslim.

By comparison, Nazism does not oppose an offending socio-cultural *status* but rather, and fundamentally, contraposes itself against an assertedly biological, and irremedial, givenness—Semite vs. Aryan. In this particular racial collision one denies the essential humanity of the other, their status as persons *qua* persons. Unlike the circumstance that governs in class conflict, Aryan-Jewish racial conflict does not allow for the conceptual or juridical separation of person and status. Indeed, this, and precisely this, is the intended sting of racial claims—no alteration in either status (now defined biologically) or person is possible. Hence, while Stalinism will seek "confessions" of wrongdoing, admissions of ideological heresy, and public acknowledgment of "wrecking," as a required, if not always successful, prologomenon to social rehabilitation and readmission to the Party, Nazism will seek no comparable acts from Jews. Jews are what they are—alien, polluting, sub-human—and cannot be another thing. In this basic sense, Nazism locates the fundamentals of the cosmic-historical struggle that it discerns as elemental to cosmic-historical progress at a deeper level than Marxism, i.e., it grounds them in immutable biological rather than mutable economic-cultural determinants. Accordingly, Marxist-Leninism-Stalinism provides programmatic, life-preserving possibilities that are absent in Nazism.

Ideology, then, was central to the self-definition of these two regimes. *Principle* had a decisive influence on what each of these states undertook to do, and, equally important, on what these states did not undertake to do. Once the *principle of race* was accepted as the primary determinant of Nazism's manichean cosmology then a war different *in kind* from that entailed by the Marxist-Leninist *principle of class* was inevitable. That is to say, the primacy of race understood as metaphysics in the syntax of Nazism leads to genocide while the primacy of class understood as metaphysics in the syntax of Marxism-Leninism does not.

The single most important historical case in the Stalinist context over-against which to test these analytical observations on ideology is that provided by the assault on the Kulaks.

Two fundamental facts about this defining event of the Stalinist era need to be highlighted at the outset of our analysis: a) Stalin murdered only a minority of the Kulaks. He could have murdered them all, but he explicitly, consciously, chose not to do so. b) Stalin's primary target in this violent confrontation, for all its deadly severity, was a contingent, "socially alien," identity, that by definition, could be altered. Whatever neurotic fears energized and accompanied this convulsive anti-peasant policy, there should be no doubt that what was elemental in this unstinting war was the Kulaks' self-interested class loyalties that had to be broken down, even if through force, in order for the general good, as defined by socialist theory, to prevail. (Stalin was not alone in holding this severe position. It was *the* view of almost the entire Bolshevik elite, including Trotsky, differences existing only as to how best accomplish this "progressive" policy.)

The need for this mass conversion was the immediate consequence of three related socialist imperatives. First, there was the axiomatic requirement that called for the elimination of all "capitalist" classes which threatened socialist hegemony. Second, only the collectivization of agriculture, following upon the shortages and economic chaos of 1927 and the 1928 confiscations of grains-that Stalin interpreted as pointing the correct way to future policy-appeared to provide a way of ending the severe grain crisis that led to food rationing in the cities in 1928-29. In 1928 grain acquisitions by the government, despite the new use of coercion, fell two percent below the poor level of 1927. This failure was symptomatic of the enduring and recurring structural weakness of Soviet agriculture. And as Stalin came to understand this weakness—i.e., the decline/absence of draft power (horses and oxen and later tractors), the inherent limits of communal land tenure, the inefficiency of subsistence farming, the variety of problems posed by the need for assured acquisition of grain by the state, the existence of faulty pricing mechanisms, the inadequate distribution and marketing networks, and what he took to be the pervasive capitalist greed on the part of the kulaks—he came to believe that only the complete and permanent collectivization of agriculture could remedy this deeply unsatisfactory situation. Third, only the forced collectivization of the Kulaks and other peasants could provide the needed capital, primarily in the form of grain exports that was to be squeezed out of the newly created collective farms in order to pay for the massive, rapid, industrialization of the Soviet Union called for by socialist theory. (This had been the governing ideological understanding of Trotsky and the so-called "left" throughout the 1920's, now it was adopted by Stalin as his own point of departure.)

In addition, ideological compulsions aside, the leadership acted, had need to act, so as to overcome the national economic crisis that now directly involved both the rural and urban sectors. Inflation, which was due in large part to a shortage of grain, dramatically eroded real urban wages between 1928 and 1932 while farm wages declined by nearly half in the same period. Though the Bolshevik leadership had, in large measure, created the present crisis something dramatic still needed to be done to overcome it. (Merely raising grain prices, and continuing with the compromises of the NEP, was considered, in this context, both practically and ideologically unacceptable.)

At the Sixteenth Party Congress held in April, 1929, against the background of another grain crisis, the First Secretary's demand for collectivization, a demand incarnating all of Stalin's profound Bolshevik voluntarism, became Party policy, thereby transforming the situation, as Stalin later said, from "a policy of limiting the exploiting activities of the Kulaks to a policy liquidating the Kulaks as a class."[4] There would now be an end to accommodations and vacillation. Stalin had convinced the Party Congress—and there were considerable segments within the Party that required little convincing—that there was only one reasoned option that it could choose and that there could be no turning back once this course was selected. The uncompromising treatment of the Kulaks, their exemplary victimization, would set the pace for the collectivization of the whole of the peasantry, and it would send the appropriate message to the entire agricultural sector, particularly the middle peasantry: the State would not countenance any deviation from or interference with this grand political objective.

"We must deal the Kulak such a blow," Molotov announced, "that the middle peasant will snap to attention before us."[5] However ill-prepared the country was for the draconian measures that were about to ensue, and it was nearly completely unprepared-as was the state apparatus that was to carry out these extraordinary initiatives-they would come to pass. Between late 1929 and March 1930, a mere five months, the percentage of all peasants-those defined as Kulaks and those not so defined-living on collective farms rose from 4.1 percent to 58 percent, i.e., from approximately 1.1 million households to 15 million households, some twelve percent of the total population. By 1934 the percentage of peasants living on collectivized farms had risen to seventy-five percent. Thus, through the harsh intrusion of the OGPU, a massive metamorphosis of Soviet peasant life, *not* its genocidal demise, had occurred.

That there was no fully genocidal intention behind the assault on the Kulaks is clear from the policy directives governing the entire action against them. Though Stalin intervened to stiffen the guidelines recommended by the special Politburo Commission on De-Kulakization that reported in December 1929, his own more radical version of this transformational program, published in the name of the Central Committee on January 5, 1930 under the title "On the Tempo of Collectivization and Measures of State Assistance in Collective Farm Construction," still allowed for a tripartite distinction among Kulaks. The first sub-class of Kulaks was defined as being composed of hardened, unrepentant reactionaries and anti-Soviet counterrevolutionaries. Such individuals were to be separated out, jailed or exiled to the Gulag and, if necessary, shot. Their families were also to be exiled. It is estimated that 50,000 to 63,000 households (300,000 to 378,000 persons) fell into this class. The second category to be established recognized the existence of less recalcitrant, though still "potentially" dangerous, Kulaks and their families who were also to be exiled, though to less distant and less ecologically extreme areas. Approximately 112,000 households (672,000 persons) were identified as belonging to this second subdivision. The third and largest group established by Stalin's edict was comprised of the less affluent, less politically active Kulaks who constituted the majority, estimated at seventy-five percent, of all Kulak families. There were between 650,000 and 800,000 households (between 3,900,000 and 4,800,000 persons) in this category. They were to be settled in their own raion but, on Stalin's insistence, outside of the collective farms. In the event, this three-part organizational plan, that involved the active participation of tens of thousands of armed state personnel, provided the national blueprint for the program of collectivization.

When the Kulak relocation program actually took place elements of a class war were unleashed involving "a positive orgy of violence which were later referred to as 'excesses.'"[6] At the same time, the conditions of exile and resettlement were much harsher than those proposed, however cynically, in the relevant official legislation. As a result the removals, as actually carried out amidst the chaotic conditions extant in the countryside—often by overzealous and ill-disciplined district level authorities,—created more exiles and more "executions" than originally envisioned. Officially, it was at first reported that a total of 240,757 Kulak families, approximately twenty-five percent of Kulak households, some 1.2 to 1.5 million people, had been exiled. Later this total was revised upwards to 381,000 families, or nearly 2.3 million persons. The actual final number, when all the deportees are included, was probably more than double this estimate, involving somewhere in the region of five million individuals. These deportations were also the cause, directly and indirectly, of between one and two million deaths, with a disproportionate number of the dead being children who were unable to survive the appalling living conditions, the severe food shortages and wretched weather that existed during the transport and the first years of resettlement.

These horrors and the enormous damage they did to the agricultural infrastructure of the country brought such a public outcry, and such monumental disorder in the countryside, including the accelerating slaughter of animals—the greatest loss taking place in February and March 1930—that even Stalin, in direct contradiction to his own desire to force the tempo of collectivization, felt constrained to criticize the deportations in his hypocritical essay, "Dizziness from Success."[7] In addition, new guidelines were now issued limiting the number and types of Kulaks to be deported. However, this respite from forced collectivization was temporary. A second wave of so-called de-Kulakization now occurred with the result that while "only twenty-six percent of peasant households participated as Kolkholz members in the spring sowing of 1930…between January and March 1931…the figures rose sharply from under thirty percent to forty-two percent."[8] And this frenzied process continued throughout the second half of 1931 so that "over half the peasant households of the Soviet Union were collectivized by the end of the 1931 sowing, and more than sixty percent by the end of the harvest season." By the spring of 1933 collectivization was a fait accompli and Stalin ordered the cessation of any further forced deportations in support of it.

As a result of these extreme governmental actions, the Minister of Agriculture was able to announce by 1931 that the Kulak population (using this term very broadly) population, *in terms of class membership*, had declined from 5.4 million in 1928 to its then present size of 1.6 million. Four years later, in 1935, an official document described this class constriction in even more dramatic terms: the 1928 Kulak population of 5,618,000 had been reduced to 149,000 on January 1, 1934. It must be stressed, however, that this precipitous drop in class affiliation, involving approximately 5.4 million individuals, does not equal a corresponding loss of life, i.e., every lost unit of class membership is not equivalent to a death. The number of Kulak deaths, from all causes, as a consequence of these tyrannical removals is estimated, as already noted, at between one and two million. This is to recognize that despite the ferocity of the attack upon the approximately 5.4 to 5.6 million persons identified as Kulaks in 1928, somewhere between 63 and 81.5 percent of this original group—some 3.4 to 4.4 million individuals—remained alive.

VI

The number of minority peoples available for repatriation in 1953 was, allowing for all the imprecision in the relevant demographic statistics, somewhere between a minimum of 280,000 and a maximum of 603,400, excluding Volga Germans and Tatars. If we add in the German and Tatar population the figures increase dramatically. The 1959 census lists the total Soviet German population at 1,619,000. And though the number of surviving Crimean Tatars is difficult to estimate with precision, their population, by the early 1950's, was considerable. Roy Medvedev, in trying to reconstruct their national odyssey, suggests that fifty percent of the original 200,000-250,000 deportees died, but this is almost certainly too high a figure, and a loss rate of approximately thirty percent, plus or minus five percent, appears more in keeping with the later data we have. Building from this post-removal base of between 140,000 and 175,000 their population advanced until it again numbered—and here I estimate in the absence of hard and reliable figures—in the region of 200,000 to 250,000 at the time of Stalin's death. At the same time, the Tatar population in the Soviet Union as a whole grew considerably in the 1950's reaching, according to 1959 estimates, 4,967,700—an increase of fifteen percent over what it had been in 1939. Though these aggregates for the Tatar community are all subject to revision, and a refined demographic breakdown that would allow us to calculate the Crimean Tartar population with more precision in any given year is unavailable, these totals readily indicate the continued existence, whatever the actual rate of growth, of this minority group, even under the rigors of exile. And when all the 1959 population estimates are added together, and the required backward (to 1953) extrapolations are done, the resultant sum (of survivors) reveals that a considerably large percentage of the minority nations were *not* murdered by Stalin either before, during or after removal and resettlement. Indeed, the total population of the five main minority peoples—excluding the Volga Germans and Tatars—in 1953 was only twenty percent smaller, of the maximum estimate cited above, than it had been in 1939 just two years before the forced deportations began. And if we include the numbers for the Volga Germans and Crimean Tatars the population of the seven deported national groups was, in fact, greater in 1953 than it had been in 1939. In effect, there were many hundreds of thousands, even millions, of minority individuals that Stalin could have killed-but, in consequence of his determinate and, ironic though it is to say it, restraining ideology, didn't. (I note that this outcome bears important structural similarities to what occurred in the United States in the event known as the "Trail of Tears"—the removal of five southern Indian tribes to Indian territory, and their subsequent growth in the West. One of the five, the Cherokee, are today the largest Indian nation in the U.S.).

VII

Let me also say a brief word about the recently much discussed Ukrainian famine of the early 1930s that claimed the lives of millions. Here, one must begin by understanding that given the importance of the independent, economically autonomous peasantry in the Ukraine's socio-economic structure(s), Stalin's plan for the extermination of national identity required—in addition to the removal of the national intelligentsia-a crusade against this "protocapitalist" strata. As Semen O. Pidhainy has described it, Stalin had to move against Ukrainian nationalism's "social base"—the individual landholdings. "Only a mass terror throughout the body of the nation—that is, the peasantry could reduce the nation to submission."[9] As long as the *selianym* (a euphemism now for all free Ukrainian peasants) existed, nationalist (and capitalist) sentiment would remain: both needed to be crushed.

The dominant method used to achieve this collective submission to socialism, and with it the elimination of the base of Ukrainian national sentiment, was the forced collectivization of the agricultural sector. At the same time, and not unimportant, such a centralized agrarian policy gave the Communist Party—in the form of the All Union Commissariat of Agriculture—control over the region's grain supply.

It was the task of this commissariat, in conjunction with the Soviet planners, to calculate, coordinate and organize the yearly grain harvest, in other words, to set and oversee the state exactions to be levied and collected. In the event, when this direct control was expressed in an overly demanding target for grain exports from the region—ostensibly justified by the increased program of industrialization that was to be financed by the agricultural surplus—it effectively translated into a manmade famine in the Ukraine in 1931 that grew worse in 1932 and 1933. For example, in 1931, the procurement quota for the region was set at seven million tons out of a total of 18.3 million tons (much of which had been lost to inefficient collective harvesting). Such a level of national procurement almost certainly spelled trouble for the local community. Matters of food supply only got worse in 1932 when the procurement total was again set at seven million tons while that year's harvest, due to drought, inefficiency and a decline in the number of acres sown—the last partly in protest to Stalinist policy came in at the very reduced level of 14.7 million tons. Although the local leadership, in the face of the total decline in tonnage, managed to persuade Moscow, at great cost to itself in the suspicions of disloyalty (and suspect nationalism) that such appeals raised, to reduce the quota to 6.6 million tons—itself a target never fulfilled—even this reduced sum was still far too high to make it possible to avoid massive starvation. Stalin, despite the mounting death toll, did not believe, or did not *want* to believe, the claim that the harvest was too small both to feed the Ukrainian people and to provide sufficient grain for export. Instead, already intensely suspicious of Ukrainian separatism and fearful of local disloyalty, he chose to interpret the failure to meet the inordinate quotas sent down from the center as deliberate acts of "sabotage," and the peasants as no better than "wreckers" of the socialist dream. Therefore, in a deliberate act intended to punish the population of Ukraine—though justified as an act of socialist self-defense—he continued to export grain from the region, if at a lower rate, 1.73 million tons in 1932 and 1.68 million tons in 1933, compared to 5.2 million tons in 1931. This export of grain, given the greatly reduced supplies, turned an already grave situation into an occasion of mass death.

Increased pressure was now also applied against the *selianym* class enemy, local party officials (37.3 percent of the new Ukrainian Communist Party members and candidate members were purged and seventy-five percent of local Soviets and members of local committees were replaced, with many of those who were replaced being arrested, for failing to produce the required quota), those involved in local agricultural middle management (many of these officials were arrested in the second half of 1932 for sabotaging Bolshevik policy), and all channels of Ukrainian economic, cultural and nutritional self-sufficiency. On December 14, 1932, the Central Committee of the All Union Communist Party accused the leadership of the Ukrainian Communist Party "of tolerating a Ukrainian nationalist deviation in its ranks," and then proceeded, on January 24, 1933, to replace it with a new ruling clique headed by Pavel Postyshev. At the same time, all available food aid to the stricken population, it is argued, was consciously denied; existing grain reserves in the region and elsewhere were not made available, and the importation of food was stopped at the border of the Ukraine—all while Stalin, in an act of depravity, continued, as already noted, to export more than 3 million tons of grain in 1932 and 1933. As a result there was massive—on this decoding *intentional*—starvation throughout the Ukraine climaxing in 1933 and 1934. Of a peasant population of upwards of twenty-five million, I estimate that up to five million persons, or twenty percent of the rural population, plus 500,000 to 750,000 persons in the urban areas of the Ukraine, died from lack of food and related medical problems in this period. In some areas, the death rate was as low as ten percent, in others nearly one hundred percent, depending largely upon local agricultural and ecological conditions, for example, and most importantly, the ability to find other sources of nutrition, such as fish or wildlife—in many places this also led to cannibalism and infanticide—to replace the lost grain supplies.

So goes the nationalist account of the Ukrainian famine interpreted as an intentional, man-made "genocide." Stalin purposely killed five million or more Ukrainians, plus hundreds of thousands of additional individuals belonging to other ethnic groups such as the Volga Germans and Kuban Cossacks, in order both to decapitate opposition to agricultural collectivization and to eradicate Ukrainian, and other, nationalist aspirations.

Now, accepting this nationalist interpretation of Ukrainian history, at least for the sake of argument, what are we to conclude about these events constituting an instance of genocide? This is neither an irrelevant nor a trivial question given the size of the human losses involved and the evil will that is asserted to have directly caused, to have been knowingly responsible for these losses. Moreover, I do not want to support any diminution or denial of this vast collective tragedy, the existence of which is not in doubt. However, and here I recognize that given the loss of millions of persons this conclusion will seem at first counterintuitive, even if the nationalist intentionalist thesis is correct, the results—at least five million deaths—do not constitute the technical crime of genocide, and the event, in its phenomenological specificity and totality, is not, for all of its murderous ferocity and demographic enormity, comparable to the Shoah. I would argue—assuming the correctness of this account—that the ruthless campaign against Ukrainian nationalism that destroyed a majority of the indigenous Ukrainian cultural and political elite, in addition to a significant segment of the peasant population of the region, is most correctly categorized as an instance of nationalist conflict and internal colonialism rather than as an example of genocide. Stalin did not intend to exterminate the entire population of the Ukraine.

This conclusion finds immediate support from the apposite statistical indicators: though the human carnage was enormous—approaching the number of Jewish victims during the Second World War—the portion of the Ukrainian peasant population lost was somewhere near twenty percent (plus or minus five percent), and the losses for the Ukrainian population as a whole were in the area of fifteen percent. These demographic results resemble (if being slightly higher than) the figures for population decline in those Eastern European countries overrun by the Nazis, and in both cases the numbers do not indicate that a policy of total population eradication was pursued. Had Stalin in Ukraine—as Hitler in Eastern

Europe—sought to pursue a genocidal war, given the destructive possibilities that lay open to him, more than fifteen percent of the national community would have been done away with. More people were not killed because, amid the murder that did occur, there was, odd as this may seem, restraint. There was restraint because Stalin did not want to eradicate the people of Ukraine; he wanted to exploit them. Eliminating the whole of a vanquished helot population makes no more sense than slaughtering one's slaves. However, in contrast, eliminating a conquered people's controlling elite, leaving it leaderless, anxious, and vertiginous, is a rational and functional strategy, long pursued by conquerors and adopted by Stalin, in order to achieve both enduring subordination of the subjugated and political stability in one's empire. This is not a humane imperial strategy—a regular course of action to be recommended as a form of empire maintenance—but neither is it genocide.

Ironically, this judgment is confirmed by the heartrending condition of the children, especially infants and the newborn. Throughout Ukraine, youthful cadavers lay strewn across the landscape; the entire territory had become a crude necropolis for children under the age of twelve who were unable to obtain enough nourishment to stay alive. Yet even here, in the midst of the most intense human suffering, the relevant population statistics require careful decipherment. The latest demographic data indicate that fewer than 760,000 children died, largely from starvation, between 1932-1934. This represents, depending on one's estimation of other relevant demographic variables, between 6 percent and 33.5 percent of the age cohort, and a significant percentage of the total population decline. However, recognizing the great tragedy that occurred here, even the maximum loss rate of 33.5 percent does not support a genocidal reading of this event. For, on these numbers, that is, a loss rate of between 6 and 33.5 percent, 66.5 percent of Ukrainian children, at a minimum, survived. Once the famine was past its peak in May 1933, the surviving two out of three children were not singled out for further harassment or worse. Most of those who survived the crisis of 1932-33 survived.

This historical outcome regarding the children is not trivial. What makes the Ukrainian case non-genocidal, and what makes it different from the Holocaust, is the fact that the majority of Ukrainian children survived and, still more, that they were *permitted* to survive. Even the mountain of evidence pertaining to Stalin's evil actions produced by the proponents of the nationalist, genocide thesis, for example, James Mace and Robert Conquest-does not indicate an intent to eliminate, or any motive that would plausibly justify the extermination of, the Ukrainian biological stock. Though the number of Ukrainian children who died and, under the intentionalist reading, were murdered, was almost as high as (or higher than) the number of Jewish children who were exterminated, their deaths were the consequence of, represented, and intended, something wholly different from what the murder of Jewish children at Auschwitz and Treblinka represented and intended. In the Ukrainian case, the focused object of the violence and death was national enfeeblement and political dismemberment. In the Shoah, the focused object, given its racial determinants, was physical genocide. Stalin intended that after the famine there should still be Ukrainians, though not Ukrainianism; Hitler intended that after Auschwitz there would be neither Jews nor Judaism. The loss of every child in both contexts, employing the calculus of the talmudic sages, was the loss of a world. The death of each child was an act of equal immorality. Nonetheless, there is an important, nonreductive, phenomenological difference to be drawn between mass murder (including children) and complete group extinction (including children), between a war for political and territorial domination (including children) and a war of unlimited biological annihilation (including children).

VIII

The Armenian tragedy was an enormous historical outrage. As I understand this event, the controlling ambition, the collective civic agenda, behind Turkish inhumanity was primarily nationalist in character and, in practice, limited in scope and purpose. The Armenian massacres were an indecent, radicalized manifestation of a most primitive jingoism activated by the exigencies of war from without and the revolutionary collapse of the Ottoman Empire from within. Turkish nationalism—the extreme nationalist elites in control of the Turkish state—now under the violent cover of war, envisioned and pursued the elimination of [*not* the murder of] *all* non-Turkish elements—and most especially and specifically the eradication of the Armenian community—from the national context. The anti-Armenian crusade was therefore, for all its lethal extravagance, a delimited political crusade. Of course, mixed into the noxious brew that represented itself as national destiny were other obsessions: a loathing of Christians if not all non-Muslims, xenophobia, greed, jealousy, fear, desire and the like. But, above all else, the "war against the Armenians" was a vulgar and desperate manifestation of raw nationalist politics.

This is to argue that contrary to, for example, Helen Fein's contention that the Armenians were "enemies by definition," that is, on a priori ideological or racial grounds—thereby allowing her erroneously to equate the action against Jews and Gypsies in World War II with that against the Armenians in World War I—the Armenians were "enemies" to the degree that they were enemies in this context, on practical and political grounds centering around long-standing policies of internal colonialism, the implications and machinations of national self-determination and the provocative issue of loyalty in time of war. Accordingly, the objective of Turkish action, when it came in 1915-1916, was the destruction, once and for all, of Armenian national identity. The criminality of the Armenians did not require (as I shall show in detail in a moment) the biological extinction of every Armenian man, woman, and child—especially if such individual and collective survival took place outside Turkish national boundaries and, therefore, made no claims upon Turkish sovereignty or national territory.

At this juncture of our argument, three seminal factors that are central to the morphological *disanalogy* between the Armenian tragedy and the Holocaust need to be introduced. They are: (a) the possibility of Armenian Christian conversion to Islam as a way of avoiding deportation and worse; (b) the specific character of the forced deportations; and (c) the *nontotalistic* nature of the anti-Armenian crusade.

As regards the mediating role of conversion to Islam, the eyewitness accounts of the tragedy repeatedly mention this lifesaving, though communally destructive, possibility. Both "willingly" and unwillingly, large numbers of Armenians became Muslims. In particular, there appears to have been extensive, forced proselytization of Armenian women and children. It is difficult to ascertain just what role official Ittihadist ideology played in these coerced prophylactic rituals, though it is clear that the Committee of Union and Progress (CUP), devoid as it was of a racist ideology, did not oppose such recreative, death-deflecting, actions. Indeed, to the degree that Islamicization constructively reinforced the Young Turks' normative political agenda—Islam being a fundamental buttress of Turkification (whereas Christianity was the key element in Armenian self-identity)—this survivalist (flagrantly inhumane) program was consistent with CUP ambitions; and it found wide instantiation. So wide, in fact, that Johannes Lepsius again and again excoriates the Turkish government for allowing, even encouraging, this tyrannical policy, and Arnold Toynbee accusingly refers to "survival being purchased by apostatizing to Islam."[10] Likewise, the German, U.S., British and other governments are on record as protesting this unwelcome practice.

In that neither Islam nor Turkism are predicated on inelastic, biologistic concepts, both possess absorptive capacities that create existential as well as socio-political possibilities unavailable in Nazism. Accordingly, the "other" is not only defined differently by the Ittihat elites than in Hitler's Reich—not genetically and without reference to metaphysical canons of ontic pollution and decadence—but the required response to the "other" allows for the is the remaking of the "other," primarily through the mysterious rite of conversion, so as to obviate still more complete—that is, exterminatory—forms of overcoming. We have evidence that the children in Christian orphanages were converted en masse. It was not only women and children who were forcibly converted. Lepsius, for example, records that the entire male medical staff of the German Mission Hospital in Urfa was coerced into becoming Muslim, as were Armenian Army physicians at Sivas. In Aleppo, the entire Armenian labor battalion was converted in February 1916, and further large-scale conversions of Armenian men occurred in March and April 1916. Lepsius also reports that "all Armenian villages in the Samsun area and in Unich have been Islamicized. No favors were granted to anyone, apart from renegades."[11] In fact, Lepsius conservatively estimates that 200,000 men, women and children, approximately 12 to 13.5 percent of the entire Armenian community, were forcibly converted and thereby saved, however objectionable the instrument of their salvation. In this respect, Turkish policy reproduces medieval procedures of cultural homogenization, not modern procedures of physical genocide. As such it kept Armenians, if not Armenianism, alive.

Secondly, the Armenian deportations were not uniform events of total annihilation. Though these Armenian removals, carried out under the most brutal conditions, were regularly occasions of mass death that sealed the fate of hundreds of thousands, several hundred thousand Armenians did survive these horrific journeys. Lepsius, for example, (under) estimates the remnant at 200,000 individuals. Toynbee cites a total of 600,000 Armenian survivors up to early 1916—the combined total of those who lived through the deportations and those who fled into Russian territory. He summarizes:

> In general, wastage [death during the deportations] seems to fluctuate, with a wide oscillation, on either side of 50 percent; 600 out of 2,500 (24 percent) reached Aleppo from a village in the Harpout district; 60 percent arrived there out of the first convoy from the village of E. (near H.), and 46 percent out of the second; 25 percent arrived out of a convoy from the village of D. in the same neighborhood. We shall certainly be well within the mark if we estimate that at least half those condemned to massacre or deportation have actually perished.[12]

Supporting these large estimates of the number of those who were *not* killed during these forced evacuations are the figures for Armenians who found refuge in Arab countries and then, later, in Western Europe and the United States. Richard Hovannisian, writing of their acceptance in the Arab world, indicates that:

> Many of the deportees suffered a cruel fate at the hands of certain Bedouin tribes in the Syrian desert, but most were accorded sympathetic asylum by the Arab peoples, who had themselves endured four centuries of Ottoman domination. In all, the number of Armenian deportees who found refuge in Arab lands, by 1925, is estimated at well over 200,000.[13]

This figure excludes the 50,000 who found refuge in Iran. More specifically, Hovannisian breaks these refugee figures down as follows: Syria accepted 100,000 Armenian refugees; Lebanon, 50,000; Palestine and Jordan, 10,000; Egypt, 40,000; Iraq, 25,000; and Iran, 50,000, making a total of 275,000 survivors. These numbers are supported by later governmental statistics issued by the respective Arab countries. Census data released between 1931 and 1945 by the individual Middle East states indicate that Syria had an Armenian population of 125,550 (1945); Lebanon, 72,797 (1944); Palestine, 3,802 (1931); and Egypt, 19,596 (1937). Moreover, in addition to these aggregates, we also have evidence in various national census counts of the inter-war period of sizable new Armenian communities, in France, Greece, Cyprus, Bulgaria and the United States, with additional small populations in Czechoslovakia, Switzerland, Greece, Hungary, Austria, Yugoslavia, Italy and Canada. (The population figures for these communities overlap with Hovannisian's figures for the Arab World—though to what exact degree is uncertain.) Therefore, if we put the number of survivors of these inhumane transfers at between 300,000 and 400,000, we shall be on secure grounds—or at least grounds that are as secure as possible given all the statistical uncertainties—remembering that Hovannisian's total of 275,000 does not include any survivors in Russia, Europe, or the

United States. This translates into somewhere between a 17.7 percent (300,000 out of 1,700,000) and 26.6 percent (400,000 out of 1,500,000) survival rate. Then, too, beyond the mathematics alone, these substantial statistics indicate that the Turkish oppressor did not require nor demand the death of all Armenians. The Turks had all these individuals, this entire defenseless population, within their control and could have murdered them all, despite the practical difficulties in murdering an entire people in a country as large as Turkey, had they so desired. Evidently, this was not necessary.

Thirdly, the enacted policy of deporting Armenians was not universally applied even within the borders of Turkey. The Armenians of Constantinople, numbering up to 200,000, and the Armenians of other large cities—for example, Smyrna, where between 6,000 and 20,000 Armenians lived, Kutahia, and, to some degree, Aleppo—were not uprooted en masse during the entire war period. Lepsius estimated (and, in his own words, perhaps "overestimated") that the number of Armenians so protected represented one-seventh to one-ninth of the total Armenian population, or some 204,700 persons (out of what he projected as an original Armenian population of 1,845,450). Although recent studies require that we temper Lepsius's figures and indicate that up to 30,000 Armenians were, in fact, deported from Constantinople, the need to modify all generalizations as to Turkish intentions, given the very real limitations placed upon evictions from Constantinople and elsewhere, stands.

To gain a complete picture of all the relevant statistics bearing upon the question of Armenian survival we must also add in the 250,000-300,000 or so Armenians who retreated with the Russian army back into Russian territory after the final defeat at Van in the summer of 1915 and the 4,200 individuals who survived the famous battle of Musa Dagh and were rescued by the French in mid-September 1915. Accordingly, the comprehensive demographic accounting regarding Armenian casualties and survival:

1914 Armenian Population	1,500,000–1,700,000
Converts to Islam	200,000–300,000

Survive Deportations (outside Turkey)	300,000–400,000
Survive in Large Turkish Cities	170,000–220,000
Survive in Russia	250,000–300,000
Survivors of Musa Dagh	4,200–4,200
TOTAL SURVIVORS	924,200–1,224,200
TOTAL DEATHS (1915-1918, based on 1,700,000 total)	475,800–775,800

Ultimately, the Armenian tragedy, for all its horror, was, in defining ways, phenomenologically different from the Shoah.

IX

Conclusion

The spatial limits imposed on this paper prevent further comparative review and analysis. However, I believe that in all the other cases that are said to parallel the Holocaust, close study would show that they also are dissimilar insofar as they too would not be examples of an unlimited war that required complete annihilation—the death of every man, woman and child—of the victim population. The Holocaust is a unique historical reality.

Endnotes

1. Given the length of this paper, I have elected to avoid all footnotes except for citations involving direct quotations. The full supporting evidence for the arguments presented here will be provided in the extended and detailed discussion to be found in the second, forthcoming, volume of the *Holocaust in Historical Context* (Oxford University Press, New York).

2. Robert Conquest, *Kolyma: The Arctic Death Camps* (New York, 1979), p. 47.

3. Iosef Stalin, *Collected Works,* vol. 11, p. 48 (London, 1955).

4. Lynne Viola, "The '25,000ers:' A Study in a Soviet Recruitment Campaign during the First Five-Year Plan," *Russian History/History Russe,* vol. 10, pt. 1

(1983), p. 23.

5. Cited from Robert C. Tucker, *Stalin in Power: The Revolution from Above, 1928-41* (New York, 1990); p. 139.

6. Moshe Lewin, *Russian Peasants and Soviet Power* (Evanston, IL, 1968), p. 490; and Lynne Viola, *The Best Sons of the Fatherland: Workers in the Vanguard of the Stalin Revolution* (New York, 1987), pp. 108-112.

7. *Pravda,* March 2, 1930. An English translation of this essay can be found in J. Stalin (ed.), Leninism (Moscow, 1940), pp. 333-339.

8. Sheila Fitzpatrick, *Stalin's Peasants: Resistance and Survival in the Russian Village After Collectivization* (New York, 1994), p. 65.

9. Robert Conquest, *The Harvest of Sorrow: Soviet Collectivization and the Terror-Famine* (New York, 1986), p. 219.

10. Arnold J. Toynbee, The Murderous Tyrrany of the Turks (New York, 1917).

11. Johannes Lepsius, *Deutschland und Armenien, 1914-1918* (Potsdam, 1919), pp. LXXIIff, p. 105.

12. A. Toynbee in Viscount Bryce, *The Treatment of the Armenians in the Ottoman Empire: Documents Presented to Viscount Grey of Fallodon, Secretary for Foreign Affairs by Viscount Bryce* (London, 1916), p. 650.

13. R. Hovannisian, "The Ebb and Flow of the Armenian Minority in the Arab Middle East," *Middle East Journal,* vol. 28, no. 1 (Winter 1974), pp. 19-32; p. 20.

Chapter 2

The Genocidal Mind: In Search of a Definition

Paul Vincent

> *"God, I thank thee, that I am not as other men are...."*
> Luke 18:11

The question before us is both stimulating and challenging: what exactly is a genocidal mind? We can all agree that genocide occurred in Europe between 1939 and 1945. Indeed, using Yehuda Bauer as our guide, we might argue that the Holocaust was in fact "a radicalization of genocide: a planned attempt to physically annihilate every single member of a targeted ethnic, national, or racial group."[1] We can quantify and classify and, in most cases, name its victims. Moreover, beginning with the ground breaking work of Christopher Browning, we are increasingly able to identify and classify—and, in numerous cases, name—the perpetrators.[2] But when we tackle the issue of defining a genocidal mind, we leap into murky waters—waters which, while seeming to assume a deterministic definition of humanity, are largely outside either deductive or empirical verification. What are the characteristics of a genocidal mind? Is it possible to assume certainty in this area? If we bring ourselves to surmise something other than the immediate experience of 1933-45—e.g., to theorize absent events and people, to eliminate the person of Hitler and his closest cohorts, or to conceive of other unrealized possibilities—what happens to our supposed definition? Must we assume that, given other circumstances, the person sitting next to us is capable of genocide? Can we accept that free agency is inherent in the very nature of human behavior? And if so, what is the possibility of knowing other minds?

When I first chose to tackle this question, I soon concluded that a strong dose of prejudice must be a central ingredient of the genocidal mind. A simple murderer, if I may use that characterization, need not be prejudiced to kill. The killing may be driven by rage or hatred, it may result from the challenge or entertainment of the process, or it may be the act of a mercenary hit man or the aberrant behavior of a serial killer. But while the killers who made up the *Ordungspolizei,* the *Einsatzgruppen* or who comprised the guards at Treblinka or Belzec may have shared some of these characteristics, the evidence suggests that their involvement in mass murder was ultimately induced by something more. Can we assume with any certainty that the prejudice of anti-Semitism is the missing ingredient? I believe that the evidence brings us up short.

Poland has come under increasing scrutiny in recent years due to the high degree of anti-Semitism in that country, both before and during the Second World War. There is, for example, the recent work of Jan T. Gross, detailing how townspeople and farmers from the Polish village of Jedwabne turned on their Jewish neighbors, torturing them and then burning them alive.[3] It is, in fact, often overlooked that a contributing factor in the events leading up to the *Kristallnacht* pogrom was the Polish government's decision in October 1938 to deprive Polish Jews of the right of return from territories under German rule. Given a strong strain of anti-Semitism in Poland, much has been made, and properly so, of Zegota, the only organization in wartime Poland—indeed, in Europe as a whole—whose sole purpose was the saving of Jewish lives. Yet Zofia Kossak-Szczucka, a well-known writer of historical novels and the Catholic founder of Zegota, was herself an ardent anti-Semite, and she repeatedly expressed her wish that the Jews she was aiding and abetting would disappear from Poland after the war. How does one differentiate between Kossak-Szczucka and the townspeople of Jedwabne? Clearly, to be an anti-Semite, even one who wishes the Jews to all disappear, does not necessarily make one a mass murderer.

Expressions of distaste for the Jews from individuals we might otherwise respect and honor are not limited to Kossak-Szczucka, who was added to the Righteous Gentile Registry of Yad Vashem in 1982. In the immediate aftermath of World War II, anti-Semitism increasingly riddled the diary entries of George S. Patton. "The dissolution of Germany was a plot," he wrote, "organized by American Jews." He accused Henry Morgenthau and Bernard Baruch of "Semitic revenge against Germany," and even described those Jews who had survived the extermination camps as "lower than animals." In September 1945, General Patton launched into a tirade against Jews to an exasperated General Eisenhower, who had paid his subordinate a visit upon learning that Patton had appointed former SS men to guard an enormous DP camp. While being debriefed by his commander, Patton bemoaned that the Jews were "pissing and crapping all over the place."

> I've never seen a group of people who seem to be more lacking in intelligence and spirit. There's a German village not far from here, deserted. I'm planning to make it into a concentration camp for some of these goddamn Jews.[4]

Is this the bombast of a genocidal mind? Given the right circumstances—suppose, for example, that Josef "Sepp" Dietrich and George Patton had traded places in 1929—would Patton have been one of Hitler's "willing executioners?" We will never know.

In December 1948 T.S. Eliot was awarded the Nobel Prize for Literature. A highly regarded poet—perhaps the most influential of the twentieth century—Eliot had delivered a series of lectures in 1934 at the University of Virginia. Later collected and published as *After Strange Gods,* the lectures included Eliot's statement that modern society could not achieve cultural and spiritual unity so long as there were Jews in its midst. Eliot went on that "reasons of *race and religion* make any large number of free-thinking Jews undesirable" (my italics). It would be appropriate, he argued, if a fairly homogeneous Anglo-Saxon Christian community could humanely take its Jewish neighbors and place them "beyond the borders of the city."[5] Now, if uttered by anyone else, one would certainly deem this an anti-Jewish statement—indeed, given the reference to race, an anti-Semitic statement. Was Eliot anti-Semitic? Did he have a genocidal mind? He once remarked, by the way—in an echo of Friedrich Nietzsche—that "the urge to destroy is creative."

In presenting the remarks of Patton and Eliot, I aim not to single out something unique. Indeed, expressions of anti-Judaism or anti-Semitism were endemic to western society, and had been for hundreds of years. Johann Gottfried von Herder, among the leading intellectuals of the late eighteenth century, remarked that the "Jewish race is and remains in Europe an Asiatic people alien to our region." Whether or not it belongs in Germany was no longer a religious issue but a question of whether and to what degree "this alien race…may be dispensed with, how many are useful or detrimental to *this* and not to any other state—that is the problem."[6] Goethe, certainly among the major intellectual figures in early nineteenth-century Europe, expressed considerable skepticism over attempts to emancipate the Jews and integrate them into European society. Although he never hitched his reputation to either side of the "Jewish Question," he noted that the Jews of antiquity impressed him, while those who were his contemporaries were but a race of vulgar and unscrupulous traders and moneylenders. What he opposed most strongly was the legalization of mixed marriages, which he claimed made nonsense of established religion. To marry "a Jewess" demonstrated "contempt for religious feeling;" however, he added, "I do not hate Jews."[7]

One may continue *ad nauseum* to quote the distasteful remarks of otherwise highly respected individuals—that is, I am not making reference here to Houston Stewart Chamberlain, Arthur de Gobineau, Paul de Lagarde, Julius Langbehn, Richard Wagner, or the legion of other racist pundits who often made their reputation on the basis of their hatred for Jews. The fact remains that, while contempt for and resentment of Jews was a crucial ingredient of the Nazis' genocidal campaign, it was insufficient in itself to trigger the massive and systematic killing of the Holocaust. Were that not the case, Europe's Jews would have vanished from the continent well before the twentieth century. To quote David Vital, what we must recognize is that however "hostile public and private thinking about the Jews might" have been "in important social, political, and intellectual circles in" pre-Nazi "central and western Europe, nowhere was the state as such the *declared* enemy of the Jews." While "no western or central European state was necessarily friendly to Jews, nowhere had the Jews reason to distrust, let alone fear the state and its instruments."[8]

Given these facts, we must conclude that something both decisive and exceptional happened in twentieth-century Germany once Hitler took power. A key interaction during the Eichmann Trial of 1961, an exchange between Eichmann and Benjamin Halevi—one of the three Israeli judges who presided over the trial—opens a crucial window on just what that "something" might have been. After Eichmann read, at Halevi's request, a particularly damning segment of Heinrich Himmler's infamous Posen speech of 4 October 1943—the one in which the Reichführer-SS remarks on the extermination of the Jews as being a glorious page in German history—Halevi provided some explication characterizing the essence of what Himmler was saying.

> At that time, when Himmler gave authoritative expression to the prevailing National Socialist point-of-view, and in particular to the duties of the SS, …it was considered a glorious act to destroy Jews; that Jews were looked upon as a germ which had to be destroyed, just like any other disease.[9]

Once Halevi stopped, Eichmann responded: "Yes, that is correct. That I must admit." These were probably the most remarkable words that Eichmann expressed during the course of the trial; they served also as a fatal confession. When it came to purifying and preserving the "body of the *Volk*," murder became the principal means of therapy.

In discussing *Aktion T-4*, the children's euthanasia program in Nazi Germany, Michael Burleigh argues that the

> most salient fact…is that we are dealing with a group of people who believed in the rectitude of what they did, even if they did not care to share their reasoning with the confused, traditionalist mass of humanity through some form of explicit legal sanction.[10]

Although he is discussing the mass murder of mentally ill and physically disabled people, Burleigh's paradigm treats the issue of "racial hygiene." As such, it must be expanded to include anyone whom the Nazis feared, stigmatized, and then earmarked for extermination. What separates the "routine" murderer or the casual anti-Semite from the genocidal mentality is an unqualified belief in the moral necessity to destroy *"Leben unwertes Leben,"* and then the deliberate and methodical determination to put that belief into practice. It is not surprising that many employed in the T-4 euthanasia program later moved on to work in the extermination camps of *Aktion Reinhard*. With the dogmatism that so often attaches to bureaucratic efficiency, the killing of the mentally ill or physically disabled gradually became "routine and systematic;" such killing was, Burleigh argues, "an act of moral and intellectual conviction on the part of a closely knit group of like-minded individuals."[11] In an interview with Gitta Sereny, Franz Suchomel—an SS photographer assigned to the euthanasia program—remarked that

> the people who were involved in the actual killing process in the institutes, those who worked in the crematoria—we called them *die Brenner* [the burners]—became calloused, inured to feeling. And they were the ones who were afterwards the first to be sent to Poland.[12]

One of these, the pediatrician Ernst Wentzler—a physician who had been heavily involved in the killing of handicapped children—recalled in testimony given in 1963 that "I had the feeling that my activity was something positive, and that I had made a small contribution to human progress."[13] If we wish to discern the genocidal mentality, we must reckon not only with the increased callousness of the killers but also with their misguided conviction that they were engaged in something advantageous to humanity.

On the basis of the available record, few people better encapsulate the personality of what we might wish to call the genocidal mind than Otto Ohlendorf, one of the principal Nazi administrators responsible for carrying out the Nazi extermination policy. Born near Hanover in 1907, he had studied at three universities, completing a doctorate in jurisprudence.[14] Nevertheless, he deemed himself first and foremost a research economist. In 1925, at the age of 18, he joined the NSDAP; the following year he entered the SS. In 1941, at age thirty-four, he assumed command of *Einsatzgruppe D* with the rank of *SS-Brigadeführer* (major general). He was quietly brought back to Berlin's Wilhelmstrasse in June 1942 to serve on the Central Planning Board of the Department of Overseas Trade in the Economics Ministry. During the year in which he commanded Einsatzgruppe D, he was responsible for the liquidation of ninety thousand Jews. Walter Funk, Economics Minister and supervisor of Ohlendorf, was unaware of his subaltern's activities.

Next to Göring, Ohlendorf was perhaps the most compelling of the defendants at the various Nuremberg trials.[15] Handsome, suave, and exceedingly well poised, his voice was carefully modulated, and he came across as graceful and self-confident. During the trial for his life in 1947, women spectators sent flowers to his cell. Ohlendorf was interrogated by Lieutenant Commander Whitney Harris, an American naval officer. When asked how many men, women, and children were killed under his command, he shrugged his shoulders and calmly replied "ninety thousand." The Soviet judge, I.T. Nikitchenko, asked why children were massacred, and Ohlendorf stated: "The order was that the Jewish population should be totally exterminated." It was a matter of self-defense, he continued. The Jews posed a continuous danger for the German occupation troops and might some day attack Germany. Clearly angered by this response, the prosecutor asked: "Will you explain to the tribunal what conceivable threat to the security of the Wehrmacht a child constituted?" Ohlendorf, surprised by the question, replied "I believe I cannot add anything to your previous question. I did not have to determine the danger but the order said that all Jews including the children were considered to constitute a danger to the security of this area." The prosecutor continued, however, to press the defendant. "Will you agree that there was absolutely no basis for killing children except genocide and the killing of races?" Ohlendorf, retaining his composure, replied: "This order did not only try to achieve a temporary security but also a permanent security, for the children were people who would grow up and, surely, would constitute a danger no smaller than that of their parents."[16] What one must understand from this statement is that the ninety thousand Jews, including the children, were but a passionless abstraction to Ohlendorf. During his trial he insisted that he had no special hatred of Jews, but that the order for their execution was absolutely necessary militarily and had to be obeyed.

It is logical to conclude that one's age impacted one's commitment to Hitler's genocidal program. Alfons Heck, the once fanatical member of the *Hitlerjugend* featured in the HBO film *Heil Hitler: Confessions of a Hitler Youth,* remarks at the conclusion of that excellent production that "children are like empty vessels: you can fill them with good, you can fill them with evil; you can fill them with hate and you can fill them with compassion." What the Nazi regime did, beginning in both the schools and the *Hitlerjugend* organizations, was to indoctrinate Germans into abandoning faith in their own judgment. Did it always succeed? Of course not. Nevertheless, it succeeded all too frequently. Heck, in his autobiography, states that, unlike their parents, "we, the children of the '30s, knew nothing of the turmoil or freedom of the Weimar Republic."

> As soon as the Nazi regime came into power, it revamped the educational structure from top to bottom, and with very little resistance. Our indoctrination, therefore, did not begin with admission

to the *Jungvolk* at age ten, but from our very first day in the *Volksschule,* the elementary school. We five and six-year-olds received an almost daily dose of nationalistic instruction, which we swallowed as naturally as our morning milk.[17]

Heck began elementary school in the spring of 1933. His first teacher, a Herr Becker, was both a Nazi Party member and a pious Catholic—"not at all an unusual combination in my hometown," Heck observes.[18] Becker, he notes, never hid his conviction that the Jews were "different," a fact he elucidated in his weekly instruction in "racial science."

As we consider the significance of teaching racial science to a ten-year old in 1933, we should recognize that the same child will be eighteen in 1941. Hitler and his closest cohorts did, in fact, engineer a revolution: a cultural revolution, a moral revolution. The Germany that invaded the Soviet Union in 1941 was *not* the same country in which Hitler assumed power in 1933. When Goebbels claimed, shortly after Hitler took power, that with "the Nazi revolution, the year 1789 is stricken from history," we need to reflect on what he meant.[19] For all its eventual shortcomings, the French Revolution aimed to make reality of the liberal and universal ideals of the Enlightenment. But such concepts as human freedom and equality were, Goebbels argued, no longer valid; racial conflict would now gird German society. And the racial enemy, who had to be contained if not destroyed, was the Jew. To transcend the tensions of history, and thereby live in peace, Germany had to be *Judenrein*—cleansed of Jews.

Nevertheless, the problem of defining a genocidal mind remains a puzzle. If we can so define Hitler, what do we make of the secondary or minor actors within the Nazi regime? How do we classify the enigmatic Albert Speer, or the members of the *Einsatzgruppen,* or the doctors and nurses in the euthanasia program, or the guards at the extermination camps, or—and this is aimed to make us all uncomfortable—the *Sonderkommandos,* those "privileged prisoners," Primo Levi tells us, who "were a minority within the Lager population, yet represented a potent majority among survivors?"[20] If from our viewpoint we identify Hitler as a world historical figure—i.e., someone whose role in history outshines that of contemporaries, upon whom s/he has an uncommonly important impact—how, then, do we evaluate his followers? Historians are generally prepared to recognize that independent thought and action among the masses is severely hampered when such individuals as Alexander the Great or Napoleon Bonaparte arrive upon the scene. Is this any less true of the average German in Hitler's Third Reich? Where do we draw the line between the overawed follower, the individual unwilling to risk his way of life, and the true believer—the clearly genocidal personality? One might surmise that there is no clear line. Indeed, the committed follower of 1936 may have been at the center of opposition in 1944. We must always recognize that, rather than some permanent standard, human beings are given to temporary reactions, shifting from apparent objective truths to subjective feelings, with little conscious understanding of what precisely is driving their perceptions. Primo Levi reflects on the various industrial concerns that were commissioned by SS commanders to supply installations or significant quantities of merchandise to the Polish camps. These orders must have aroused some suspicions. Yet they "were stifled by fear, the desire for profit," by "blindness and willed stupidity,…and in some cases (probably few) by fanatical Nazi obedience."[21]

With this perspective as backdrop, I should like to underscore the great "however." We may speak of the power of rampant anti-Semitism or the attempted programming of an entire national community to anticipate utopia once all the Jews, and others categorized as *Leben unwertes Leben,* are removed from society. These topics must be studied and acknowledged as contributing to the so-called genocidal mind. Yet, as a historian firmly planted in the humanistic wing of his profession, I believe that human beings are ultimately unique among God's creatures in their capacity for moral choice. Behavioral science stresses, with some justice, the extent to which human beings are subject to the laws of nature. It also posits the degree to which human beings might be programmed by an ideology that breeds illusions, fantasies, and forms of irrational behavior. But when it comes to the evil of refusing to recognize the humanity of another human being, I remain convinced that individual human beings are not mere marionettes—notwithstanding the row upon row of goose-stepping soldiers in Leni Riefenstahl's *Triumph of the Will*. We may be shaped by our class position, our race, our religion, our education, our gender, or our cultural and political traditions; yet, as individuals, each of us retains the capacity for moral choice. Thus, while I tend to believe that any definition of the genocidal mind remains just beyond our reach, I also believe that, as a historian, I must allocate praise or blame for individuals in Nazi Germany for their historical conduct. If we reject this notion, how can we condemn the Nazi in the dock who claims "I was just following orders?" Yehuda Bauer, in explaining his biases, has staked out this position quite well. "I am against antisemitism and racism of any sort," Bauer says,

> I believe, on the strength of the historical evidence, that the Nazi regime was just about the worst regime that ever disfigured the face of this earth. Worst from what point of view? From a basically liberal point of view that, in line with Jewish and other traditions, sees human life as a supreme value. Morality, in this context, is based on the idea that acts or intentions that run counter to the right of individuals and groups to exist, to live fully, also run counter to the existence of human life altogether, hence their unacceptability. Morality as here presented is an absolute value, then—absolute, that is, as long as one posits the continuation of the human race as a desired condition.[22]

To be sure, the historian faces an important barrier when it comes to establishing verdicts of right and wrong, good and evil. It has long been held that historians are directed to describe and explain, not to pronounce verdicts. In this sense the historian is a detective, not a judge; s/he provides the evidence and it is up to the reader to form a moral conclusion. This is a good and necessary warning against historical narratives that resemble moralizing polemics. Yet the historian must be careful not to interpret too literally Ranke's stipulation that we write our history *"wie es eigentlich gewesen"*—that is, to conform to the standard used by the exact sciences. History employs few concepts, categories, or special techniques that are peculiar to itself. Attempts to construct a special paraphernalia such as may be found in sociology or psychology—let alone physics—have generally led to wooden and spiritless narrative. To a considerable degree, a physicist can speak with different voices as a scientist and as a human being. Although this may be less true with the economist or psychologist, it is patently absurd when applied to the political, social, or cultural historian. To be sure, all historical work must be based on empirical evidence. Yet, to stipulate that we suppress all moral evaluation, which is inevitably involved when studying human beings as creatures with purposes and motives, is to confuse the aims and methods of the humane studies with those of the natural sciences. The conclusions of historians differ from those of scientists in that the judgments they entail—be they moral, political, cultural—are intrinsic to their subject matter and not, as in the sciences, external to it.

In seeking the roots of the Holocaust, I must first take for granted some general propositions. Assuming that the generally accepted physical laws of the world apply, I can accept that all men require and seek food, clothing, shelter, and a degree of protection for their persons. I might also assume that human beings are prone to various passions—greed, envy, lust for power—and that some men are more ruthless, ambitious, cunning and fanatical than others. These are assumptions based on both my study of history and personal experience. But are they capable of being formulated in the manner of theories or laws such as those used by scientists? The idealized models used by physicists, economists, and sociologists are of little use here. History must be embedded in the concrete; however, it is also an inexact discipline that relies upon vagueness, ambiguity, and suggestiveness. And whereas scientific method is crucial in fields upon which solid history must rely,[23] it is never sufficient to develop historical narrative. Historians focus on specific events or people because they believe them to have attributes of overriding importance or significance. It is not always possible to measure or quantify those attributes in the fashion utilized by scientists, or even social scientists. Moreover, expressions of moral judgment—i.e., with respect to issues of good and evil, or right and wrong—such as enter into our deliberations when we are evaluating the events and individuals at the center of the Holocaust, are quite beyond the laws, systems, and terminology devised by the natural sciences.[24] With respect to Hitler's appointment on 31 January 1933, there is general agreement that this was an event of monumental significance; however, there is ongoing debate as to whether Franz von Papen was an evil man in view of his role in engineering that appointment. Moreover, and perhaps more to the point, we can all agree that Hitler represents a category of individual that the profession identifies as "a world historical figure," and we might also agree—indeed, we *should* all agree—that he possessed a genocidal mind. How else can we classify a man who likened himself to the bacteriologist Robert Koch, zealously engaged in a battle against lethal pathogens—which, as it happens, were fellow human beings—thereby ordering and perfecting the human race through genocide?[25] When Yehuda Bauer underscores his moral bias with respect to Nazism and racism by stating that morality, in this particular context, "is based on the idea that acts or intentions that run counter to the right of individuals and groups to exist, to live fully," are unacceptable, he underscores his belief that morality is "an absolute value" that "posits the continuation of the human race as a desired condition."[26] In other words, there comes a time when historians *must* make moral judgments about the topics that they study.

What I am suggesting is that, rather than conceiving some generic genocidal mind, we must recognize that, in viewing the human condition, we are studying individual men and women engaged in the business of choosing the way that they live and the things that they do. Assuming an environment that provides equality with respect to freedom of choice, we admit an individual's right to make choices and then be guided by those choices. *But if the state interferes,* that interference must be seen as a limitation on such freedom of choice, however that limitation might be justified—and it sometimes can be justified—or is unjustified. Sometimes, when examining the Nazi regime with the benefit of hindsight, we are tempted to believe that it was easy to distinguish good from evil. But when so many Christian leaders believed that National Socialism was restoring authority and morality following the drift of the Weimar years, how can we postulate that the average German perceived the Nazis with greater clarity? If a specific culture leads an individual to give up much of his or her freedom for the sake of joining a religious community, a military organization, or a rigid political party—and we must recognize that such organizations hold the promise of bringing value to their members—then the limitations on further choice so stipulated by such action must be taken into account. Nazi Germany was such a state, and its impact on those prepared to grant it fanatical allegiance was both profound and deadly. Any human being is capable of extraordinary cruelty and great compassion; indeed, the Holocaust proves that man—i.e., the human species—is capable, as Primo Levi tells us, of constructing "an infinite enormity of pain."[27] A regime that embraced the pseudo-science of eugenics, that promoted vegetarianism, and that, when it came to animals, advanced the most far-reaching anti-cruelty laws that the world has known to date, and yet earmarked a specific group of people for annihilation, bears special reflection.

It would be unjust, and thus wrong, to ignore the circumstances under which Nazi Germany's police, bureaucrats, soldiers, doctors, nurses, lawyers, businessmen, industrialists, architects, and others found themselves during the final several years of the Third Reich. We might—indeed we should—contemplate whether or not Albert Speer, who as Minister of Armaments held responsibility for the use and abuse of approximately four million forced laborers, would have been engaged in genocide had he, say in 1932, landed a principal position with the Boston architectural firm of Shepley, Bulfinch, Richardson and Abbott. This suggestion may seem absurd, but is it without logic? Yehuda Bauer, in a masterful argument against mystifying the Holocaust, warns us to remember that the perpetrators were human. Those who both ordered and carried out acts of mass murder and genocide were human beings, Bauer reminds us. "We all have within us," he states,

> instincts that under certain circumstances of birth, education, society, social history, and the like might lead us to actually understand them. German historical theorists of the nineteenth century argued that "understanding" lies beyond "explanation;" and we can "understand" only when we can place ourselves, instinctively or existentially, in the shoes, so to speak, of the historical actors. What do we mean when we say that we can place ourselves in the shoes of Heinrich Himmler? Naturally, most of us will reject such placement with disgust: we could *never* act like that. But we protest too loudly. He was human, and so are we.[28]

In the end, however, I would argue that an individual's life is by no means totally predetermined by the environment. What we find in Nazi Germany—and perhaps in any totalitarian state that bases itself on a combination of ideology and terror—is moral cynicism and a fundamental contempt for ordinary human beings. But we are still focusing our inquiry on human beings. Those of us who, as part of our professional responsibilities as historians, instruct Western Civilization since the Renaissance, generally introduce our students to Giovanni Pico della Mirandola, a fifteenth century humanist, whose *Oration on the Dignity of Man* has long been held up as a humanist manifesto. Pico's work is, thus, a primary source for understanding the Renaissance and the further evolution of modern European intellectual history. Pico argued that God has bestowed on human beings a unique distinction: the power to choose the form and value our lives will acquire. He expresses this by constructing a monologue in which God tells Adam how he differs from the other creatures in the Garden of Eden:

> The nature of all other beings is limited and constrained within the bounds of laws prescribed by Us. Thou, constrained by no limits, in accordance with thine own free will, in whose hand

> We have placed thee, shalt ordain for thyself the limits of thy nature.... [W]ith freedom of choice and with honor, as though the maker and molder of thyself, thou mayest fashion thyself in whatever shape thou shalt prefer. Thou shalt have the power to degenerate into the lower forms of life, which are brutish. Thou shalt have the power, out of thy soul's judgment, to be reborn into the higher forms, which are divine.[29]

At last year's Scholars' Conference, Michael Berenbaum spoke of the pain experienced by those who spend their lives teaching, researching, or thinking about the Holocaust. "Everyone who works with this material pays a price," Berenbaum said; "one does not touch fire without being burned."[30] The essential truth of this statement is something that I regularly underscore with my students. Good historians spend at least some of their time reliving the era of their studies—and good history requires each of us to cross time and space, thereby reenacting events as if they had not yet occurred. When it is Nazi Germany that one is reliving, the consequences can be—indeed, *should be*—troubling if not horrifying. Jacob Neusner has written that, in a way, however superficial, those of us who devote ourselves to the study of the Holocaust relive the terror-filled years in which about half of Europe's Jews were wiped out—*and we attempt to do something about it*.[31] When we consider the assertions of Berenbaum and Neusner, we should also ask ourselves—those of us who are not Jews—which side of the wire would we be standing on.

It is precisely in this context that Pico della Mirandola's description of the human condition becomes significant. For the fact remains: we, as human beings, are not *entirely* shaped by the circumstances of birth, education, society, and social history. The society that produced Albert Speer also produced Dietrich Bonhoeffer. While it brought the world Heinrich Himmler and his genocidal minions, it also produced the likes of Wilhelm Canaris, Hans Oster, Helmuth James von Moltke, Hans von Dohnanyi, Adam von Trott, Martin Niemöller and Hans and Sophie Scholl.[32] Alfons Heck, a man who has taken enormous strides to come to grips with his activities as a leader in the *Hitlerjugend*, describes in his autobiography the deportation of the Jews from his hometown of Wittlich.

> Early one morning…as I came home from serving the six o'clock mass, the remaining 80 Jews of Wittlich, all dragging heavy suitcases, were marching to the station, guarded by a single SA man…. Most townspeople did not doubt that the regime would deport them to Poland, into the enclave known as the *General Gouvernment*. Our conquest of Poland had solved the Nazis' problem of where to ship the Jews. When I told my grandmother that eventually they all would atone for their crimes by working the land for us, she shrieked in a rage, triggered by her own feelings of shame, "How would you like to work as a slave on a lousy farm in godforsaken, lice-ridden Poland, *Du dummer Idiot?*" That was our concept of the "Final Solution." Not even the most fanatic Hitler youth leader believed that the term indeed meant annihilation.[33]

Although there are those who view every German of the Nazi era as somehow programmed for genocide—in essence, eighty million "Manchurian Candidates"—the facts are not so black and white. Were this the case, there would be less need for conferences such as this, or for programs of Holocaust studies at our colleges and universities. We could simply outline those factors that generated the Holocaust and, ipso facto, contrive a neat formula for preventing genocide. The last two centuries teach us, however, that formulae and systems designed for explaining the human condition—whether designed by Hegel, Comte, Marx or, indeed, Hitler—are inevitably defective because they were conceived by human beings. Time after time it has been demonstrated that to buy into such a system is to resign our responsibility to act as human beings. At least one fundamental lesson that our students should take from their study of the Holocaust is that free will is at the core of the human condition. Every man and woman is responsible for what they say and do, because they are free to do so. Moreover, this is not a precept that originates in the writings of Pico della Mirandola. The earliest lessons found in the scriptures that Jews and Christians hold in common—and that the great majority of Germans, be they Catholic or Protestant, understood in the 1930s and 40s—relate that the moral range of a human being is far greater than that of any other living creature; being torn between good and evil, we possess the capacity to be both beasts and angels. The choice is ours, and therein is our autonomy both blessing and curse. As Isaiah Berlin expressed so eloquently, it requires "more than infatuation with a programme to overthrow some of the most deeply rooted moral and intellectual habits of human beings."[34] By examining Bonhoeffer as well as Speer, we come to realize that—again, to quote Berlin—"no perfect solution is, not merely in practice, but in principle, possible in human affairs, and any determined attempt to produce it is likely to lead to suffering, disillusionment and failure."[35]

In conclusion, I should underscore my own opinion that this paper is necessarily inadequate—necessarily because I believe the task of deciphering the genocidal mind is beyond our capacity. Johan Huizinga, among the twentieth century's leading medievalists, once wrote that for the historian the facts will always be

> a series of events that happened at a given time [and], it must be added, that could have happened differently.... The sociologist...searches for the way in which the result was already determined in the facts. The historian, on the other hand, must always maintain towards his subject an indeterminist point of view. He must constantly put himself at a point in the past at which the known factors still seem to permit different outcomes.... Only by continuously recognizing that possibilities are unlimited can the historian do justice to the fullness of life.[36]

We must evaluate those who would be killers and the steps taken toward the Holocaust with Huizinga's paradigm in mind. When we do, we are apt to settle on Immanuel Kant's persuasive observation: "Out of the crooked timber of humanity no straight thing was ever made."[37]

Endnotes

1. Yehuda Bauer, *Rethinking the Holocaust* (New Haven: Yale University Press, 2001), p. 12. Although genocide is a topic with broad application, this paper focuses narrowly on Nazi Germany.

2. Christopher R. Browning, *Ordinary Men: Reserve Police Battalion 101 and the Final Solution in Poland* (New York: HarperCollins, 1992).

3. Jan T. Gross, *Neighbors: The Destruction of the Jewish Community in Jedwabne, Poland* (Princeton: Princeton University Press, 2001).

4. Carlo D'Este, *Patton: A Genius for War* (New York: HarperCollins, 1995), pp. 755 & 762-63.

5. Quoted in Michael Ignatieff, *Isaiah Berlin: A Life* (New York: Metropolitan Books, 1998), pp. 186-187.

6. Quoted in Paul L. Rose, *Revolutionary Antisemitism in Germany from Kant to Wagner* (Princeton: Princeton University Press, 1990), p. 103.

7. Alfred D. Low, *Jews in the Eyes of the Germans* (Philadelphia: Institute for the Study of Human Issues, 1979), pp. 67-86.

8. David Vital, *A People Apart: The Jews in Europe, 1789-1939* (New York: Oxford University Press, 1999), p. 248. The qualifier "central and western Europe" is significant. For most of the nineteenth century, Jews had reason to both distrust and fear Czarist Russia; certainly, the pogroms of the 1880s and later underscored how the Czarist regime could use its power against the Jewish community. And while a policy of genocide did not originate in Russia, either under the Czars or under the Soviets, the cooperation of Ukrainians and other Eastern Europeans in Nazi genocide underscores the impact of centuries of private distrust and official condemnation of Jews in areas once under Czarist rule.

9. Quoted in *The Trial of Adolf Eichmann* (Burbank, CA: ABC News Productions and Great Projects Film Company, 1997).

10. Michael Burleigh, *Death and Deliverance: "Euthanasia" in Germany, 1900-1945* (New York: Cambridge University Press, 1994), pp. 97-98. To my knowledge, no other study so forcefully and systematically examines the Third Reich's euthanasia program.

11. Ibid., p. 111.

12. Quoted in Gitta Sereny, *Into That Darkness: An Examination of Conscience* (New York: Random House, 1974), p. 83.

13. Ibid., p. 100.

14. One should note that high levels of education should not be equated with enhanced morality. The upper reaches of the SS ranks contained numerous indi-

viduals possessing doctorates. Einsatzgruppe A was commanded by Dr. Franz Walther Stahlecker; Einsatzgruppe C, responsible for the Aktion at Babi Yar, was commanded by Emil Otto Rasch, holder of doctorates in law and political science.

15. Ohlendorf was the chief defendant in the Nuremberg Military Tribunals' Case No. 9, the so-called Einsatzgruppen Case, which opened on 15 September 1947. The judges found him guilty and sentenced him to death on 10 April 1948; he was executed on 8 June 1951. In January 1946 he appeared as a witness at the trial of the major war criminals.

16. Quoted in Nora Levin, *The Holocaust: The Destruction of European Jewry, 1933-1945* (New York: Schocken Books, 1973), pp. 242-243.

17. Alfons Heck, *A Child of Hitler: Germany in the Days when God Wore a Swastika* (Frederick, CO: Renaissance House, 1988), p. 2. The Deutsches Jungvolk was the junior branch of the Hitler Youth, open to boys aged ten through thirteen.

18. Ibid., p. 12. Heck was raised in Wittlich, a Rhineland town located in the Mosel valley, scarcely twenty-five miles east of the French border.

19. Quoted in Karl A. Schleunes, *The Twisted Road to Auschwitz: Nazi Policy toward German Jews, 1933-1939* (Urbana: University of Illinois Press, 1990), p. 48.

20. Levi, *Drowned and the Saved*, pp. 40-41. To be sure, when speaking of the Sonderkommandos, one must acknowledge that these were individuals with little or no choice. Indeed, their choice was to place their survival ahead of that of others.

21. Ibid., pp. 15-16.

22. Bauer, *Rethinking the Holocaust*, p. 3.

23. One might consider here the study of the engineer Richard H. Levy in "The Bombing of Auschwitz Revisited: A Critical Analysis," in *The Bombing of Auschwitz: Should the Allies have Attempted It?* ed. by Michael J. Neufeld and Michael Berenbaum (New York: St. Martin's Press, 2000), pp. 101-126; or the forensic evidence assembled by the pharmacist Jean-Claude Pressac and the architectural historian Robert J. van Pelt in "The Machinery of Mass Murder at Auschwitz," in *Anatomy of the Auschwitz Death Camp*, ed. by Yisrael Gutman and Michael Berenbaum (Bloomington: Indiana University Press, 1994), to demonstrate that Zyklon-B gas was, indeed, used in the Auschwitz gas chambers to kill human beings.

24. Isaiah Berlin tells us that science and history are both able to identify so-called non-moral categories of value as being "important," "trivial" or "significant." For example, the ending of the ice age was significant, and the hurricane of 1938 or the cloning of the sheep Dolly was important. Similarly, the historian might point to the storming of the Bastille or the appointment of Adolf Hitler to the German chancellorship as significant. See Berlin, "Historical Inevitability," in *The Proper Study of Mankind: An Anthology of Essays* (New York: Farrar, Straus, Giroux, 1998), pp. 168-169.

25. See Hugh R. Trevor-Roper, ed., *Hitler's Table Talk, 1941-1944* (New York: Oxford University Press, 1988), entry dated 22 February 1942.

26. Bauer, *Rethinking the Holocaust,* p. 3.

27. Levi, *Drowned and the Saved,* p. 86.

28. Bauer, *Rethinking the Holocaust,* pp. 18-19.

29. Quoted in *The Renaissance Philosophy of Man,* ed. by Ernst Cassirer, Paul Oskar Kristeller and John H. Randall, Jr. (Chicago: University of Chicago Press, 1948), pp. 224-225.

30. "Recent Attacks on Holocaust Education: Some Comments and Rejoinder," The 31st Annual Scholars' Conference on the Holocaust and the Churches, 4 March 2001.

31. Jacob Neusner, *The Way of Torah: An Introduction to Judaism,* 6th ed. (Belmont CA: Wadsworth, 1997), p. 232.

32. In identifying perpetrators and resisters, one should not lose track of the fact that bystanders—many of whom were in fact collaborators—predominated.

33. Heck, *The Burden of Hitler's Legacy,* p. 77.

34. Berlin, *The Proper Study of Mankind: An Anthology of Essays* (New York: Farrar, Straus and Giroux, 1997), p. 187.

35. Berlin, *The Crooked Timber of Humanity: Chapters in the History of Ideas* (New York: Knopf, 1991), p. 48.

36. Johan Huizinger, "Historical Conceptualization," in Fritz Stern, ed., *The Varieties of History* (New York: World Publishing, 1956), p. 292.

37. Quoted in Berlin, *Crooked Timber,* p. 48.

Chapter 3

Early Warning: Perverting the Lessons of the Holocaust—The Protocols of the World Conference Against Racism

Shimon Samuels

While the United States and the Soviet Union were competing in the race to the moon, South Africa decided to join in, but announced that they would launch their rocket to the sun.

The U.S. and the Soviet Union remonstrated, "Are you crazy? The rocket will be burnt to cinders."

South Africa responded: "We are not so stupid, we are launching our rocket at night."

* * *

Last fall, I experienced two nightmare weeks in the South African night. My thirty-year professional involvement in combating antisemitism and racism paled in the fetid air of Durban.

Some three years ago, I was elected to the Board of the European Network against Racism (ENAR) an umbrella for six hundred and sixty anti-racist movements, supported by the Moroccans of Luxemburg, Tunisians of France Iraqis of Spain (as Moslems and Jews were common targets of the extreme right). Through ENAR, I was elected to the twenty member all-powerful Stalinist-controlled International Steering Committee (ISC) of the World Conference Against Racism (WCAR). As I was also chair of the Jewish Caucus of non-governmental organizations (NGOs) in the Durban process, I attended all UN preparatory meetings in Geneva, Strasbourg, Warsaw and Santiago. In contravention of my UN status, however, I was denied a visa for the Teheran Preparatory Committee. It was there that the wheels fell off and the writing of a new Protocol of Zion began.

The two years leading up to Durban witnessed an incremental process of semantic theft. Let us play the Passover game:

- Who knows three? Three are the *Holocausts:*

    - The twin holocausts of the trans-Atlantic slave-trade and the subsequent period of slavery in the Americas characterized as extermination i.e. a campaign baseline for reparations.
    - The third holocaust visited by Israel upon the Palestinians, the "Naqba."

In Teheran, "(H)olocaust" education in the Draft Resolutions was replaced by "(h)olocaust(s)"

- Who knows two? "Anti-Semitism and the hyphen problem"— we have unhyphenated the word "Antisemitism about fifteen years since the Russian neo-Nazi "Pamyat" group redefined "Semitism" as "Arabophobia" at a Moscow trial. "Antisemitism," which was recognized by the UN in 1992, at our UNESCO Conference, as directed exclusively against Jews, was not assimilated into "Arabophobia;" the erstwhile Jewish victim is replaced by the Arab target. viz. Professor Hadi Adhem of New York, who said in Teheran that:

    The two antisemitic myths that stereotyped Jews in Europe and North America are the images of "the banker Jew" of the West and "the subversive Jew" of the East.

The Holocaust, European guilt and the Zionist lobby had, by 1948, succeeded in eradicating modern Jewish antisemitism. But antisemitism is alive and well, the hook-nosed Jew is replaced by the hook-nosed Arab, the "banker Jew" by the "oil-rich Sheikh," the "subversive Bolshevik Jew" by the "fundamentalist Arab terrorist." Thus, antisemitism becomes anti-Arabism and Zionism becomes antisemitism.

Even before the launch of the Intifada, there was a superimposition of the classical antisemitism of Western colonialists upon traditional complex stereotypes of Jews, as taught in growing numbers of Jihadist Koranic Schools. These are essentially three big lies:

- The medieval blood libel, as in Syrian Defence Minister Mustafa Tlas' 1988 book, *The Matza of Zion* (the revival of the 1848 Damascus calumny of the Jewish ritual murder and bleeding of French priest, Father Thoma);
- *The Protocols of Zion* (I sit in my hotel in Geneva transfixed each night as I watch the Stürmer-like presentation on Syrian television of Jewish control of the globe);
- *Holocaust Denial* (Norman Finkelstein and Roger Garaudy are heroes throughout the Moslem world), a phenomenon personified by Ahmed Huber (a Swiss-German convert to Islam and representative of Bin-Laden's Al Taqwa Bank in Zurich, financier of the German neo-Nazi NPD and organizer of the Beirut and then Amman symposium on Holocaust denial, together with Swiss-German revisionist Jürgen Graf, a fugitive from Swiss justice, now resident in Teheran.

Durban turned what seemed to be the marginal thinking of a few such fanatics into a mainstream campaign that exploited the means of television, Internet, universities, churches, non-governmental organizations (NGOs) and, above all, the United Nations—a campaign for the demonization of the Jewish State and the Jewish people.

Major human rights groups (Amnesty International, Save the Children, Franciscans International, etc.) expressed alarm at the inflammatory language but, when I was expelled by the ISC in the presence of the United Nations Human Rights Commissioner

(UNHRC), Mary Robinson, as a "Zionist agent," they would not speak out in solidarity with its Jewish targets.

When the daily "Voices Tribune," held under the patronage of Mary Robinson, excluded our Jewish candidate from the daily featured victims of racism, or, when the Jewish Caucus official Commission on Antisemitism was physically invaded and occupied by one hundred and fifty threatening Palestinians (who claimed to be the authentic Jews!), Human Rights Watch refused to protest, arguing that "calls for violence were justified if against apartheid or on behalf of the Intifada."

Paragraph 14 of the NGO Draft Declaration was adopted after considerable struggle, but its condemnation of anti-Semitism was removed at the demand of the representative of the World Council of Churches—at that point, the Jewish Caucus walked out.

The huge protest march against racism did not converge upon Durban Town Hall, but at the Jewish Club synagogue on Friday night, where fifteen thousand demonstrators handed out flyers of Hitler asking "what if I would have won," together with *The Protocols of Zion* and the Arab Lawyers Union's cartoon pamphlet straight out of *Der Stürmer*. Anti-Zionism ended at the gates of Durban's synagogue, and a new anti-Semitism was spawned under the cover of human rights, denying sovereignty only to the Jewish people, i.e., the right to live equally among the family of nations. The demonstrators reached a paroxysm of Orwellian absurdity as the Dalit delegation howled that the Jews were even responsible for the caste system in their native India.

Human rights thus became the new secular religion, in which:

- Israel is the anti-Christ, the poisoner of wells, an "apartheid" state (a word that greatly resonates in South Africa);
- Israel is the enemy of labour (ILO), of health (WHO), of culture (UNESCO), of women (UN Conference on Women), of children (UNICEF), the enemy of mankind (UN Human Rights Commission);
- Israel is a war criminal and author of crimes against humanity (the 4th Geneva Convention met last December, the first time

in its fifty years of existence, only to attack Israel and from which I was physically ejected while reviled as "the World Jew");
- As Israel is the source of original sin, the UN injustice of 1948 must be rolled back; and
- Israel is the enemy of G-d (the UNHRC Conference on Religious Tolerance in Madrid where, on 11 November, the Syrian Ambassador asked for the exclusion of "a certain religion of arrogance that considers itself chosen").

Despite my appeals, no NGO would agree to protest with me! The critical mass of NGO conferences pillorying Israel and the Jews is taking its toll and growing in volume.

The Durban process has a built-in ten-year implementation program. Its way stations include Durban 3, Durban 5 and Durban 10. SANGOCO (the South African NGO Coalition), which took control of the ISC in Durban, produced a document detailing this plan; it discussed a headquarters in Pretoria, regional offices in Europe, Asia, the Americas, sources of funding and a "World Movement Against Racism" under its leadership.

By Durban 3, the solidarity campaign against the "last bastion of apartheid" i.e., the State of Israel, would be in full swing. By Durban 5, the eight-point blueprint for dismantling the Jewish State will have been achieved, i.e., what I would call genocidal anti-Semitism.

- A UN educational campaign on the crimes of Israel to establish a global solidarity campaign against "the new apartheid" modelled on the 1970-1980's struggle against "old apartheid" in South Africa.
- Cases to be brought to all possible tribunals against Israeli citizens for crimes against humanity, especially the new International Criminal Court.
- The repeal of the Law of Return for Jews;
- The adoption of a Law of Return for all Palestinians; and
- The launch of a complete trade boycott (based on the Sullivan embargo on apartheid in South Africa).

This was launched in Damascus in January and we have already had to deal with such firms as Zara, Kinder, Panthene, Motorola, Fuji, Selfridges and Harrods etc.

- The imposition of a tourism, cultural, sport, military, telecommunications embargo on Israel;
- The breaking of diplomatic relations with Israel; and
- The ostracism of those states refusing to break relations.

By Durban 5, with a Palestinian state in place, the World Movement Against Racism will change its name to the World Movement for Reconciliation which, for the next five years, will focus on the United States for its crimes of hegemony and globalization and the campaign for reparations; i.e., the move from "the small devil" to "the Great Satan," from Israel to America.

The next step is the UN Human Rights Commission session this month in Geneva, from which, after fifty-three years of membership, the United States is now excluded, and which is now controlled by such human rights paragons as Syria, Sudan, Iran, Iraq and Algeria. The campaign will continue next August in Johannesburg at the UN Summit on Sustainable Development.

Israel is not above the law, but human rights standards must be applied equally, i.e., equitably before the law. At present, Israel's only right is to sit in the dock. It is the only state of one hundred ninety, which is not a full member of any UN regional group and thus cannot stand for election to any function throughout the UN system. On the other hand, Syria, Iran, Iraq, Sudan, etc. have exculpatory immunity. For example, Damascus, the slaughterer of thirty thousand of its own citizens in Hama, sits this year on the fifteen-member Security Council.

Seventy-two hours after the close of the Durban hate-fest, its violence struck at the strategic and financial centres of its main target, the United States. If Durban was "Mein-Kampf," then September 11th was "Kristallnacht"—a prelude. Simon Wiesenthal said that, in the 1920s, he "was not so much concerned by the number of

Nazis, as by the absent voices of the anti-Nazis." The hate speech of Durban set the tone for the hate crimes of New York and Washington and was challenged by too few voices of sanity.

To return to the Shoah and to contemporary antisemitism, the volume of antisemitic assaults around the world since the Intifada Middle-East related violence began in October 2000, has included over one hundred synagogue burnings, mostly in France. Extreme left organizations mark "Kristallnacht 38" with anti-Israel marches, ignoring contemporary anti-Jewish violence.

Can the commitment to the memory of the Shoah hold integrity without a commitment to living Jews? Ceremonies last October and November to honour Righteous Gentiles in Poitiers and Marseilles were marred by their municipalities' exclusion of the Israeli Ambassador. The de-Judaization of the Holocaust and of antisemitism is not an empty intellectual exercise. Its bottom line is:

- If the Holocaust was a lie, let's make it a reality; and
- To create, by attrition, a climate of tolerance for anti-Semitism.

But, since the Holocaust, antisemitism really has nowhere to hide. Tolerance of antisemitism is tolerance of genocide and it is in the world's own enlightened interest to contain it, for, remember "What starts with the Jews almost always ends as a scourge for general society." We should have learned the danger of not challenging assaultive speech as the first early warning, so elegantly formulated by Abraham Joshua Heschel: "Auschwitz was not built with bricks, it was built with words." As Holocaust scholars, I call upon your commitment as an interested party to make your voices heard against media prejudice, UN hypocrisy and, above all, the ganging up of former perpetrator and bystander nations against the survivor state of the Holocaust.

Durban was, as I began, South Africa's rocket launch at night. It was a lost opportunity to celebrate South Africa's post-apartheid achievements; it discredited the UN and hijacked the anti-racist movement from its true responsibilities: neo-Nazi skinheads, extreme right violence, racism in sport, hate on-line etc. It is *our* responsibility to fight this diplomatic intifada, rebuild alliances with loyal friends in the NGO community and set the human rights movement back on course.

One scintilla of light broke through the darkness when a South African black Moslem friend in Durban asked me a Jewish riddle: "a rabbi and his students were discussing when does night end and day begin? One student said, "when you can distinguish between a lamb and a goat." A second student suggested, "when you can distinguish between a fig-tree and an olive-tree." The rabbi responded: "No, when you see a black woman and a white woman, when you see a rich man and a poor man and you *cannot* distinguish between them, then you will *know* that day has begun."

When the UN World Conference against Racism makes that its objective, then we will know that the true battle against xenophobia and hate has been launched.

CHAPTER 4

Canada Attempts to Curb Hate Mail: The Lessons of the Zündel Case

Frederick M. Schweitzer

While The action by the Canadian Human Rights Tribunal, January 18, 2002, barring Ernst Zündel from the Internet, has the potential to be a landmark decision. The case against the neo-Nazi Zündel, a notorious antisemite and Holocaust denier, was brought initially by Sabina Citron and the Mayor of Toronto, and taken up by the Canadian Human Rights Commission with the support of other interested parties, B'nai B'rith, the Canadian Holocaust Association, the Canadian Jewish Congress, and the Simon Wiesenthal Center. Rather than a trial, there was a hearing before a tribunal of three (later two, when one academic member had to return to his university) with no jury, which ran fifty-five contentious days, spun out from 1996-2001, largely because Zündel's counsel sought to quash the proceedings by a medley of objections and motions to terminate the proceedings. In particular, he claimed the action against Zündel violated free speech and was therefore unconstitutional. Although he never spoke or took the witness stand, Zündel was invariably present at the sessions, sitting through them impassively until February 2001, when he apparently gave up and left the country. One can only surmise why Zündel is so brutish an antisemite, for it is impossible to imagine that he believes the fantasies he peddles; much more likely he relishes the notoriety, has sadistic pleasure in inflicting pain and suffering on people, and makes lots of money as an antisemitic entrepreneur and denial huckster. As a person, Zündel is repugnant and oafish; although not unintelligent he is half educated at best. He is of secular cast of mind rather than religious, certainly not Christian. Some find him to be "charismatic;" if so, none of it emerged in a court chamber.

I

Zündel was born in Germany in 1939 to a very pious mother, immigrated to Canada in 1958, where he settled in Montreal and then in the mid-1960s relocated to Toronto. He ran a successful photo retouching business for magazines, a career for which he had been trained in Germany and won awards. Zündel became a devotee of Adrien Arcand, the Canadian fascist who had spent World War II in jail; the "Canadian Hitler," the admiring Zündel said, "made a German of me" by imparting a classic education in antisemitism and Holocaust denial as well as linking him up to a worldwide network of Nazi zealots. Zündel emerged as the self-styled "führer" of Concerned Parents of German Descent and co-wrote a biography with Eric Thomson, *The Hitler We Loved and Why,* which was published in 1977 by White Supremacy Publishing in West Virginia. That book portrays Hitler as "this humble, totally dedicated savior" who had "the vision to create a happy and sound society," meaning *Judenrein;* Hitler "saved White civilization" and so this idolization of the führer closes with "WE LOVE YOU, ADOLPH [sic] HITLER."

As he made his antisemitic way, Zündel held protests and demonstrations against the TV series "Holocaust," the film *The Boys from Brazil* that depicted Joseph Mengele and featured a clone of Hitler, and the life imprisonment of Rudolf Hess. For a time this P.T. Barnum promoter took up UFO's, which he represented as Hitler's "secret weapon," saying that research has been going on since the 1930s and is still being conducted underground and, apparently, in Antarctica. His proclamation of his belief in flying saucers is on a par with his proclamation of his disbelief in the mass murders of the Holocaust; he began in an appropriate business, retouching photographs, a kind of falsification that may have opened the door to

Holocaust denial and, indeed, systematic misrepresentation.
 As early as 1981 Zündel was subjected to a mail ban that lasted for a year. He founded the "German-Jewish Historical Commission," another instance of his posturing and fakery. The same applies to his choice of name for his publishing business, Samisdat. He was behind the nasty prank of Ernst Nielsen, a Zündel surrogate and unreconstructed Nazi, who first audited and the next term registered for the Holocaust course given by Michael Marrus and Jacques Kornberg at the University of Toronto; the intention, in addition to a publicity stunt, was to disrupt the class and protest to the department chair that the course did not include "revisionist" works and was "nothing but hate literature." It ended with Nielsen's expulsion, twice, but not before Zündel's pseudonymous publications appeared.
 By the early 1980s Zündel's violent antisemitism, Holocaust denial, and Nazi activities were out in the open and attempts to prosecute him began. Sabina Citron and the Holocaust Remembrance Association took the initiative in a private case, but after some hesitation it was taken over by public authority. In 1985 Zündel was tried in criminal court for knowingly spreading "false news" that was likely to do harm to a recognizable group of people, specifically for Zündel's dissemination of that denialist chestnut, *Did Six Million Really Die?* by Richard Harwood. Always the exhibitionist, Zündel showed up wearing a bulletproof vest and other outlandish garb (at a later proceeding he sported a yarmulke). Zündel himself testified and the prosecution showed, or attempted to show, that Zündel did not believe his own antisemitic propaganda but used it maliciously to justify his Nazi ideology and rehabilitation of Hitler. His counsel, Douglas Christie, is a veteran defender of Canada's antisemites, such as James Keegstra, and an unsuccessful politician. He is coarse and brutal in cross-examination, especially of Holocaust survivors. He ludicrously garbles witnesses' names, mocks them in every way, and tries to trap them in seeming inconsistencies or falsities. He used these tricks on Raul Hilberg—who had to establish the truth of the Holocaust, since the court did not accept it as a given—with regard to casualty statistics, and Christie, in his sensationalism and

caustic provocation, may have undermined the effectiveness of the historian's testimony, as he did that of some survivors. Nevertheless, the jury found Zündel guilty of spreading "false news" and he was sentenced to fifteen months in jail.

Pending appeal, Zündel was free on bail. In 1987 the Appeals Court found that the law making "false news" punishable was constitutional but granted a retrial on grounds of irregularities by the judge. The second trial in 1988 was a reprise of the first. This time, however, no survivors testified and Christopher Browning served as the leading historical expert for the prosecution. David Irving made his debut as a denier and witness for Zündel. Again Zündel was found guilty and sentenced to nine months imprisonment. In 1990 the Appeals Court upheld the decision, the sentence, and the constitutionality of the "false news" law. In 1992, however, the Canadian Supreme Court overturned Zündel's conviction on the grounds that the "false news" law was too vague and therefore unconstitutional.

Zündel was jubilant and celebrated his victory for "free speech." No doubt, his egomania and exhibitionism were, if possible, further inflated. Reputedly Zündel the media mogul was/is the largest distributor of antisemitic and Holocaust denial propaganda in the world—books, pamphlets, newsletters, tapes, and videos, his own and those of others. One item that he underwrites is the idiotic Leuchter Report. His antics in Munich, Germany, led to his arrest in 1991 for inciting race hatred and other offences. Not surprisingly, he went on spewing out more than ever his antisemitic hatred and fabricated denial trash, such as this on Kristallnacht: The Jews did it!

> Mysterious people wearing SS uniforms suddenly appeared out of nowhere [in November 1938], set fire to the synagogues and just as suddenly and mysteriously vanished. The same tactics as the Zionists [a term he often employs to avoid the legal category of "a recognizable group"] used against Germany as partisans, maquis and as members of the Jewish Brigade: false uniforms, false documents, etc.

Mrs. Citron decided to try again.[1]

II

I was invited by counsel for the Commission to testify on antisemitism, and in the course of eight days in April 1998 spelled out a series of nine lethal stereotypes: Jews as "Christ killers" and an eternally criminal people in the service of Satan, the anti-Christ Jew, the Talmud Jew who is required as a religious obligation to inflict harm and loss on non-Jews, the exploitative Shylockian capitalist Jew and bolshevik anti-capitalist Jew, the racial menace Jew, the *Protocols-of-the-Elders* Jews who conspire to dominate the planet and destroy all other religions, and finally the liar and extortionist "Holocaust Jew," almost the invention of Zündel and a recapitulation of all the preceding ones. I helped to demonstrate, first, a correlation over two millennia between specific periods of antisemitic propaganda and violence against Jews; second, how Zündel's diatribes replicate all the classic antisemitic motifs; third, that what had caused suffering to Jews in the past was likely to do so again in Zündel's rendering.

That Zündel does in fact threaten Jews will be clear from a few examples. Zündel said in his "Power Letter" of July 1996 that "The day of reckoning is dawning. The Jewish century is drawing to a close. The Age of Truth is waiting." I commented that his perverted way of characterizing the twentieth century meant that it was dominated by the Jews in the manner of the *Protocols,* thus a reprise of classic antisemitic themes, as is the "age of truth" reference, signifying that the Jewish age was that of the lie; I said that, like so much of Zündel's verbiage, such a "vague, ominous assertion" was a repetition of antisemitic motifs that had often been translated in the past into action, "namely harm to Jews in one form or another, whether mild with restrictions like quotas or expulsion, murder, and so forth." I also referred the Tribunal to the "Power Letter" of January 1997, which states: "There is always the straw that breaks the camel's back. I predict that once again the tribe's near total victory will end in near global disaster for them. In the affairs of men, and in nature, NOTHING LASTS FOREVER." I noted that the passage is eerily similar to Hitler's predictions in a speech of January 1939, prophesying the demise of world Jewry—heads will role in the sand. In a

"Power Letter" of March 1997 Zündel wrote, "I fear for the 'Little Jew' who has no voice in this matter, but ultimately will have to suffer the fallout" (invoking the ninth *Protocol* that cites antisemitism as a device by which the Elders coerce humble Jews into obedience, and the like); in the "Power Letter" of September 1997, Zündel booms out that "the hour of reckoning has struck." Such blasts, I testified, were "ominous in the context of passages" previously cited and in the light of the nine lethal stereotypes spelled out earlier. I had presented the Tribunal an aide-memoir with two columns, one showing antisemitic theories/rhetoric and propaganda since 1100, paralleled by antisemitic outbreaks and violence. In concluding my testimony at that stage, I remarked that

> Words are not merely words. Many writers have said that words are more powerful than bombs and bullets. I see ample evidence of that¼. Since the Crusades and into the twentieth century, well before the Holocaust, Jews have suffered simply because they were Jews, placed upon the bull's-eye of fear and hatred by ideological stereotypes. Such were the harvests of hate.

I reminded the Tribunal of Rabbi Abraham Joshua Heschel's reflection that "Auschwitz was not built so much of bricks and mortar as of words and ideas."

Zündel most reveals himself, I think, in the following passage: "This is the reason why I have dedicated my life to excise the virulent lie that is killing the soul of my kin and race." Virulent is synonymous with infection, disease, and pathology, an age-old antisemitic motif, as is lying. It is the "Holocaust lie" that holds the German people prostrate in shame and payment of reparations, inflicting some form of cruel destruction upon the Germans, at the least a spiritual death upon them. Further along, Zündel writes: "In the following I shall introduce my friends to my turbulent life history. This was, and is, my life and my struggle," which I rendered in German for the Tribunal as, "Das war und ist mein Leben und mein Kampf," remarking that it is a quotation and paraphrase from *Mein Kampf,* as is the rest of the passage, "¼ for the honor and future of my poor deformed homeland Germany, bled dry by international leeches." I said that the Tribunal should understand that Herr Zündel represented himself as a second Hitler, that he aspires to be Adolf II, who would redeem Germany from the "Holocaust lie" as Adolf I putatively did from defeat in war and the Treaty of Versailles. For confirmation one need only recall Zündel's biography, *The Hitler We Loved and Why*.

On the witness stand I followed Gary Prideaux, a professor of linguistics and discourse analysis at Alberta University, who characterized Zündel's writings as "unabashedly polemical" and using rhetorical devices calculated to denigrate Jews and expose them to hatred and danger. Examples he presented include:

> The use of epithets such as the "Jewish," "Holocaust," "Zionist" or "Marxist" Lobby; the constant use of scare quotes to express doubts in regard to the "Holocaust" or "survivors;" unsubstantiated assertions of Jewish control and influence; inversion strategies where those widely understood as the victims of Nazi Germany become the aggressors, and the aggressors become the victims; ascribing, or implying, negative attributes to all Jews upon reference to a single individual who it is asserted possesses those characteristics.

In February 2001, at the time when counsel for the opposing sides presented final written submissions to the Tribunal, Zündel left Canada, which had repeatedly denied him citizenship as a security risk, for the United States, where his website has been located all along. Now married to an American citizen and thereby the holder of a Green card, he continues to disseminate hate literature on the Internet and in other media with impunity. Situated in Tennessee, he avoids a contempt citation by the Tribunal for not complying with its order to cease and desist, and also avoids likely deportation to Germany where he would be jailed. So the proceedings ended up rather as an anti-climax. Nevertheless, the Decision, a judgment formulated by a public body following judicial procedures and applying evidentiary rules, places a stigma on him as a dangerous falsifier, as it does on those "experts," also Holocaust deniers and as notorious as he, summoned to testify on his behalf, all of whom were roundly rejected by the Tribunal: Robert Countess, Robert Faurisson (who is barred from teaching in his native France), Tony Martin (a professor of Black studies at Wellesley College where he has student read Farrakhan's and the Nation of Islam's spurious treatise *The Secret Relationship of Blacks and Jews*, purporting to prove that Jews initiated the slave trade and were its principal exploiters, promoters and profiteers), and Mark Weber. Weber in particular was rejected "as a historian" but allowed to testify because of his familiarity with Holocaust denial, as well he might, since he is director of the bogus Institute of Historical Review and editor of its rag, *The Journal of Historical Review*. I have a further satisfaction in that I evaluated the credentials and "Anticipated Evidence" of Countess, Faurisson and Weber for the Commission's attorneys, helping them to tear these "experts" to shreds in cross-examination. I tracked the footnote citations of their pseudo-scholarship, and found many instances in which the "source" was either fabricated or quoted so elliptically as to distort the original meaning or assert the opposite of what the document says in the plainest language. For example, in Weber's essay "Auschwitz: Myth and Facts," the familiar denial piffle is put forward in plausible language, decked out with an apparatus of scholarship and the predictable citations of ranking Holocaust scholars. As in the usual denial charade, Weber cites primary sources to back up his claim that there were no gas installations at Auschwitz, that inmates knew nothing and could know nothing about gassings in Auschwitz, that murder by gassing was mere rumor, and so on. As evidence, Weber cites the affidavit of Sergeant Charles Joseph Coward, a British prisoner of war in Auschwitz for nearly three years, who testified in the 1947 IG Farben Case. When one reads the affidavit, however, Nuremberg document NI-11696, one will see how false and brazen the director of the Institute of Historical Review and editor of its *Journal of Historical Review* is. Paragraph 6 is worth quoting at length; it reads:

… Although I [Coward] had heard that conditions were bad, I at first did not believe it. I made it a point to get one of the guards to take me to town under the pretence of buying new razor blades and stuff for our boys. [Coward was the leader of the British POW's.] For a few cigarettes he pointed out to me the various places where they had the gas chambers and the places where they took them down to be cremated. Everyone to whom I spoke gave the same story, the people in the city of Auschwitz, the SS men, Concentration camp inmates, foreign workers, everyone said that thousands of people were being gassed and cremated at Auschwitz, and that the inmates who worked with us and who were unable to continue working because of their physical condition and were suddenly missing, had been sent to the gas chambers. The inmates who were sent to be gassed went through the procedure of preparing for a bath; they stripped their clothes off, and walked into the bathing room. Instead of showers, there was gas. All the camp knew it. All the civilian population knew it. I mixed with the civilian population at Auschwitz. I was at Auschwitz nearly every day. The population at Auschwitz was fully aware that people were being gassed and burned. On one occasion they complained about the stench of the burning bodies. Of course all of the Farben people knew what was going on. No one could live in Auschwitz and work in the plant, or even come down to the plant without knowing what was common knowledge to everybody.

Even among the Farben employees to whom I spoke, a lot of them would admit they knew about the gassing. Others who were pretty scared to say anything would admit that they heard about the gassing but then would say it was all propaganda. I am sure that Duerrfeld [the IG Farben executive] who was always walking around the factory knew about the gassings and the burnings. It would be utterly impossible not to know. Everybody knew from the civilians to the top dogs. It was common talk. Even while still at Auschwitz we got radio broadcasts from the outside speaking about the gassings and burnings at Auschwitz. I recall one of these broadcasts was by [British Foreign Secretary] Anthony Eden himself. Also, there were pamphlets dropped in Auschwitz and the surrounding territory one of which I personally read, which related what was going on in the camp at Auschwitz. These leaflets were scattered all over the countryside and must have been dropped from planes. They were in Polish and German. Under those circumstances, nobody could be at or near Auschwitz without knowing what was going on.

Clearly Weber was shown to be an obvious fraud as were others of Zündel's so-called experts and Zündel himself, although the Tribunal was too polite and formal to dismiss them as such, letting it suffice to reject them as "unqualified and unreliable."

The longest section of the Decision (total 110 pages) addresses the constitutional issue of free speech. Under the rubric of "hate messages," the Canadian Human Rights Act of 1985 specifies that

> It is a discriminatory practice for a person or a group of persons acting in concert to communicate telephonically ¼ repeatedly, ¼ any matter that is likely to expose a person or persons to hatred or contempt by reason of the fact that that person or those persons are identifiable on the basis of a prohibited ground of discrimination.

These include "race, national or ethnic origin, colour, religion, age, sex" and so on. The Tribunal had to reconcile its judgment that Zündel did so expose Jews to hatred and contempt and therefore danger, with Canada's Charter of Rights and Freedoms, by which everyone enjoys "freedom of thought, belief, opinion and expression, including freedom of the press and other media of communication," subject only to "reasonable limits prescribed by law as can be demonstrably justified in a free and democratic society." Noting that hate mail does double damage, to the "listener" and the party attacked, and that preventing "serious harms caused by hate propaganda remains a matter of pressing and substantial importance," the Tribunal justified its infringement of Zündel's freedom of expression as "minimal impairment." Canada's guarantees of freedom of speech are almost as fundamental as in our Constitution, but it is much more aware that, as the Tribunal stated, "There are indeed limits to freedom of expression…that hate propaganda presents a serious threat to society," and requires preventative action. One of the judges in the Keegstra case of 1991 spelled out an eloquent justification for Canada's efforts to curb the public expression of hatred:

> Parliament has recognized the substantial harm that can flow from hate propaganda, and in trying to prevent the pain suffered by target group members and to reduce racial, ethnic and religious tension in Canada, has decided to suppress the willful promotion of hatred against identifiable groups. Parliament's objective is supported not only by numerous study groups, but also by our collective historical knowledge of the potentially catastrophic effects of the promotion of hatred.

Unfortunately, we have no remedies such as Canada's Human Rights Law affords against a real danger. Zündel in Tennessee is now our problem and embarrassment. The 32nd Annual Scholars' Conference on the Holocaust and the Churches was dedicated to pondering and defining "The Genocidal Mind." I suggest we need go no further than Zündel for an example of the genocidal mind in full measure. He is a would-be Adolf II. So dangerous a person should be muzzled. The marketplace mechanism, which is supposed to assure a sifting out process by which truth and good ideas will endure and falsehood and bad ideas will fall by the wayside, does not work very dependably.

The lack of publicity about the tribunal's decision is surprising. To my knowledge, the only newspapers that reported the story were in Toronto. No major paper in the United States or Europe has published anything beyond, perhaps, a bare bones mention of the event. *The New York Times* did, indeed, publish a quite substantial article about the case on August 1, 1998. Yet my attempts to remind them of that in an op-ed article, an email to the managing editor, and finally "a letter to the editor," came to nothing. Ernst Zündel would have another laugh at our expense.

Endnotes

1. The sources for this paper are the transcript of the hearing before the Canadian Human Rights Tribunal and its Decision; for background on Zündel, I have consulted the following: Marilyn F. Nefsky, "Current State of Three Canadian Hate Mongers" in *From Prejudice to Destruction: Western Civilization in the Shadow of Auschwitz*, ed. G. Jan Colijn and Marcia Sachs Littell (Münster, Germany: Lit Verlag, 1995), 199-221; Jean-François Moisan, "Fighting Antisemitism in Canada's Unique Context: The Example of the League for Human Rights [of B'nai B'rith]" in *Parcours Judaïques IV*, ed. Danièle Frison (Paris: Centre de Recherches sur les Juifs dans les Pays Anglophone, 1998), 113-32; and Manuel Prutschi, "The Zündel Affair" in *Antisemitism in Canada: History and Interpretation*, ed. Alan Davies (Waterloo, Ontario, Canada: Wilfrid Laurier University Press, 1992), 249-77.

CHAPTER 5

The Nazification of the German Legal System: Some Lessons for Modern Constitutionalism

Alan S. Rosenbaum

In modern history the idea of the rule of law, especially in rights-based, constitutional democracies, is invariably challenged under two general sets of circumstances: (1) wartime, and (2) transfers of power. Both circumstances have recently encumbered American democracy.

In response to the September 11, 2001 terrorist attack against the American homeland in New York, Washington D.C. and Pennsylvania, the Bush administration initiated a global war on terrorism, beginning with an armed assault by an American and British led international coalition of forces against the perpetrators, their protectors and sponsors based in Afghanistan. In addition, given the probability of new terrorist attacks on America and on our overseas interests, the president issued a number of orders and decrees purportedly designed to strengthen our defenses and security, and to prosecute the individuals our government might apprehend who in any way are linked to terror against America.[1]

In wartime it is virtually inevitable that the government, in the interests of national defense and security and waging war effectively, will seek to curb some measure of basic rights and freedoms our citizens and institutions would otherwise enjoy. That is, safety and security outweigh in the short run expansive exercises of individual freedoms and rights. Nevertheless, a key issue for defining the conceptual limits of the rule of law will involve a shifting wartime balance between national security and civil liberties. This is necessary to protect and preserve our lives and our way of life, and to do so without destroying or making our basic freedoms, which we as citizens so cherish, a permanent casualty of war. Accordingly, the rule of law must ultimately overrule a *carte blanche* faith in a government's good intentions where law may conflict with the experiences of policy or practice. On the other hand, however, in a pragmatic insight attributed to Lincoln, the necessities of national security only on rare occasions ought to overrule the constitution on the understanding that it is not a suicide pact.

History is replete with illustrations of chronic violence and serious civil disruptions that accompany the transfer of power from one regime to succeeding ones or a successor regime's efforts to hold onto or extend its power. Even civil war (or a military coup presumably to prevent civil war or redirect the political process) and the suspension or official repudiation of the country's Basic Law have plagued some transitions of power.

Although the political outcome of the close, hotly-contested U.S. election of 2000 was finally resolved by judicial decision (Bush over Gore), it was certainly eclipsed by the events of September 11th. Yet, as prominent scholars may disagree about the manner in which the election was ultimately decided, our nation seems to have averted a very serious socio-political crisis of major constitutional proportion. Despite the arguable recourse to the courts to decide the outcome of the most basic political contest America has, namely, the selection of the President of the United States, the constitutionally-prescribed, co-equal branch of government, it seems post-election that our overall institutions of government remain intact, while the citizens of the U.S. are reassured above all else that the system generally "works" and that the transfer of political power from one government to the next was peaceful and relatively orderly, and that conduct of the affairs of state will continue. Hence, the question of the legitimacy of a Bush presidency, especially in the aftermath of September 11th, is to my knowledge no longer raised publicly or privately due perhaps to the arguable jurisdiction of the executive and judicial branches, and not to their respective institutional legitimacy.

The Nazi Party's coming to power in Germany in 1933, and its thoroughgoing grip on power thereafter, is a paradigmatic instance of the use and abuse of a country's legal system in order to further the Nazi's highly destructive ideological purpose. Indeed, the Nazi leadership seems to have believed that political legitimacy was secured once a veneer of legality was achieved. The crucial and overarching issue in the admittedly wildly disparate cases of the fate of civil liberties during the crisis concerning the war against terrorism and the American election (2000) cited above, and of the Nazi use and abuse of the German legal system, is whether the rule of law is justifiably viewed as "politics by other means?"[2]

In my paper I shall review some of the well-established conditions for the legitimacy of a genuine rule of law (arguing against the view that law is nothing but politics of a different sort); indicate some of the theoretical and practical changes in Germany's legal system that were introduced or utilized by the Nazi regime; and, seek to explain briefly how these alterations subverted to a great degree the legitimacy of Germany's rule of law, by making it a politicized instrument of totalitarian terror. Finally, my analysis ought to underscore the inherent danger to the legitimacy of a modern liberal democratic constitutional order when a certain mix of circumstances permits powerful political forces to use, abuse and generally politicize a country's legal system (such as the case of the Third Reich makes evident, and the cases of election 2000 and wartime America may avoid).

I

An Overview of Some Essentials of American Constitutionalism and the Rule of Law

By the phrase "rule of law," I mean not only the trilogy of basics—codes, courts and enforcement—but also the subordination of political governance, in both substance and process, to the basic "law of the land." This "basic law" defines the establishment, purpose and proper function of government respecting the diffusion and limits of governmental powers and the protection of the fundamental moral, political and legal rights of persons to live in peace and dignity in society.[3] American constitutionalism embodies, then, a western liberal ideal of the rule of law. Yet, constitution-framing stands today as one of America's most important exports to countries everywhere.

In this context, American Liberalism refers to a jural social institution by which individuals are best off when left free to live their own lives in pursuit of their self-chosen life plans, provided that they respect the same basic rights of others and the laws of society presumably fashioned to promote its liberal vision. No legitimate democracy today will find refuge from criticism about its legitimacy if its policies, rules or practices are arbitrary or are carried into effect by unfairly or wrongly disadvantaging some of its citizens in their relations with other citizens in terms of basic rights and duties. Moreover, it is an essential normative expectation for societies that citizens governed by the idea of the rule of law shall be made to suffer by an authorized judicial body a prescribed, proportionate penalty on conviction for a serious offense. This, then, is the ultimate purpose of our constitution.

To best fulfill this purpose, a system of checks and balances is established with each of three co-equal branches of government assigned or prescribed a determinate set of powers, roles and functions with regard to each other and the citizenry at large.[4] A further diffusion of power is cast in a federalized system of government where the rights of states are intended to offset the power of the national government. The current wave of debate among members of Congress, scholars and media about the essentials of constitutionalism have been ignited by the types of presidential orders issued to deal with the perpetrators of terrorism.

It is beyond the scope of this paper to explore fully the ultimate wisdom or even constitutionality of the various executive orders. However, it is central to its purpose to review briefly some of the essentials which make up the legitimacy of the rule of law as enshrined in American constitutionalism, and to determine in what ways the Nazi experience may help counsel against strategies which may delegitimize our rule of law, especially as our society confronts terrorism (the presidential order to set up clandestine military tribunals may be such a case). That said, the core principles and values of our legal heritage, from "due process" fairness to civilian control of and access to trials, especially in emergency or wartime (crisis) conditions, ought not to be abandoned or sacrificed if at all possible, in the interest of national security. The world will not respect our idea of the rule of law if, for example, America alone prosecutes terror suspects in secretive military trials constituted to convict and execute whomever comes before it. As Justice Robert Jackson once stated about organizing the Nuremberg war crimes (military) tribunals in the aftermath of the Second World War:

> The ultimate principle is that you must put no man on trial under the form of judicial proceedings, if you are not willing to see him freed if not proved guilty. If you are determined to execute a man in any case there is no occasion for a trial. The world yields no respect to courts that are merely organized to convict.[5]

As I will discuss, the Nazis' Peoples' Courts are a case on point. Thus, we must underscore the difference between the rule of law and the political rule of terror under the guise of law.

II

German Law under the Swastika

When the pre-Nazi Weimer Constitution (1919-1933) came to an end, it was never formally abrogated by the Nazi regime, though some valid laws were clearly superseded by Nazi legislation. Whatever provision it had giving supremacy to the Federal Constitutional Court regarding certain constitutional matters, neither the Weimar

Constitution nor the Federal bench nor judicial review had the opportunity to acquire political importance equal to the American Constitution and Supreme Court due to the short lived Republic. In any case, the Weimar Constitution had as its cardinal purpose to establish, under the rule of law, the principles of democracy, of ordered liberty, and social justice. However, the basic rights of German citizens were vulnerable to constitutional amendment.[6]

Therefore, the independence of the judiciary, never a major element in the political process of Weimar but nevertheless a necessity for a constitutional democracy, never had the time to mature. Article 48 of the Weimar Constitution gave the president (with some question about his powers generally) the right to declare valid emergency decrees in a case of a "clear and present danger" to the Reich. However, the German parliament, (Reichstag) if it had had the will, could have legally revoked such decrees. Under the threat of the dissolution of the Reichstag Hitler, once he became president, sought control of the Reich Chancellorship (the head of parliament, which he gained upon Hindenburg's death) and passage of the Enabling Act.[7] The parliament's passage of the Enabling Act (March 23, 1933) may be the dividing line between Weimar and Nazi Germany.

A major distinguishing facet of the transition from Weimar to the Nazi Third Reich was, unlike the American situation in Bush vs. Gore, that both the legislature (Reichstag) and the judiciary became instruments of Hitler and the Nazi ideology. In effect, the legally prescribed institutional separation of powers ceased to exist. Further, the emergency clause of the Weimar Constitution—a critical weakness—gave the president the virtually limitless expanded powers which a ruthless politician like Hitler could exploit to his advantage. To my mind, there is no similar clause in the American Constitution which would allow even under emergency or crisis situations, the President to dismiss Congress or replace (or pack) the Supreme Court (though as Commander in Chief, the president does have some exceptional powers). The arguments over election 2000 were largely about the limits of the constitutional powers of each branch of government with respect to the other, and not the total degradation of each. Also, the completed transition which made Hitler dictator meant that he, as Fuhrer, was the final authority on all matters of governance. No branch of the American government could legally have such power. Consequently, the Nazis destroyed any measure of constitutional public accountability; there was no independent judicial review nor legislative counterbalance to Hitler's decrees.

In any case, Hitler (and his Reich cabinet) was now authorized to rule by decree; his subsequent emergency legislation gave him dictatorial powers. In other words, the Enabling Act gave Hitler the ostensible "legal" basis for his dictatorship.[8]

"Next to the chancellor, the president was the authoritative figure in any potential state of emergency," and it has been persuasively argued that the legal basis for Nazi rule originated with Article 48 of the Weimar Constitution and its undue expansion of the exceptional powers it granted to the president.[9] Once Hitler was named both president and chancellor, the Nazi dictatorship was inevitable since he now held ultimate political power. In short, "he who holds power makes laws" *(potestas facit legem)*.

As an aside, although the U.S. Constitution (Article II, Section 2) provides for civilian control of the armed forces in the person of the president, his role as Commander in Chief may allow for an exceptional expansion of his power in times of emergency to combat threats to national security. However, there is some reasonable basis for serious criticism if the executive's orders are flagrant violations of the Constitution and/or are likely to undermine respect for the rule of law.

A brief look at some characteristic Nazi legislation, institutions, legal concepts and professional legal personnel offers a paradigm of how the rule of law can be degraded, leaving at best a veneer of legal form and process.

The prominence of Carl Schmitt, the crown jurist of the Third Reich (as the news media called him),[10] had promoted the respectability of his old "friend or foe" doctrine as he described it in his book *The Concept of the Political* (1927). The common distinction in Europe between "loyal opposition" and treason was collapsed into the distinction between unconditional loyalty to the state's leadership and interests, on one side, or treason, on the other. Accordingly, Schmitt's notorious doctrine of the "national emergency" where the state is threatened by "enemies from within" (note the use of his "friend or foe" doctrine) was adapted by the Nazis to justify whatever was needed to accomplish their aims. For instance, the emergency Enabling Act (2/28/33), formally called the Law to Remove the Danger to the People and the Reich and passed in response to the *Reichstag* fire (2/27-8/33) gave Hitler the power to rule by decree. And rule by decree he and other leading Nazis did, sorting out friend from foe as they went along and setting up a nationwide judicial apparatus that would deal with the enemies of the Reich under legal cover. (Even Schmitt himself personalized the distinction by rejecting his former Jewish friends in a spurt of antisemitism).[11]

The basic principle of Nazi rule, "Whatever benefits the People is Right," was accepted by Germany's courts even before the Nazis came to power.[12] Eventually, the German Supreme Court's recognition of the "defense of the state" doctrine as a warrant for murder would subvert the integrity of the legal system itself. Therefore, in placing the state and its defense above the law, the highest German court sent the "fatal message:" that "the most heinous crimes were not punishable if they were committed in the interest of the state, while legal actions were punishable if they ran counter to it."[13]

The "Reichstag Fire" decree (2/28/33) simply annulled most basic civil rights guaranteed under the Weimar Constitution;[14] it legalized extensive repressive measures against various republican groups which were legally represented in parliament (e.g., Article 159 of the Weimar Constitution legalized political freedom for organized labor); and it provided legal grounds for the national government to interfere with the relative sovereignty of individual German states[15] thereby destroying federalism and an important check on the executive power. All political and legal decisions are embodied in the Fuhrer as head of state.[16] This form of executive action declares what the law is and applies it, in effect, superseding the Weimar Constitution, "The law is the will of the leader in the form of law."[17]

Another of democratic society's institutions against a government's monopoly on public opinion, the free press (meaning not controlled by government), was also abolished by Hitler, who referred to it as "objective lunacy."

The emergency Enabling Act, together with the law regarding the rebuilding of the Reich (1/30/34), finally gave Hitler the supreme executive, legislative and judicial power. The Nazis had successfully abolished judicial and legislative independence. That is, the democratic principle of the separation of powers ceased to exist in Germany. Insofar as judicial independence is crucial to securing a citizen's legal entitlements against the arbitrary actions of a hostile government, this institution also gradually ceased to exist for a number of reasons. The legislature or Reichstag consisted of a popularly elected lower house and an upper house representing the states. The Nazification of Germany spelled the end of federalism because the "coordination" of the states made the Reichstag's upper house unnecessary.[18]

The Nazified Judiciary

During the 1930s, the jurists "coordinated" themselves by issuing a decree (on the authority of the infamous Nuremberg Laws about which I will enumerate in due course) calling for the removal of all judges who were either Jewish, democratist or "politically unreliable."[19] Most of those judges who remained expressed their willingness to decide cases in favor of the compelling interests of the Nazi "leadership" state. By the mid-1930's, over one third of the country's law professors had been dismissed for reasons of race or politics. By 1939, at least two thirds of the law faculty had been appointed after the Nazis came to power. (Eventually, most of their students assumed positions of judicial and legislative authority in the federal republic after the Allies' destruction of Nazi rule.)

Nuremberg Laws: The Legislative Assault

The notorious Nuremberg race laws were passed mainly for the purpose of isolating the Jewish population from the body of German citizenry. Not only had legislators presumed to define who was a Jew, they used personal identification and biracial criteria for making the discrimination. These laws were an instance of unveiled dominative power and gave putative legal standing to the spurious but pervasive notion of the biracial health of the so-called Aryan German community by arbitrarily excluding Jewish citizens from exercising any legal rights enjoyed by other, favored citizens of the Reich.[20]

Such laws as the Law for the Protection of German Blood and Honor, the defense laws, the Law for the Restoration of the Professional Civil Service (4/7/33), the Reich citizenship laws, all passed by 1935, exemplify the Nazi legislative assault on the legal and moral rights of German Jews.[21]

The liberal notion of universal equality, enshrined in the German Civil Code (Section I), means that every person is meant to receive full legal rights at birth. The Nazis transformed this abstract notion into the idea that legal rights can only be enjoyed by being politically serviceable to Nazi Germany.[22]

Accordingly, the idea against "race-mixing" between Germans and Jews, which already has a lengthy history in Europe,[23] had evolved in antisemitic circles from "Jewishness" as rooted in the religious background of a person's forebears (but had not yet been defined in biology). Nevertheless, since Nazi scientists were unable to certify a clear biological basis for the presumed differences between Jewishness and Germanness, they began to use the phrase "German or related blood."[24] A normative prohibition against "racial pollution" became an ideological first principle.

In their attack on Germany's Jews, Nazi judges facilitated the divorce process by awarding so-called Aryan spouses the legal "right to divorce their racially undesirable partners without proving guilt." By 1938, judicial decisions included the following among the grounds for divorce: adultery, refusal to procreate—"racial incompatibility, and eugenic weakness."[25] Clearly, a racist antisemitic ideology was at the heart of the Nazi vision of a hierarchy of races with the Aryan or Germanic master race on the top.[26]

In any case, the "legal" basis for the persecution of German Jewry started with the Law for the Restoration of the Professional Civil Service (April 7, 1933) and its infamous "Aryan paragraph" which required that non-Aryans like Jews and political enemies were to be "retired" from the German civil service.[27] The core of the antisemitic Nuremberg Laws were the Reich Citizenship Law (9/15/33), and with it a flood of supplementary decrees, and the Law for the Protection of German Blood Honor (9/5/35). These laws, along with Supplementary Decrees, began the process of eliminating Jews from German society and culture.[28] Eventually, under the cover of war, Nazi Germany officially initiated its exterminationist antisemitism (decided at the 1942 Wannsee Conference). Hitler's Night and Fog Decree (December 7, 1941) ordered the death penalty for any person who endangered the security or preparedness of the Nazi-sympathetic regimes in the occupied territories. In addition, the accused would often in fact disappear and their fate would remain unpublicized.[29]

The waves of legal measures (i.e., supplementary decrees) deliberately kept the average German citizen disoriented in terms of what clearly was expected of him, while unpublicized ordinances such as the "delivery of jewels and precious metals taken from Jewish property"[30] also confused them. The fact that these were kept secret provided some cover both from public scrutiny and possible criticism.

Immediately following *Kristallnacht* (November 8-9, 1938), the last nationwide "pogrom" against the Jews, Jewish institutions and places of worship in Germany,[31] anti-Jewish legislation stripped Jews in Nazi Germany of any livelihood, banning them from all professions like medicine and dentistry, and eliminating all titles such as "doctor." Other political, religious or racial minorities soon suffered a similar destiny. But the Nazis' main target was Jews and Judaism, and they used the law (and terror, side by side) to "Aryanize" businesses, confiscate property, impose compulsory levies and fines such as charging the victimized Jews for Nazi-executed burning of synagogues, and to force Jews to wear identification badges in the form of a yellow Star of David.

Until the final phase of unjust discrimination and persecution of Jews in Nazi Germany, the various antisemitic measures and actions assumed a veneer of legality—even prompting German jurists to comment upon them in professional conferences and publications.

The cleansed (i.e., Nazified) judiciary was "educated" to ignore the original legislative intent of the received, i.e., pre-Nazi Reichstag's, enactments and to arbitrarily interpret (or analogize from the) older Weimar and pre-Weimar legal rules (from the Civil Code of 1900, the Penal Code of 1871, and the established Laws of Procedure, etc.) which constitutes the German Basic Law. Traditional legal method was sidestepped by ideologically-guided judges who utilized such slogans as "the will of the Fuhrer," "the needs of the Volk community" and "loyalty and faith" in supposedly "finding" the law.[32] These slogans were hallmarks of the set of ideological principles which were laid down (January 14, 1936) by the head of German jurists, Hans Frank, to govern judicial decision-making and therewith to remove a formerly independent judiciary's function of judicial review. For instance, the Nazis retained the normative core of the Civil Code, but recommended "entry points" for their ideology: the point of departure for all legal interpretation (civil, criminal and constitutional) is the state as a means to preserve the "national community." The doctrine of individualism is to be cast aside,[33] for no longer would there be a distinction between public and private law, with liberty—securing guarantees for individuals. Instead, the ideological principle of "duties to the state" is central to any legal consideration.

The Reich Ministry of Justice, the prosecution staff at the national level, and special military and civilian courts were set up both within Germany and in its occupied countries and territories in order to fulfill Nazi goals.[34] Of worthy note were the Special Panel of the Supreme Court and the notorious People's Court, created in 1933 and 1934, respectively. Their task: to obliterate the enemies of the Reich under the guise of judicial process and to intimidate the general public.

The most well-known proceeding of the latter court was the trial of the conspirators involved in the failed attempt to assassinate Hitler in 1944. Their speedy conviction was a foregone conclusion. (And, of course, this is the fear many Americans have if terrorists are to be tried by clandestine military tribunals without benefit of the rules of the U.C.M.J. or civilian legal safeguards of "due process"). They were executed within hours after the verdict, the appeals process for "disloyal" defendants long having been curtailed. Guilt by association, another American constitutional prohibition, resulted in the arrests and placement in concentration camps of hundreds of friends and relatives of the so-called co-conspirators.[35]

The jurisdiction of the People's Court had gradually expanded from cases involving treason and attacks on the property of the Nazi leadership (which had come heretofore before the Supreme Court) to those involving any subversion of the "will of the Fuhrer."[36]

A lesser-known case concerned Hans and Sophie Scholl, leading members of the small and heroic White Rose Resistance group. They were prosecuted and executed on order of the People's Court for the capital crime of distributing anti-Nazi pamphlets at a university,[37] as was their mentor, a philosophy professor (Kurt Huber).[38] The prominent Germany military man Field Marshall Erwin Rommel (of the Africa Korps) was to be charged with treason and prosecuted before the People's Court. He chose instead to die by his own hand.[39]

In substance, process and consequence, the impact of the Nazi "judicial" process could not support respect for the rule of law but rather quickened fear of running afoul of the certified ideology and authority. In addition, it deprived Jews and other unfortunate people of all rights (and protections) of citizenship and personhood. The People's Court was a legal tool of Nazi terror because it degraded any claim to judicial impartiality and fairness; it placed on trial and executed almost immediately over five thousand people whom it judged (seemingly beforehand) to be enemies of the Nazi state. Its proceedings were customarily held *in camera* (like England's Star Chamber, also unaccountable), and no appeal of its sentences was permitted.[40] Defense lawyers were typically also committed Nazis. For example, as already noted, the People's Court was used to try and to convict some two hundred people implicated in a plot to assassinate Hitler. Most were executed within hours of being sentenced. These special courts, apparently consistent with legal proceedings in other German courts,

> were not subject to the usual rules. And, under the doctrines of "analogy" and the "sound of feelings of the people," it was not necessary for a conviction that a person even have violated an existing law.[41]

Alternative penalties were allowed.

Eventually, many of Germany's chief justices, prosecutors, and some leading officials of the Justice Ministry under Nazi rule were put on trial in the subsequent Nuremberg Proceedings (Case No. 3, The Justice Cases).[42] They were charged with war crimes, crimes against humanity, and membership in a criminal organization (the SS).

Some Legal Innovations under Nazi Law

Among some of its legal innovations we must include the Nazis distorted use of legal analogy against defendants. The accepted use of legal analogy, governed by the principle that "like cases should be treated alike," is to compare two distinct cases in terms of their relevant similarities (I assume that an analogy is a comparison between two objects or sets of objects that are similar in some respects, dissimilar in others). Thus, Nazi judges used "analogy" to lump together cases not covered by the plain-text meaning of the term where the dissimilarities between the cases outweighed the relevant similarities—i.e., judicial decisions were supported by an interpretation inimical to the given law that presumably was too narrow to include the cases. For example penalties were imposed by analogy (the range and severity never prescribed beforehand). In addition, the teleological method of interpretation facilitated the judicial misuse of analogy by categorizing cases in terms of an interpretation of the ideological[43] aims of the Nazi Reich often in violation of the law.[44] Judges were exhorted to "approach a case with 'healthy prejudice' and 'make value judgments which correspond to the National Socialist legal order and the will of the political leadership.'"[45]

Police agencies also eroded the autonomy and jurisdiction of traditional courts with intensive use of preventive detention, a form of punishment that may be justified, if ever, only under conditions of strict emergency, which was certainly not the case in Nazi Germany. The Nazis made abundant use of retroactive punishment for behavior that was not legally prohibited at the time it was done. Again, the right of appeal of defendants who were presumed by authorities to be "disloyal" was curtailed; some decisions "could be appealed if lodged on behalf on the Fuhrer." These appeals often resulted in the setting aside by a special appeals court (usually the Supreme Court) of a "legal verdict" by grant of a "plea of nullity" and the returning of the case to a lower court for reconsideration along lines of the requirements of a National Socialist order.[46]

In other words, the source of law was no longer "law" in the traditional usage (including statutes, precedents and sound moral and legal principles). The notorious comment made by Joseph Goebbels (the Nazi propaganda minister) about what Nazism must do may be cited: It must "erase the year 1789 from German history…repudiating basic human rights, individual rights, vis-à-vis the state…restraints on the state's right to impose punishment" and increasing the powers of the state.[47]

The German legal system under Nazism destroyed the vestiges of a just rule of law, in spite of the fact that, as has been generally observed, Germany's commercial, civil and criminal codes usually remained separate from Nazi statutes. Nevertheless the courts were inclined to integrate in practice Nazi legislation with the extant codes.

III

A Philosophical Reflection on Nazi Justice and Modern Constitutionalism

The ensuing comments about Lon Fuller, a prominent Harvard Law professor and "natural law" theorist in the 1940's, are intended to present a persuasive critique of the abuse of law that occurred in Nazi Germany, and to support the idea of the "rule of law" as envisioned by American constitutionalism.

For Fuller, at issue is the matter of the proper conceptual relationship between a system of laws and moral principles. The Nazis' perversions of law, both in promulgation and administration, pressed the issue about whether unjust or flagrantly evil "law" is truly valid (i.e., binding) law. He argues that the Nazification of Germany's legal system ultimately invalidated its institutions and rules.[48]

The resolution of this issue in Fuller's case depends upon how the role of morality is cast in the formation and enforcement of law. The acquiescence of most of Germany's legal profession (like its medical establishment) under Nazi rule was a disgrace, because they used a "legal" cover to justify their tyranny and repression. In my opinion, this approach to law vitiates respect for the law in general, if not for the body of law itself. In brief, the legitimating "being obligated to obey the law" dissipates and "being obliged" to comply becomes the delegitimizing, sole motive for obeying the law, as the legal scholar H.L.A. Hart observes (in his critique of John Austin's Jurisprudence).

Fuller cites the case of a German legal theorist (Gustav Radbruch) who rejected his own earlier, prewar positivism because he blamed Nazi legislation as being the outcome of lawmaking in the absence of respect for basic moral principles (again, the separation of law and morality). In an article cited by Fuller, Radbruch mentioned how, by a secret enactment, the Nazis claimed to legalize the extermination activities carried on in their concentration camps.[49] Fuller, like Radbruch, came to question whether law that was unpublicized (i.e., secret) or deeply offensive could be called "law." Radbruch is said to have declared that even "legality" itself must respect the "principles of humanitarian morality."[50] In Fuller's view, there are definite "implicit laws of lawmaking" or "canons of internal morality" connected with lawmaking that the Nazis disregarded, to the discredit of the "legal" quality of Nazi legislation and judicial decisions. These constraining moral conditions of lawmaking are nowhere in evidence, Fuller testifies, in the case of special Nazi criminal, military and People's courts. Defendants, accused of treason, were brought before these courts and were typically convicted by accusation alone with minimal or no show of judicial process, sometimes even in violation of the Nazis' own self-proclaimed procedures. Accordingly, it was futile for citizens to examine Nazi law to discern the nature of their legal obligations, since some apparent laws contradicted others. Also, as some laws were unpublicized or "secret," citizens could not always know what behavior was permissible or prohibited.

Another egregious illustration of the Nazi abuse of lawmaking power concerns, as I have noted, the unjust retroactivity of certain laws. For example, Ernst Rohm and about seventy other members of the SA were summarily murdered in Munich in 1934 by Hitler's forces. Hitler, as Fuhrer, arrogated to himself the highest lawmaking authority in the Third Reich and in this self-appointed capacity decreed that retrospectively these murders—carried out without judicial process—were transformed into legalized executions. Fuller denounces such retroactive legislation as an offense to both justice and to the "implicit demands of legal decency."[51] In fact, Fuller identifies at least eight conditions (or standards) for lawmaking that respect decency, security and justice in ways that allow citizens to fashion their own lawful conduct, unlike the Nazis, who abused the law by terrorizing citizens into impotence or fearful submission. These conditions include the necessity for government to publicize law; to make laws clear and understandable; to make laws general (and to avoid decision-making on an ad hoc basis; to make laws prospective (not retroactive); to make laws requiring behavior within the control of the citizens affected; and so on.[52]

Morality and Nazi Law

My own appraisal of this still interesting dispute, briefly stated, is that neither Radbruch, Hart nor Fuller is entirely correct in his understanding of Nazi "morality" but that each has, in his own respective position, captured some limited "truth." Radbruch is correct for blaming the Nazis for flagrantly disregarding morality in their administrative, legislative and judicial activities. The complicity of the legal profession (with minimal or no protest) in the unparalleled evil of the Holocaust provides ample testimony for Radbruch's concern about how legal positivism (and its leading doctrine of the separation between law and morality) may have encouraged Nazi lawmaking. But of course, other factors also were most important.[53]

Hart is also correct, in my opinion, when he observes that law, like morality, is very complex and diverse, so that no exhaustive set of a community's (moral) values can be consistently and cohesively absorbed or respected by a single legal system, nor should it be, since law would then lose its authority and integrity if any or all moral standards (some of which surely conflict) were to be applied directly in fixing the legal character of any practice, rule or principle.

And Fuller, too, is correct in a sense when he ascribes a certain inherent moral quality to a society's institution of law, because if a people could not square its profoundest moral sentiments and values with a society's legal system, the obligatoriness of law would dissipate or lose its essential hold on right-thinking citizens or else dissolve into impotent submission from mere fear of punishment for illegal conduct. (Even most thieves would probably not contest the wrongness of their actions, while expressing the need for rationalizing them, and yet they would opt for the illegal actions anyway for some expected gain they may value.)

In light of this discussion, my own view is that a primary problem with characterizing Nazi rule is not that it was bereft of all moral values (though many individuals in the Third Reich surely were). Instead, the Nazi propagandists were careful to denounce or reject certain moral values and to dramatize and underscore their preference for other "moral" values.[54] For example, Nazi philosopher Walther Darre is reported to have reformulated Kant's famous ethical Categorical Imperative as follows: "As a German, always act so that your German co-nationals could make you their paragon."[55] Kant's original articulation of this principle was intended to apply universally with respect to all rational (not merely German) beings. It states: "Act only on that maxim through which you can at the same time will that it should become a universal law."[56]

What counts here is what meaning its interpreters pack into the term "German." For Kant, moral goodness accrues to actions that respect the Categorical Imperative.

For the Nazi ideologues, goodness belongs to the racial blood of the Germanic stock. The "prophet laureate" of Nazism, A. Rosenberg (who was convicted at Nuremberg and hanged for his crimes against humanity), published a book called *The Myth of the Twentieth Century*. It was "one of the two great unread bestsellers of the Third Reich."[57] Rosenberg's writing stressed the "conflict of values" necessitated by his "racial interpretation of history."[58] In other words, there is a special "ethical" mission inherent in and known intuitively by true Germans, and much of it concerns removing the virulent threat to Germans' putative biracial superiority posed by the existence of world Jewry. In a word, it is not that the Nazis considered themselves "beyond good and evil" (to use Nietzsche's phrase), but rather they sought to define morality in terms of their own exclusivist concept of themselves. Secondly, it is how their self-selected morality or values would impact all other institutional practices that gave Nazism its immoral cast from the perspective of universal moral values and the intrinsic worth and dignity of all human persons. In this sense, I believe Fuller's view is closest to my own. However, it makes sense to raise the issue whether the Nazi "ethic" is truly a moral point of view or simply a moral pretense for brute domination (a view I think is close to the truth), an idea at least as old as the discredited argument of Thrasymachus, immortalized by Plato in the *Republic*. It holds that "might makes right," or that justice (or goodness, rightness) is whatever is in the interest of the stronger (or presumably superior) party.[59]

An Overview of Law under Nazi Rule: Two Perspectives

I return to a question raised earlier about a possible misconstrual of law under Nazism based strictly on American (i.e., non-German) legal and moral standards—the notion that "only Germans can fairly judge Germans." In my opinion, although it is true that certain important differences exist(ed) between pre-Hitlerite Nazi Germany and America (e.g., the principle of the binding value of precedents or stare decisis, the nature of "jury" trials, and so forth), these cannot excuse the kinds of irrational discriminatory, racist and unfair laws, courts, judicial proceedings, interpretations and findings, and ultimate Nazi "values" that the German legal system only too readily embraced. Furthermore, it was the Nazi government itself, along with the still unbelievable sympathy and support it continued to receive from the German people generally, that spearheaded the effective nazification of the legal order. By placing itself (and its proponents) above "the law," its leaders and functionaries would not be held legally accountable by its own institutions for their atrocities. In mobilizing the German people for the purpose of fulfilling the aims of Nazism, Nazi totalitarianism forged a society that was determined to reject the rational, universalistic, and human values that some from German history itself had made the centerpiece of the European Enlightenment (e.g., as in Kantian ethical philosophy). In their place, arbitrary vicious discriminations based on race, religion, ethnicity, national origin, and sexual preference were given legal standing; the end result often being individual murders, organized extermination of an unwanted or "undesirable" people, and the overall corruption of civilization's stabilizing institutions. In this regard, the undeniable complicity of the German legal profession in furthering Nazism stands as a monument to the institutional subversion that an intolerant militaristic rights-denying, irrational society made possible. Moreover, there are no accessible rational and empirical grounds that would qualify those of so-called Germanic "stock," "character" or "mind-set" to be the sole authoritative interpreters of German history, institutions, policies, and behaviors. Indeed, Kant's ethical philosophy, the centerpiece of the European Enlightenment, stands as an enduring internal monument against such insidious thinking.

The supreme "rule of law" morally upholds the American democratic liberal tradition of constitutionalism by mandating that citizens will be ideally (or reasonably) secure in the possession and enjoyment of their basic rights and will be protected from civil and criminal wrongs committed against them or their society. In principle, it mandates that the wrongdoer will be legally brought to account and compelled to make satisfaction in one or another way as prescribed by law either to the victim or to the public whose community is harmed by the prohibited behavior. In the protection of these basic rights generally, it also mandates that certain procedures must be observed in order to prevent unjust infringements on the possessor's substantive rights in the administration or enforcement of the law. Granted, there are many different sorts of rights, principles and values that engage a system of law in a variety of ways. But, as Fuller explains, it is much too simplistic to conclude, then, that in general, law remains law as in the case of Nazi law, regardless of its link to immorality, injustice, indecency or evil.

Given the rights, principles and values which are the foundations of modern constitutionalism, it should be axiomatic that they provide our citizens' chief[60] defense against the misuse of law and the slide towards tyrannical rule. For this reason, public scrutiny of governmental policies and rules, even during times of national emergency or crisis, is an essential condition for respecting the rule of law in the long run. For concessions to questionable exercises of government power, without explicit "due process" and sunset provisions, for example, in times of war, will likely lead to the very excesses of government and the abridgement of basic freedoms and rights which modern constitutionalism abhors.

Endnotes

1. *Origins of the Bill of Rights* (New Haven: Yale University Press, 1999); pp. 8, 16.

2. For specifics, see *The NewYork Times* (12/2/01), p. 14.

3. These are the words of C. von Clausewitz said in connection with his view of war in Ian Clark, *Waging War* (Oxford: Clarendon Press, 1990), p. 55.

4. Burns Weston, Richard Falk and Anthony D'Amato, *International Law and World Order* (St. Paul: West, 1980), p. 189; also, Louis Henkin, *The Rights of Man Today* (Boulder: Westview Press, 1978), p. 32.

5. See Morton White, Philosophy, "The Federalist," and the Constitution (New York: Oxford University Press, 1987), pp. 159-166.

6. Cited by Whitney R. Harris, "Justice Jackson at Nuremberg," *International Lawyer*, Vol. 20, No. 3 (Summer, 1986), p. 869.

7. See Louis Henkin and Albert Rosenthal, eds. *Constitutionalism and Rights* (New York: Columbia University Press, 1990), pp. 210-211.

8. Hans Mommsen, *The Rise and Fall of Weimar Democracy* (Chapel Hill: The University of North Carolina Press, 1996), pp. 397, 460.

9. Karl A. Schleunes, ed. *Legislating the Holocaust* (Boulder: Westview Press, 2001), p. 105 n 20.

10. Mommsen, p. 57; also, Carl Schmitt, *The Crisis of Parliamentary Democracy* (Cambridge: The M.I.T. Press, 1985), p. XXIX.

11. Mark Lilla, *The Reckless Mind* (New York: New York Review Books, 2001), pp. 50-1.

12. See Joseph W. Bendersky, *Carl Schmitt* (Princeton: Princeton University Press, 1983), pp. 227-229.

13. Ingo Muller, *Hitler's Justice: The Courts of the Third Reich* (Cambridge: Harvard University Press, 1991), pp. 10-11, 22, 24.

14. Muller, pp. 23-24.

15. Michael Stolleis, *The Law Under the Swastika* (Chicago: The University of Chicago Press, 1998), p. 12.

16. Mommsen, p. 542.

17. Also, it is called the Fuhrerprinzip, in Mommsen. p. 323.

18. Franz Neumann, *The Rule of Law*, (Dover: Berg, 1986), p. 289.

19. Stolleis, p. 1.

20. Muller, pp. 39.

21. David W. Zisenwine, ed. *Anti-Semitism in Europe* (New York: Behrman House, 1976), pp. 31-34.

22. Muller, pp. 29, 60, 72, 74, 97.

23. Neumann, p. 298.

24. David I. Kertzer, *The Popes Against the Jews* (New York: Alfred A. Knopf, 2001), pp. 9-10.

25. Schleunes, pp. 16-21; also see George L. Mosse, *Toward the Final Solution* (Madison: The University of Wisconsin Press, 1985), p. 208.

26. Claudia Koonz, *Mothers in the Fatherland* (New York: St. Martin's Press, 1987), p. 192.

27. Yehuda Bauer, *Rethinking the Holocaust* (New Haven: Yale University Press,

2001), pp. 44-5, 53.

28. Schleunes, pp. 52, 154.

29. For an English translation of these laws, see Schleunes, pp. 154-180.

30. Whitney R. Harris, *Tyranny on Trial* (Dallas: Southern Methodist University, 1970), pp. 221-224.

31. Schleunes, pp. 66-72.

32. Raul Hilberg, *The Destruction of the European Jews* (New York: Harper Torchbooks, 1961), pp. 20-29.

33. Stollis, p. 15.

34. Stollis, p. 14, 76.

35. Muller, p. 154.

36. Muller, p. 148.

37. Muller, pp. x, 224.

38. Peter Hoffman, *German Resistance to Hitler* (Cambridge: Harvard University Press, 1988), pp. 109-110.

39. William L. Shirer, *The Rise and Fall of the Third Reich* (New York: Simon & Schuster, 1960, p. 1023.

40. Shirer, pp. 1077-1078.

41. Shirer, pp. 269; also, Hoffman, p. 125.

42. John A. Appleman, *Military Tribunals and International Crimes* (Westport: Greenwood Press, 1971), p. 158.

43. Appleman, pp. 158-162.

44. The term here means "…the values that form the basis of political action" and legal argumentation. Stolleis, p. 211 n 2.

45. Muller, pp. 74, 238.

46. Muller, p. 73.

47. Muller, pp. 41, 129-130.

48. Muller, p. 70.

49. Lon L. Fuller, "Positivism and Fidelity to Law: A Reply to Professor Hart," in J. Feinberg and H. Gross, eds. *Philosophy of Law* 3rd ed. (Belmont: Wadsworth Publishing Co., 1986), pp. 98-102.

50. Feinberg and Gross, p. 98.

51. H.L.A. Hart, "Positivism and the Separation of Law and Morals," in R.M. Dworkin, ed. *The Philosophy of Law* (Oxford: Oxford University Press, 1979), p. 31.

52. Kenneth I. Winston, *The Principles of Social Order: Selected Essays of Lon Fuller* (Durham: Duke University Press, 1981), pp. 159-167.

53. From Lon Fuller's *The Morality of Law* (1964), quoted in John Arthur and William H. Shaw, eds. *Readings in The Philosophy of Law* (Englewood Cliffs: Prentice-Hall, 1984), pp. 54-55.

54. Muller, p. 296.

55. Muller, p. 10.

56. Aural Kolnai, *The War Against the West* (New York: Viking Press, 1938), p. 279.

57. Quoted in H.J. Paton, *The Moral Law* (London: Hutchinson, 1981), p. 29.

58. Robert E. Conot, *Justice at Nuremberg* (New York: Harper & Row, 1983), p. 216.

59. Peter Viereck, *Meta-Politics: The Roots of the Nazi Mind* (New York: Capricorn Books, 1961), pp. 232-235.

60. *The Republic of Plato* trans. F.M. Cornford (New York: Oxford University Press, 1964), p. 18.

CHAPTER 6

The Complicity of Modern Philosophy in the Extermination of the Jews

David Patterson

When struggling to identify the elements of Western civilization and German culture that contributed to the Holocaust, often the last place we look is the philosophical tradition of the Enlightenment. After all, from the Enlightenment we have the principles of democratic government, civil rights, scientific inquiry, organized education, technological advancement, and so on. How could such a movement have anything at all to do with the Holocaust? And yet it is well known that the slaughter of European Jewry was planned and implemented by highly educated people who were thoroughly versed in the art, literature, and philosophy of the German Enlightenment. Indeed, with the same clarity of vision that led him to declare that those who burn books will end by burning people, in 1834 Heinrich Heine wrote:

> The German revolution will not be milder and gentler because it was preceded by Kant's *Critique*, by Fichte's transcendental idealism, and even by the philosophy of nature. These doctrines have developed revolutionary forces that wait only for the day when they can erupt and fill the world with terror and admiration. There will be Kantians forthcoming who will hear nothing of piety in the visible world, and with sword and axe will mercilessly churn the soil of our European life, to exterminate the very last roots of the past. Armed Fichteans will enter the

lists, whose fanaticism of will can be curbed neither by fear nor by self-interest.... But the most terrible of all would be natural philosophers..., [who] can call up the demoniac energies of ancient Germanic pantheism.... A play will be performed in Germany that will make the French Revolution seem like a harmless idyll in comparison.[1]

It turns out that, *in part,* the Holocaust happened not due to any breaking away from "these doctrines," as Heine calls them, but precisely because its chief instigators were so thoroughly versed in the German intellectual and cultural history as that history emerges from the German Enlightenment.

Emphasizing the self's autonomy, authenticity, and resolve, the thinking that arose in the German Enlightenment and contributed to the Holocaust follows a clear line of development from Kant to Heidegger. If the Cartesian *cogito* situates being within the thinking ego (I think, *therefore* I am), the Kantian critique deduces everything from the thinking ego and thus, as Franz Rosenzwieg astutely points out, "'reduces the world' to the perceiving self."[2] Far from glorifying the human being, however, the reduction of the world to the perceiving self is radically dehumanizing. "Corresponding to the Copernican turn of Copernicus which made man a speck of dust in the whole," says Rosenzweig,

> is the Copernican turn of Kant, which, by way of compensation, placed him upon the throne of the world, much more precisely than Kant thought. To that monstrous degradation of man, costing him his humanity, this correction without measure was, likewise, at the cost of his humanity.[3]

Refashioning himself after his own image, the human being loses his human image and ends by dehumanizing the *other* human being.

With the advent of this thinking, all values, moral and otherwise, are viewed as a product of either natural accident[4] or human will, and nothing outside the self has any inherent or absolute value. Recognizing here the basic ingredients of what is now termed "post-modernism," one soon realizes that the "post-modern period" does not arise in the "post-Holocaust period;" rather, it begins with a mode of thinking that contributed to the Holocaust. With the emergence of Martin Heidegger—who is more concerned with authenticity, mortality, and freedom than with responsibility, morality, or justice—thinking is already post-modern because the holy has already been thought out of the picture. And with Heidegger's entry into the Nazi Party, post-modernism and Nazism become bedfellows. The point is not that either German idealism or post-modernism is the same as Nazism, but rather that Nazism is an offshoot of both.

It is no accident that many of the post-modern thinkers have responded to the scandal of Heidegger by fervently defending the Nazi philosopher. In *De l'esprit*, for example, Jacques Derrida suggests that Heidegger's turning to Nazism in the early 1930s was a sign of his involvement not with that incarnation of evil but with metaphysics; once Heidegger renounced metaphysics, argues Derrida, he renounced Nazism and moved beyond philosophy.[5] Although Heidegger never uttered a word of regret or retraction, Derrida views his silence as a form of renunciation and repentance; thus the philosopher's saying nothing gets deconstructed into confession and expiation. Derrida adds his own silence to the silence of Heidegger, however, for he never mentions Heidegger's comment on "the inner truth and greatness" of Nazism, which appears at the end of the 1953 edition of the *Introduction to Metaphysics*.[6]

What Heidegger refers to as "the inner truth and greatness" of Nazism is an outlook traceable to Kant's notion of the autonomous will, culminating in Nietzsche's insistence on the will to power, and exemplified in Heidegger's emphasis on resolve as the mark of human authenticity. "Dasein is its own self," he maintains, "in the original isolation of silent resolve."[7] Here, as Hans Jonas points out,

> Decision in itself is the greatest virtue…[Heidegger] identified the decisiveness (of the Führer and the Party) with the principle of decisiveness and resoluteness as such. When I realized, appalled, this was not only Heidegger's personal error but also

somehow set up in his thinking, the questionability of existentialism as such became apparent to me.[8]

Of course, a key category in existentialism is freedom, where freedom lies in doing anything one can find the resolve to do within the contexts of a self-legislating autonomy—and not in response to a divinely given Law, as Jewish teaching maintains. The thinking that began with Kantian Idealism and culminated in Heideggerian post-modernism *has to seek* the elimination of heteronomous Jewish thought, inasmuch as such thought embraces the absolute authority of the Holy One, who is known only through His uncompromising commandment. That embrace is what Heidegger complained of when he complained about the "Jewification" of the German mind.[9] And so the philosopher joined the Party that would see to a final solution to the Jewification problem.

Philosophical Aspects of the Nazis' Assault on the Jews

The Nazis' annihilation of the Judaism that defines the Jews is not so much about Judaism's understanding of G-d as it is about G-d's understanding of the human being as one who is forever implicated in his relation to his neighbor. From the standpoint of Judaism, the human being is an insertion of something greater than the all into the midst of the all. Created in the image and likeness of the Holy One, the human being harbors the presence of what sanctifies all of being from beyond being. In a word, the human being is a breach of being. The demand placed upon me, therefore, arises not from the dictates of reason or from the will to power but from the cry of my neighbor, through whom I receive the commandment of G-d. And *every* human being is my neighbor—indeed, is my relative, descended as we are from a single human being. There are no races, and we are all "blood."

If such a view characterizes Jewish thinking about G-d and humanity, then "the adjective Jewish," as Henri Crétella correctly states it, does not designate an ethnic group. On the contrary, it signifies that there is no true humanity without being related to divinity—as the Jews have shown us. In other words, it is not blood and soil which properly define us, but rather the possibility of emancipating ourselves from this very blood and soil.[10]

Opposite the Jewish outlook we have this assertion from the notorious Nazi philosopher Alfred Rosenberg:

> This heroic attitude [of National Socialism], to begin with, departs from the *single* but *completely* decisive avowal, *namely from the avowal that blood and character, race and soul are merely different designations for the same entity.*[11]

Therefore Nazi philosopher Max Wundt is quite right when he asserts that the Jewish view of world and humanity "stands opposed to the folkish world view as its total antithesis."[12] If the Nazis are to be Nazis, then they *have to* eliminate the notion of a higher, divine image within the human being that places upon each of us an infinite responsibility for the *other* human being. And to do that they have to eliminate the people whose presence in the world signifies such a teaching.

Emil Fackenheim observes that, once they took the word of the Führer to be law, the Nazis made the rejection of the divine image a matter of law. "The law itself," he writes,

> came closest to the self-fulfilling prophecy aimed at in the murder camp. The murder camp was not an accidental by-product of the Nazi empire. It was its pure essence. The divine image in man *can* be destroyed. No more threatening proof to this effect can be found than the so-called *Muselmann* in the Nazi death camp…. The *Muselmaenner* are a new way of human being in history, the living dead.[13]

The *Muselmann* is the incarnation of the human being who has no trace of a divine image, of the human being as the one who is simply and indifferently there—of the human being as *Dasein*. This assault on the divine image of the human being was conceived by philosophers and carried out by the SS. First conceptual and then actual, it is an assault on divinity, humanity, and the people chosen to attest to the divine chosenness of every human being.

Here we have a defining feature of what we have termed the "philosophical aspects of the Nazis' assault on the Jews"—at least as it is understood from the standpoint of the Jews. Rashi, for example, maintains that "whoever attacks Israel is as though he attacks the Holy One."[14] Numerous Holocaust diaries, in fact, attest to this connection between G-d and Israel and the assault on both.[15] In these testimonies we see that, in its metaphysical dimensions, the Holocaust is an attack not only on human beings but also on the Holy One who sanctifies humanity. This singularity manifests itself in the calculated destruction of Jewish souls and Jewish prayers, of Jewish texts and traditions, of synagogues and cemeteries. Judith Dribben recalls one Nazi's remark as he gazed upon a synagogue filled with Jews as it went up in flames: "The Jewish G-d is burned to ashes!"[16] Not only were the places of prayer and the people who pray to be destroyed, but prayer itself had to be demolished. On the eve of Tisha B'Av 5700 (1940), for example, Chaim Kaplan writes in his Warsaw Ghetto diary, "Public prayer in these dangerous times is a forbidden act. Anyone caught in this crime is doomed to severe punishment. If you will, it is even sabotage, and anyone engaging in sabotage is subject to execution."[17] For prayer—something that Kant held in contempt,[18] since it is contrary to the rational inquiry of a free, autonomous being—is as dangerous to civilized Germany as the Jews are.

In addition to the prohibition against prayer, the use of the mikveh, or ritual bath, was forbidden, so that there could be no purification of the body of Israel before it was reduced to ashes. Further, in a diary entry dated 2 February 1941, Emmanuel Ringelblum reports that "a group of Jews were locked up in the synagogue until they hacked the holy ark to bits."[19] Like the synagogue and prayer, the ritual bath and the holy ark are components of the sacred center upon which the Jewish community is founded. Tied to that center and sanctified by it is the sanctity of the home. Therefore, in their assault on G-d, the enemy launched an attack on the symbol that consecrates the home: the *mezuzah*. "At the beginning of the Ghetto period," writes Ringelblum, the Nazis "tore down the *mezuzot* from the doorposts of Jewish apartments."[20] This destruction of the *mezuzah* has nothing to do with the desecration of this home or that but was an undermining of the very notion of home and family as a sanctuary for the sacred. Indeed, every Jew in Europe was rendered homeless—not only because every Jew was in a camp, in a ghetto, or in hiding but because every space that could be designated as a home was transformed into a cramped and crowded emptiness.

Because Jewish ritual objects represent a way of thinking that is antithetical to Nazi thought, they were subject to destruction. For the same reason, religious ways of dressing and grooming oneself were also targeted. Among Jewish men, for instance, the symbol that distinguishes the face as a face turned toward G-d is the beard. And so, writes Warsaw diarist Michael Zylberberg, the Jews "were ordered to shave their head and face completely, to remove every symbol of Jewishness."[21] Similarly, Rabbi Shimon Huberband notes in his diary, "If a bearded Jew was caught, his life was put in danger. They tore out his beard with pieces of flesh, or cut it off with a knife and a bayonet."[22] And, describing an *aktion* staged in the Lvov Ghetto, David Kahane writes, "First they seized old men with beards and sidelocks. Not even a work card could save a bearded Jew."[23] Why were the Nazis not content simply to murder the Jews? Why did they have to get rid of synagogues, *mikvehs, mezuzas* and beards? Because in murdering the Jews they set out to murder a teaching and tradition that included a view of the *absolute* sanctity of the other human being and an *absolute* prohibition against murder. And such metaphysical absolutes had to be eliminated if the Nazis' ontological absolute was to rule.

Thus, in its philosophical implications, the Nazis' annihilation of the Jews and Judaism was not simply a case of scapegoating or racism run amok. In keeping with a major line of philosophical development from Kant onward, the Nazis sought the destruction of the G-d of Abraham and everything He signifies through the destruction of G-d's chosen. And Germany's philosophers were generally with the program.

German Philosophy's Role in the Murder of the Jews

By 1940, when the Nazis' intentions toward the Jews were clear, nearly half the philosophers of Germany were members of the Nazi Party. Given the history of the philosophers' involvement in the Party, such a statistic, while startling, is not surprising. In 1923, for example, Herman Schwarz, a thinker influenced by Meister Eckhart and Jacob Boehme, distinguished himself by becoming the first philosopher to publicly support the Nazis. He was followed by Bruno Bauch, Max Wundt, Hans Heyse and Nicolai Hartmann, all of whom were Kantian Idealists; then there was the noted Hegelian Theodor Haerung and the Nietzscheans Alfred Bäumler and Ernst Krieck. The most renowned of them all, of course, was Martin Heidegger. What these thinkers have in common is their embrace of a philosophical tradition that is fundamentally hostile toward Judaic theism and that takes individual autonomy to be the measure of human freedom and authenticity. To be sure, in 1922 Heidegger proclaimed that what attracted him to philosophy was "the full-blown antireligious attitude of the German *Geist* ripened from German Idealism."[24]

But how exactly does this antireligious stance "ripen" from German Idealism? It begins with Immanuel Kant. Insisting that religion derives from morality, and not the other way around,[25] Kant embraces a rationalist theology that is opposed to anything resembling a revealed religion such as Judaism. Indeed, in *The Conflict of the Faculties* Kant declares, "The euthanasia of Judaism is the pure moral religion."[26] Of course, the euthanasia of Judaism amounts to the elimination of the G-d of Abraham, Isaac, and Jacob. Kant takes a step in that direction in his *Universal Natural History*, where he asserts that the only thing dependent upon G-d's will is the creation of matter.[27] Once matter is the only thing that comes from G-d, G-d soon becomes superfluous, except as the projection of one's own psyche, as in Feuerbach,[28] or as what one aspires to become in a self-apotheosis, as in Nietzsche.[29] Contrary to the embrace of anything like a divine commandment, the human being is "determinable," says Kant, "only by laws which he gives to himself through reason."[30] Judaism is the opposite of Kantian Idealism—that is why Kant wanted to see it eliminated.

Like Kant, G.W.F. Hegel was a rationalist who associated freedom with human autonomy. His writings, as Paul Lawrence Rose has noted, "conform to the basic Kantian idealist and moralist critique of Judaism. Judaism is seen as the epitome of an unfree psyche."[31] Unlike Kant, however, Hegel draws on the Christian notion of the Christ as the Incarnation to develop a view of G-d that denies the otherness of the divinity. In Hegel, Fackenheim explains, "divinity comes to dwell, as it were, in the same inner space as the human self."[32] Resisting this internalization, Jews live an "animal existence," as Hegel sees it; they are in a "state of total passivity, of total ugliness," and are to blame for refusing to "die as Jews."[33] The perceiving self that had appropriated the world now appropriates the divinity. The philosophical result of this incarnation of G-d in the self and the subsequent deprecation of the Jews unfolds in the thinking of atheistic neo-Hegelians such as Feuerbach and Marx, where, says Fackenheim, "divinity vanishes in the process of internalization, to be replaced by a humanity potentially infinite in its modern 'freedom.'"[34] Because it is infinite, the "modern freedom" eliminates the Infinite One, so that human beings now may do whatever they have the will to do. Indeed, they are justified by will alone.

Proceeding in this logical sequence, Nietzsche determines that the will to power is a will to freedom, where freedom is understood as an autonomy beyond any law, resolute and decisive. Indeed, "the expression 'will to power,'" says Heidegger in his study on Nietzsche, "designates the basic character of beings; any being which is, insofar as it is, is will to power. The expression stipulates the character that beings have as beings."³⁵ Here Heidegger emulates Nietzsche's assertion that "German philosophers" are *"commanders and legislators: they say, 'Thus is shall be!'… their will to truth is—will to power."*³⁶ And so after Nietzsche's will to power defines the *character* of beings, Heidegger's resolve defines the *authenticity* of beings. For resolve is the height of autonomy and freedom.

Emmanuel Levinas accurately states the implications of this ontological thinking that begins in Kant and culminates in Heidegger:

> A philosophy of power, ontology is, as first philosophy which does not call into question the same, a philosophy of injustice…. Heideggerian ontology, which subordinates the relationship with the Other to the relation with Being in general, remains under obedience to the anonymous, and leads inevitably to another power, to imperialist domination, to tyranny.³⁷

Grounding freedom in the autonomy and authenticity in the resolve of the self, this strain of German philosophy situates freedom beyond the Law and is therefore lawless. It is, as Levinas rightly argues, "the outcome of a long tradition of pride, heroism, domination and cruelty" that "continues to exalt the will to power."³⁸ Such is the philosophy of *Volk* and *Führer*, which insists, as Heidegger did, that "the *Führer* himself and he alone is the present and future German reality and its law."³⁹ This sentiment articulates a theme that runs throughout a pamphlet published by the National Socialist German Teachers' Union in 1933; the pamphlet contains various statements on the "new order," such as this one:

> To know means to us: to have power over things in reason and to be ready to act…. The National Socialist movement is not merely the taking over of an already existing power …, but this revolution means a *complete* revolution of our German existence.⁴⁰

This and other statements in the pamphlet bore the signatures of nine university professors, including Heidegger's.

On 27 May 1933—by which time Hitler had assumed dictatorial powers, Jews were removed from civil service jobs, Dachau was in operation, and Jewish businesses had been boycotted—Heidegger delivered the infamous Rectorial Address at the University of Freiberg. Extolling the "magnificence and greatness" of Nazism,[41] he declared that "all abilities of will and thought, all strengths of the heart, and all capabilities of the body must unfold *through* battle, heightened *in* battle, and presented *as* battle"[42]—where any contemporary German listener would immediately associate the word *battle*, or *Kampf*, with Hitler's manifesto *Mein Kampf.* Thus the philosopher joins his discourse to the discourse of the *Führer.* Indeed, from the Rectorial Address it is evident that Heidegger considered himself "the born philosopher and spiritual leader of the new movement."[43] This view of himself was not merely a matter of intellectual conceit. More than that, Heidegger believed he was addressing a philosophical vacuum that threatened the new movement and the German *Volk.*

What was to fill that vacuum? Not, according to Heidegger, a "Jewified" philosophy of values. Opposing himself to Nazi philosophers of values—such as Bauch, who sought to ground values in race—Heidegger understood the Nazi order to be one that "would find secure grounding not in values but in a new unconcealment of Being, a new truth of Being."[44] The "unconcealment of Being" arises when the individual takes on the resolve to become his own ground of truth and meaning through an allegiance to his *Volk* and the *Führer.* Thus Heidegger saw in Nazism the new comprehension of Being that finally frees itself from the appeal to an infinite or divine being, from all revelation of values from on high, from every remnant of "onto-theology." "Existential ontology," he declared, "has as its sole objective the explication of the primordial transcendental structure of the *Dasein* in man," which, in turn, "manifests itself as need of the comprehension of Being,"[45] and not as, say, the need for a moral relation to another (person or G-d), the responsibility for the life of one's neighbor, or the like. Hence neither Heidegger nor his Nazi colleagues thought they were doing a moral good by pursuing the Nazi agenda; on the contrary, they believed they were doing an ontological good beyond good and evil, with its corollary *social, political* and *cultural* good—all of which are among the shibboleths of post-modernism.

In 1936 Karl Löwith expressed a concern to Heidegger, namely there was an essential "partnership" between National Socialism and Heidegger's philosophy. "Heidegger agreed with me [about this]," says Löwith, "without reservation and elucidated that his concept of 'historicity' was the basis of his political 'engagement.' He also left no doubt about his belief in Hitler."[46] Thus Heidegger himself understood that he was not a philosopher who happened to be a Nazi; no, he was a Nazi who happened to be a philosopher. His Nazism was not a personal shortcoming or a character flaw but a central feature of his ontological thinking, a thinking influenced by Kant, Hegel, and Nietzsche. One of the central features of the Heideggerian thinking that *characterizes both Nazi ideology and post-modern thought* is the elimination of the other human being from its concern. *"Das Dasein existiert umwillen seiner,"* Heidegger declares: *"Dasein* exists for the sake of itself."[47] Ideologically extended, this existence for the sake of oneself becomes an existence for the sake of the *Volk;* one can be only with others who are like oneself, that is, who are German. Here the other is excluded—and ultimately annihilated—from consideration.

Diametrically opposed to this being-for-oneself is the being-for-the-other represented by Jewish teaching and tradition—what Heidegger deprecated as "Jewified" thought and Hegel regarded as a slave mentality.[48] Whereas Heideggerian ontology sees the death that concerns me, for example, as *my* death,[49] the Jewish view of ethical obligation to and for the other person takes the death that concerns me to be the death of the other human being—the widow, the orphan, and the stranger, who are of no concern to Heidegger. Kant's "moral philosophy," moreover, cannot be held up as a response to Heidegger because, as we have seen, it led to Heidegger. To be sure, what is the mark of contradiction that guides the rationale of the categorical imperative? It is a contradiction to *self-interest.*[50] What must be opposed to Heidegger is precisely the Jewish metaphysics that the Nazis opposed: not the autonomy of the self but the sanctity of the other, not the universal maxims of reason but the uncompromising commandments of G-d, not freedom but justice, without which freedom itself is reduced to sheer power.

One of Heidegger's chief contributions to post-modern thought is the erasure of vertical, "logocentric" categories, which leaves us merely with what "is there" or what is "at hand." With the removal of the dimension of height, in other words, we are left only with the horizontally defined power struggles of culture and politics that now determine who and what we are. Opposed to post-modernism's erasure of absolutes is the Jewish insistence on absolutes that are not culturally or politically determined but are given from on high. This height, and not our resolve or our power, is what opens up truth, meaning, and the good in life. In the words of Levinas,

> Height introduces a sense into being. It is already lived across the experience of the human body. It leads human societies to raise up altars. It is not because men, through their bodies, have an experience of the vertical that the human is placed under the sign of height; because being is ordained to height the human body is placed in a space in which the high and the low are distinguished and the sky is discovered.[51]

To be sure, in Jewish thought the capacity to make such distinctions—between high and low, G-d and humanity, good and evil, sacred and profane—forms the basis of every notion of the Holy, from which the sanctity of human life is derived. As Heidegger ushers in post-modernism, however, being loses the dimension of height that imparts meaning to it and is leveled into a flatland of neutrality. This leveling of all into the same is characteristic of the post-modernist thought that went into the making of the concentrationary universe, where the living were ultimately indistinguishable from the dead.

Heidegger himself illustrates this post-modern leveling of life into death by equating technologically driven agriculture with the technologically driven murder of the Jews.[52] Commenting on

Heidegger's view in this regard, Jürgen Habermas wrote, "Under the leveling glance of the philosopher of Being, the extermination of the Jews, too, appears as a happening, where everything can be replaced as one likes with anything else."[53] The world in which everything can be replaced as one likes with anything else is precisely the post-modern world, and the murder camps are part of the landscape of that world. Since everything is all the same, anyone can take the place of another, and everyone is expendable. Thus the human being is rendered faceless. And since, in the words of Levinas, "the face is what forbids us to kill,"[54] with the post-modern loss of the dimension of height, we also lose the absolute prohibition against murder. That is why Fackenheim declared the murder camp to be the essence of National Socialism. That is why the murder camp is a logical outcome of a line of German thought traceable from Kant's idealism to Heidegger's post-modernism.

Conclusion

We now see the truth of Levinas's insight and better understand its implications, when he asserts,

> Heideggerian philosophy precisely marks the apogee of a thought in which the finite does not refer to the infinite (prolonging certain tendencies of Kantian philosophy: the separation between the understanding and reason, diverse themes of transcendental dialectics), in which every deficiency is but weakness and every fault committed against oneself—the outcome of a long tradition of pride, heroism, domination, and cruelty. Heideggerian ontology subordinates the relation with the other to the relation with the neuter, Being, and it thus continues to exalt the will to power, whose legitimacy the other alone can unsettle, troubling good conscience.[55]

In the case of Holocaust studies, the other who unsettles and troubles good conscience is the Jew. That is why many of us seek to eliminate the Jew from our study of the Holocaust; that is why many of us follow the post-modernist fashions and fads spawned by Heidegger. We do not deal with the Jews because we do not want to deal with the flesh and blood of Jewish life, which is rooted in Judaism. We do not want to look into the faces that put to us the question of what is ultimate in life, from beyond life. Instead, we prefer to level the Jew annihilated before and after his death into the sameness of just another victim. And so the study of the Holocaust becomes increasingly *Judenrein*. Rather than speak of Jews and Judaism, we speak of coping and trauma, dialogue and healing, representation and remembrance, textual analysis and ethical implications—everything except the singular assault on Jews and Judaism.

If we view the Holocaust in terms of the murder of the Jews, then in order to understand the Holocaust, we must address the question of what the Jews signify *by their very presence in the world*, so that we may have some inkling of what was targeted for destruction. And whatever the Jews may signify, it has been shaped by the Torah and Talmud of Judaism. There can be no understanding of the Holocaust, then, without an understanding of the Judaism—of the sacred tradition of Torah and Talmud—that the Nazis marked for extinction upon the extermination of the Jews and that Western ontological thought, from German idealism to post-modernism, has sought to eliminate. Making these connections is nothing less than a matter of life and death. For making these connections is a matter of arriving at the talmudic insistence that I must sanctify G-d's name in a *Kiddush Hashem* rather than commit murder. Unless we can come to *this* absolute, we shall be left either with the egocentric idealism or with the relativistic post-modernism that have proven to be equally incapable of achieving anything more than the position of bystander.

Endnotes

1. Heinrich Heine, "The German Revolution" in *Works of Prose*, tr. E.B. Ashton, ed. Hermann Kesten (New York: L.B. Fischer, 1943), pp. 51-53.

2. See Nahum Glatzer's introduction to Franz Rosenzweig, *Understanding the Sick and the Healthy*, tr. Nahum Glatzer (Cambridge: Harvard University Press, 1999), p. 24.

3. Rosenzweig, Franz Rosensweig's "The New Thinking," tr. and ed. Alan Udoff and Barbara E. Galli (Syracuse, NY: Syracuse University Press, 1999), p. 96.

4. Kant, too, ascribes certain features of the human being to natural accident, and not to the faculty of reason or will. See his *Anthropology from a Pragmatic Point of View*, tr. Victor Lyle Dowdell, ed. Hans H. Rudnick (Carbondale: Southern Illinois University Press, 1978).

5. See Jacques Derrida, *De l'esprit* (Paris: Éditions Galilee, 1987), pp. 11, 12, 64, 66, 155, 156.

6. See Martin Heidegger, *Introduction to Metaphysics*, tr. Ralph Mannheim (New York: Doubleday, 1961), p. 199.

7. Heidegger, *Sein und Zeit* (Tübingen: Max Niemeyer, 1963), p. 322. Translations from works in German are my own.

8. Hans Jonas, "Heidegger's Resoluteness and Resolve" in *Martin Heidegger and National Socialism*, ed. Guenther Neske and Emil Kettering, tr. Lisa Harries (New York: Paragon, 1990), pp. 202-03.

9. Reported in Die Zeit, 29 December 1989; see Theodore Kisiel, "Heidegger's Apology: Biography and Philosophy and Ideology" in *The Heidegger Case: On Philosophy and Politics*, ed. Tom Rockmore and Joseph Margolis (Philadelphia: Temple Univ. Press, 1992), p. 12.

10. Henri Crétella, "Self-Destruction" in *Martin Heidegger and the Holocaust*, ed. Alan Milchman (Atlantic Highlands, NJ: Humanities Press, 1966), p. 159.

11. Quoted in Max Weinreich, *Hitler's Professors: The Part of Scholarship in Germany's Crimes Against the Jewish People* (New Haven: Yale University Press, 1999), p. 26.

12. Max Wundt, *Deutsche Weltanschauung* (Munich: J.F. Lehmans, 1926), p. 75; see also Hans Sluga, *Heidegger's Crisis* (Cambridge: Harvard Univ. Press, 1993), p. 113.

13. Emil L. Fackenheim, *The Jewish Return into History* (New York: Schocken, 1978), p. 246.

14. Rashi, *Commentary on the Torah*, Vol. 4, tr. M. Rosenbaum and A.M. Silbermann (Jerusalem: Silbermann Family, 1972), p. 146.

15. See, for example, Yitzhak Katznelson, *Vittel Diary*, tr. Myer Cohen (Tel-Aviv: Hakibbutz Hameuchad, 1972), p. 122; Emmanuel Ringelblum, *Notes from the Warsaw Ghetto*, tr. Jacob Sloan (New York: Schocken, 1974), p. 80; and Zelig Kalmanovitch, "Diary of the Nazi Ghetto in Vilna," *YIVO Annual*, 8 (1953): 52.

16. Judith Dribben, *And Some Shall Live* (Jerusalem: Keter Books, 1969), p. 24.

17. Chaim A. Kaplan, *The Warsaw Diary of Chaim* A. Kaplan, tr. A.I. Katsh (New York: Collier, 1973), p. 179.

18. In a letter to Johann Caspar dated 28 April 1775 Kant refers to prayer as "the so-called worshipful supplications which have perennially constituted the religious delusion." See Ernst Cassirer, *Kant's Life and Thought*, tr. James Haden (New Haven: Yale Univ. Press, 1981), p. 377.

19. *Ringelblum*, p. 127.

20. Ibid., p. 152.

21. Michael Zylberberg, *A Warsaw Diary*, tr. M. Zylberberg (London: Valentine, Mitchell & Co., 1969), p. 21.

22. Shimon Huberband, *Kiddush Hashem*, tr. D.E. Fishman (Hoboken: Ktav, 1987), p. 35.

23. David Kahane, *Lvov Ghetto Diary*, tr. J. Michalowicz (Amherst: Univ. of Massachusetts Press, 1990), p. 45.

24. See Kisiel, p. 34.

25. For a good discussion of Kant's views in this regard, see Allen W. Wood, "Rational Theology, Moral Faith, and Religion" in *The Cambridge Companion to Kant*, ed. Paul Guyer (Cambridge: Cambridge University Press, 1992), pp. 394-416.

26. Immanuel Kant, *The Conflict of the Faculties*, tr. Mary J. Gregor (New York: Abaris, 1979), p. 95.

27. Cited by Frederick C. Beiser, "Kant's Intellectual Development: 1746-1781" in Guyer, p. 39.

28. Recall, for example, Feuerbach's insistence that G-d "is the manifested inward nature, the expressed self of a man," in Ludwig Feuerbach, *The Essence of Christianity*, tr. George Eliot (New York: Harper & Row, 1957), pp. 12-13.

29. This is the meaning of his statement, "In man creature and creator are united," in Friedrich Nietzsche, *Beyond Good and Evil*, tr. Walter Kaufmann (New York: Vintage Books, 1966), p. 154.

30. Kant, *The Critique of Practical Reason*, tr. Lewis White Beck (New York: Macmillan, 1985), p. 101.

31. Paul Lawrence Rose, *German Question/Jewish Question* (Princeton, NJ: Princeton Univ. Press, 1990), p. 109.

32. Fackenheim, *Encounters Between Judaism and Modern Philosophy* (New York: Basic, 1993), pp. 190-91.

33. See G.W.F. Hegel, "The Spirit of Christianity and Its Fate" in *Early Theological Writings*, tr. T.M. Knox (Chicago: Univ. of Chicago Press, 1948), pp. 201-05.

34. Fackenheim, *Encounters*, p. 191.

35. Heidegger, "Will to Power as Art" in *Nietzsche*, Vol. 1, tr. D. Krell (San Francisco: Harper, 1979), p. 18.

36. *Nietzsche*, p.136.

37. Emmanuel Levinas, *Totality and Infinity*, tr. Alphonso Lingis (Pittsburgh: Duquesne University Press, 1969), pp. 46-7.

38. Levinas, *Collected Philosophical Papers*, tr. Alphonso Lingis (Dordrecht: Martinus Nijhoff, 1987), p. 52.

39. From the *Freiburger Studentenzeitung*, 3 November 1933 (see Neske and Kettering, p. 45).

40. Quoted in *Weinreich*, p. 14.

41. *Neske and Kettering*, p. 13.

42. Ibid., p. 12.

43. *Sluga*, p. 4.

44. Heidegger, "Martin Heidegger: A Philosopher and Politics: A Conversation" in *Neske and Kettering*, p. 217.

45. Heidegger, *Kant and the Problem of Metaphysics*, tr. J.S. Churchill (Bloomington: Indiana Univ. Press, 1962), p. 244.

46. Karl Löwith, "Last Meeting with Heidegger" in *Neske and Kettering*, p. 158.

47. Heidegger, *Vom Wesen des Grundes*, 5th Ed. (Frankfurt am Main: Klostermann, 1965), p. 38.

48. In his commentary on the creation of the human being in the image of the divine being, for example, the great sage Rabbi Ovadiah ben Yaacov Sforno teaches that only through a life devoted to one's fellow human being can the meaning of being created in the divine image be realized. See Sforno, *Commentary on the Torah*, Vol. 1, tr. Raphael Pelcovitz (Brooklyn: Mesorah, 1987), p. 25.

49. *Heidegger, Sein*, p. 118.

50. See, for example, Kant, *Grounding for the Metaphysics of Morals*, tr. James W. Ellington (Indianapolis: Hackett 1981) pp. 30-2.

51. Levinas, *Collected Philosophical Papers*, p. 100.

52. See John D. Caputo, "Heidegger's Scandal: Thinking and the Essence of the Victim" in *Rockmore and Margolis*, p. 265.

53. Quoted by *Neske and Kettering*, p. xxxi.

54. See Levinas, *Ethics and Infinity*, tr. Richard Cohen (Pittsburgh: Duquesne University Press, 1985), p. 86.

55. Levinas, *Collected Philosophical Papers*, p. 52.

CHAPTER 7

Adorno and Lifton: Subjectivity and the Psychology of Genocide

Gary A. Mullen

Within the mainstream of philosophy, there is a general aversion to taking up genocide as a fundamental problem, as an event that calls for a radical reassessment of methods and concepts. The tendency is to treat genocide, when it is treated at all, as a political/ethical aberration, far distant from, and alien to the safe house of sound reasoning. Perhaps it is because one does not come away from the intellectual confrontation with genocide enriched with a new set of puzzles presented and solved. More importantly, after such a confrontation one is less likely to be charmed by any suggestion of progress—and the sense of disillusionment is intensified the more one cannot resist harboring hope for humanity. One risks being dismissed out of hand as a pessimist for even broaching the subject at all and one risks becoming the sacrificial victim of those who take offense at having their accustomed habits of thought revealed as instruments of genocide.

This has been the legacy of Theodor W. Adorno within mainstream philosophy. Adorno was among the first to take up genocide as his central philosophical problematic. He was the first to risk the proclamation that there is no aspect of philosophy or of culture that does not require radical reassessment in the wake of the Holocaust.[1] For this reason, his account of the psychology of genocide is unique for its cultural breadth. In Adorno's work, genocide does not remain within social psychology, but sees this as only one moment of a constellation that includes metaphysics, epistemology, aesthetics and ethics—for the problem of genocide is rooted in subjectivity itself. Hence it is impossible to discuss Adorno's account of the psychology of genocide without cutting across the boundaries of other disciplines, for which, according to Adorno, genocide is no less fundamental a problem.

Recognition of the importance of Adorno's thought has been obscured not only by the unpopularity of his position but also because of the difficulty of his writing, which assumes a thorough familiarity with Kant, Hegel, Nietzsche, Marx, Heidegger and others. Adorno's particular treatment of the psychology of genocide is dealt with in his discussions of the collapse of the scientific modern subject into the irrationality of anti-Semitism and fascist ideology.[2] Reading this in parallel with Robert Jay Lifton's account of the doctors who took up a central role in the genocidal machinery of Auschwitz (and who transformed the healing science into a killing science) offers a vivid concrete account of the psychology of genocide that is in many ways complementary with Adorno's account of the genocidal tendencies of the modern subject. Despite the disciplinary and methodological differences that separate Adorno and Lifton their work converges in the shared affirmation that the Holocaust is an event in the wake of which philosophy and psychology must reassess their most basic assumptions and goals.[3] This convergence carries through to their prescription that intellectual confrontation with genocide requires the integration of a sense of human vulnerability into our modes of knowing ourselves and our world.

On Adorno's view, modernity has left us with a subjectivity that understands itself as invulnerable, standing above and in opposition to its own materiality, its own embodiment and situation in the natural world. An invulnerable subjectivity is precisely what is described by Lifton in his psychological study of the Nazi doctors who took part in the genocidal machinery of Auschwitz. According to Lifton, the central psychological characteristic of the Nazi doctors was their failure to integrate a sense of their own embodiment and mortality into their understanding of themselves and others.[4] Lifton sees the same structural flaw in the genocidal psyche that Adorno sees in the modern subject, namely, the failure to integrate mortality and vulnerability into one's sense of self. Adorno's structural treatment of the flaw in modern subjectivity and Lifton's empirical study of the doctors of Auschwitz reveal the way in which the genocidal psyche externalizes and projects its own mortality onto a "threat" that must be eliminated. This is the lethal dynamic that cuts away the embodiment (objectivity) of the self and the embodiment (objectivity) of others, the political expression of which is epitomized in Nazi ideology—a pure fantasy of general hostility projected onto a group targeted for annihilation.

Adorno: Philosophy and Suffering

The "finale" passage at the close of Adorno's *Minima Moralia* is among the most famous in all of his works. While it has often been said, and with some accuracy, that Adorno's work has no central idea that stands above and orders all of his works, the passage captures one of the many ubiquitous themes that are all equally present in every facet of the constellation of themes that makes up Adorno's corpus:

> The only philosophy which can be responsibly practiced in face of despair is the attempt to contemplate all things as they would present themselves from the standpoint of redemption. Knowledge has no light but that shed on the world by redemption: all else is reconstruction, mere technique. Perspectives must be fashioned that displace and estrange the world, reveal it to be, with all its rifts and crevices, as indigent and distorted as it will appear one day in the messianic light. To gain such perspectives without velleity or violence, entirely from felt contact with its objects—this alone is the task of thought.[5]

Fashioning perspectives that displace and estrange the world is the endeavor of critical thought, of any philosophy worthy of the name. In *Negative Dialectics*, Adorno provides an elaborate strategy for forming such perspectives and for re-establishing the bond between rationality and human emancipation. According to Adorno, freedom is forged through the articulate response to human suffering. As Adorno writes:

> Freedom follows the subject's urge to express itself. The need to lend a voice to suffering is a condition of all truth for suffering is objectivity that weighs upon the subject; its most subjective experience, its expression is objectively mediated [*vermittelt*].[6]

The articulate response to human suffering is the visceral sense[7] that the violent exploitation and destruction of life is not the necessary condition of life or a tolerable condition for human coexistence. The need to lend a voice to suffering occupies a space in Adorno's thought tantamount to the place occupied by *thoumadzain* (wonder) in Plato. Unlike Plato, Adorno's "wonder" is shock—and provokes an interrogation into the conditions that frustrate and destroy human life. In a reversal of Plato's famous allegory, the index leading out of the distortion of the cave is not a light seen by turning away from the humans in bondage; instead the way out of the cave is intimated through the sounds of longing in the agony of a trapped humanity. The aim of negative dialectics is to use concepts to unearth what the usual habits of conceptual thought have buried.[8] Negative dialectics is nothing more than the attempt to integrate vulnerability (not merely human vulnerability, but also the vulnerability of nature as a whole) into how we conceptualize the world. Adorno situates thought in its immanent social context, thereby revealing the contingency and fragility of our hold upon truth, and our susceptibility to horrific, genocidal ideological distortions of the world and each other.

Identity Thinking, Self-Preservation of the Disembodied Self

What Adorno referred to as identity thinking or instrumental rationality is a disembodied form of reason that serves as the central instrument in the hands of the "master and possessor of nature" (to paraphrase Descartes). The identity principle prevents the acknowledgment of vulnerability within the subject. The search for invariant, stable structures that secure the place of the intellect over its changing objects (a search funded by the identity principle) has shaped the goals of Western philosophy since Parmenides. Under the rubric of identity thinking the features of the subject's embodiment in material life are subordinated and overcome by the labor of conceptual thought (nature, femininity, vulnerability) construed as hostile to reason and to the preservation of the self.

This opposition within the subject is fertile ground for racial ideology. The closed subject does not see what is heterogeneous and alien as an impetus for self-questioning; instead, the alien is construed as a threat that must be annihilated. The hostile tension between the subject and its own perishable nature is externalized, projected onto those persons and things that are different and foreign. The explosion of this tension onto the stage of history in Nazi Germany was, for Adorno, the shocking display of the failure of modern philosophy. The Holocaust announced the need to formulate a different epistemological standpoint that would be able to illuminate the vulnerability of the subject to horrifically destructive ideological distortions.

Only a critical understanding of the embodied locus of thought could detect and remedy the distortions generated by the hierarchical arrangement of subject and object. In a critical materialist epistemology, the subject and object are on the same plane, shaped by and vulnerable to the same socio-historical forces. Such an epistemology would allow us to work out of our current situation, in which the subject's own objectivity, and its corporeal contact with the object are occluded. For it is precisely this contact, and the impulses out of which it is woven, that the modern subject violently suppresses as hostile reminders of nature. Adorno's philosophy is nothing less than a reshaping of the problem of what evokes thought, of what demands philosophical concern. The shock that gives rise to reflection is not generated subjectively, it is evoked by our objectivity, by the sense that we are embodied, that the errors we make in how we conceive the world take their toll on human lives. We are driven to reflection because we live in the nexus of decisions and actions that are not reversible and so require all the seriousness and gravity of decisions whose effects create unrecoverable losses.[9]

The Modern Subject and Nazi Anti-Semitism

The modern subject's drive for security leads it to identify cognition with control—progress with technological advance. Adorno offers us an analysis of how the subject's hyperbolic desire for security played a central role in Nazi anti-Semitic ideology.[10] Adorno's analysis shows that, what is at work in the Nazi myth of Jewish world domination, is the projection of a subjectivity no longer capable of reflecting upon and criticizing its own projections.[11] Because the subject is woven out of an exaggerated drive for self-preservation, it easily identifies with the ambient set of social bonds and categories in which it lives and thinks. This strong identification produces suspicion toward anything outside these limits. To threaten the categories of the subject is to threaten its very existence. Anything either within the subject itself or in others that grates against the limits of the subject must be seen as the enemy, as unconquered and hence dangerous nature.

The potential for mobilizing this hostility in the political realm was exploited by Fascist ideology, but the potential lies within modernity generally. The danger of Fascism is not limited to the seductiveness of a particular racist ideology; instead, Fascism is a product of the tendency of the modern subject to assault what does not fall under the category of the norm.[12] The modern subject itself is structured in such a way that racism and genocide become its perennial products. While there are determinate historical reasons for why the Jews were singled out for annihilation by the Nazis,[13] Adorno points out that Judaism is not the sole or the necessary target of annihilation by the modern subject.[14] The resurgence of myth in the subject can direct its violence toward a variety of different objects:

... since the victims are interchangeable according to circumstances—gypsies, Jews, Protestants, Catholics, and so on—any one of them may take the place of the murderers, with the same blind lust for blood, should they be invested with the title of the norm (DE, p. 171).[15]

Because of its sharpening of the principle of identity and self-preservation, the modern subject has uniquely intensified the tensions between identity and non-identity and, against all of its attempts at enlightenment, has rendered its inclinations and desires more obscure to consciousness and reason.

Lifton on the Genocidal Psyche

Whereas Adorno's work shows us the genocidal potential of modern rationality, Robert Jay Lifton's study of the Nazi Doctors offers a vivid account of the genocidal agency of rational, well-educated men of science. Lifton's study is remarkable in this context for how closely its details fit with Adorno's account of the genocidal potential of the modern subject. The doctors of Auschwitz, because of their medical training, were better able to distance themselves from any feelings of empathy or guilt in the face of the human carnage they produced and presided over daily. These doctors were better suited to the callous task of genocide, and Lifton notes, showed far fewer signs of psychological trauma than their less educated counterparts in the *Einsatzgruppen*.[16]

In the Nazi doctors' adaptation to the death-industry of Auschwitz they developed a set of behaviors and responses severed from the affectivity of their own embodiment. In effect they developed a self that branched off from the affective network that informs ethical responsibility (the dimension of human feeling that they had to diverge from in order to effect an adaptation to the death-filled environment of Auschwitz). Lifton refers to this dark adaptation as psychic doubling: "... the division of the self into two functioning wholes, so that a part self acts as an entire self."[17] Just as the concept is the death of the particular, the double "represents one's own death." Lifton writes:

> ... the Auschwitz self of the Nazi doctor similarly assumed the death issue for him but at the same time used its evil project as a way of staving off awareness of his own "perishable and mortal part." It does the dirty work for the entire self by rendering that work "proper" and in that way protects the entire self from awareness of its own guilt and its own death.[18]

This doubling of the Nazi doctors into a deathless self is not construed as an a-historical mechanism, but is buoyed up by the immersion of German culture in Nazi racial ideology, an ideology particularly attractive to a certain social-Darwinist view of biology and genetics not uncommon among German medical students. Many Nazi doctors viewed the elimination of the Jews as a matter of cultural, racial hygiene. The Jews were characterized as vermin, disease, a malady requiring the strongest medicine. Lifton notes that eliminating this boundary between killing and healing was crucial to the passage from discrimination and periodic acts of anti-Semitic violence to systematic genocide: "At the heart of the Nazi enterprise ... is the destruction of the boundary between killing and healing."[19] This boundary could be crossed (and an irrational, paranoid ideology could invade the practices of the healing science) because of the self's propensity to eclipse its own mortality, to eradicate the last remnant of its vulnerability; this urge to flee from our own vulnerability, while being inextricably bound to the body (the particular), is also an avoidance, a denial of embodiment (particularity). The disembodiment of our urge for self-preservation, the failure to integrate the concept of self-preservation and the embodiment of the very self that we strive to preserve, is the source of genocidal distortions. According to Lifton, the source of doubling lies in the disintegration of the modern personality:

> ... that disintegration leads to a need for self-perpetuation in one's own image—what I would call a literalized form of

immortality ... the Nazi movement encouraged its would be artist-hero, the physician, to remain, like Narcissus, in thralldom to his own image.[20]

Adaptation that extends beyond the body (as with self-preservation extended beyond the particular) and attaches the self to an abstract image—even to the point at which the self is willing to die and to kill without limit for the sake of defending "the cause" or "Reich" from annihilation—is the core accomplishment of ideology. It effects the false overcoming of death through the symbolic "killing" of death.

Lifton remarks that the Aztecs "pursued as their sacred duty a course of endless warfare in order to obtain prisoners to offer in sacrifice 'to preserve the universe from the daily threat of annihilation.'"[21] While the differences between the Nazis and the Aztecs are not insignificant, they are similar in that

> ... both groups went on killing in the face of increasing evidence that the killing itself interfered with the survival of the state: with the war, in the case of the Nazis; and with the entire social and economic existence of an exhausted empire, in the case of the Aztecs. Both had to continue "killing" death. For it was as true of the Nazis as of the Aztec that each "could insist on offering blood in return for life until his whole religion become an emotional bulwark around the specter of death."[22]

Conclusion

Although this parallel discussion of Adorno and Lifton is presented as a complementary study (an intersection between an empirical extension of Adorno's philosophy and a philosophical extension of Lifton's psychology), the accomplishment lies in what this intersection tells us about the intellectual confrontation with genocide. That genocide cannot be thought or resisted without the integration of vulnerability into our thinking and into our sense of selfhood is the common thread woven through both Adorno and Lifton. This common thread marks their shared commitment to a post-Holocaust standard for veracity in the human sciences: that human phenomena can no longer be studied from the perspective of an undisturbed observer; the truth cannot be understood through concepts unmoved by human suffering; and the resistance to the repetition of genocide cannot be staged by a subject (or a self) without a body.

Endnotes

1. Theodor Adorno, *Negative Dialectics*. E.B. Ashton, trans. (Continuum: New York, 1994), p. 361.

2. It would be a mistake, however, to see his account as limited to German fascism. What made the Germans susceptible to fascist ideology is an inheritance shared by modern industrial society—and that inheritance is no less fundamental than the way in which the self or subject is constituted.

3. Lifton notes the impossibility of approaching the Holocaust from the perspective of a morally neutral observer and he resists the tendency to reduce to a simple mechanism the complexity of the psychology of human evil. Hence, his study follows the principle "that certain events elude our full understanding, and we do best to acknowledge that a partial grasp, a direction of understanding, is the best to be expected of any approach;" this amounts to "… a rejection of psychological reductionism: the collapsing of complex events into single, all-embracing explanations, in ways that sweep away rather than illuminate the interlocking structures and motivations behind those events." Lifton, Nazi Doctors (Basic Books: New York, 1986) p. 13.

4. Lifton, Nazi Doctors, pp. 441-442.

5. Theodor Adorno, Minima Moralia. trans. E.F.N. Jephcott (Verso: New York, 1994), p. 247.

6. Theodor Adorno, *Negative Dialectics*, trans. E.B. Ashton (Continuum: New York, 1994), pp. 17-18. Gessamelte Schriften VI, p. 29. Translation altered.

7. In his Aesthetic Theory, Adorno uses the term "shudder" [Ershütterung] or "shock" in the face of events that destroy life.

8. "The cognitive utopia would be to use concepts to unseal the nonconceptual with concepts, without making it their equal." Adorno. Negative Dialectics, p. 10.

9. For an excellent treatment of the materiality of the subject in relation to post-Holocaust political discourse, see Garth J. Gillan. *Rising From the Ruins: Reason,*

Being, and the Good After Auschwitz. (Albany: SUNY Press, 1998), pp. x-xi; 65-85.

10. We should not discount as a mere coincidence that Adorno's most lengthy discussion of mimesis takes place within the context of an analysis of Nazi ideology. It is important to note the political context of Adorno's discussion of mimesis, as its capacity to shed light on political possibility (a capacity Adorno never doubted) is typically missed in interpretations of Adorno; for example, see, Sheyla Benhabib, Critique, Norm, and Utopia (New York: Columbia University Press, 1986), p. 219. Also, Nigel Gibson offers a thorough account of how Adorno's interpretation of Hegel prevents him from offering a satisfactory Hegelian-Marxist politics in "Rethinking an Old Saw: Dialectical Negativity, Utopia, and Negative Dialectic in Adorno's Hegelian Marxism" in Adorno: A Critical Reader. Nigel Gibson and Andrew Rubin eds. (Malden, MA: Blackwell Publishers, 2002), pp. 257-291. While the reading of Adorno as a political quietist remains prevalent, a close attention to the political context in which Adorno discusses the central themes of his philosophy reveals the centrality of the critique of fascism in Adorno's work. Russell Berman (in "Adorno's Politics" Adorno: A Critical Reader, pp. 110-131) merges this approach with biographical details from Adorno's personal confrontation with fascism and his interaction with the German student movement in the late 1960s.

11. DE, pp. 183-184.

12. DE, pp. 169-170/GS3, pp. 193-194.

13. See, Dialectic of Enlightenment, pp. 173-176.

14. Adorno clearly claims that any group might be singled out for annihilation or might assume the position of the annihilators, as the potential for racism is exacerbated by modernity itself. However, elsewhere in Dialectic of Enlightenment, and in many other works, he suggests that there are elements of Judaism that are especially recalcitrant to the forces of modernity (see, Dialectic of Enlightenment, pp. 23, 177-8). There are many other texts as well that strongly suggest this, and it is precisely the elements of Judaism that are recalcitrant to the dominating tendency of modernity that Adorno calls upon in his criticism of modernity.

15. Ibid. GS3, p. 195.

16. Lifton, *Nazi Doctors*, pp. 15, 159.

17. Lifton, *Nazi Doctors*, p. 418.

18. Lifton, *Nazi Doctors*, p. 421.

19. Lifton, *Nazi Doctors*, p. 14.

20. Lifton, *Nazi Doctors*, p. 421.

21. Lifton, *Nazi Doctors*, p. 484.

22. Lifton, *Nazi Doctors*, p. 485.

GENOCIDE AND RELIGION

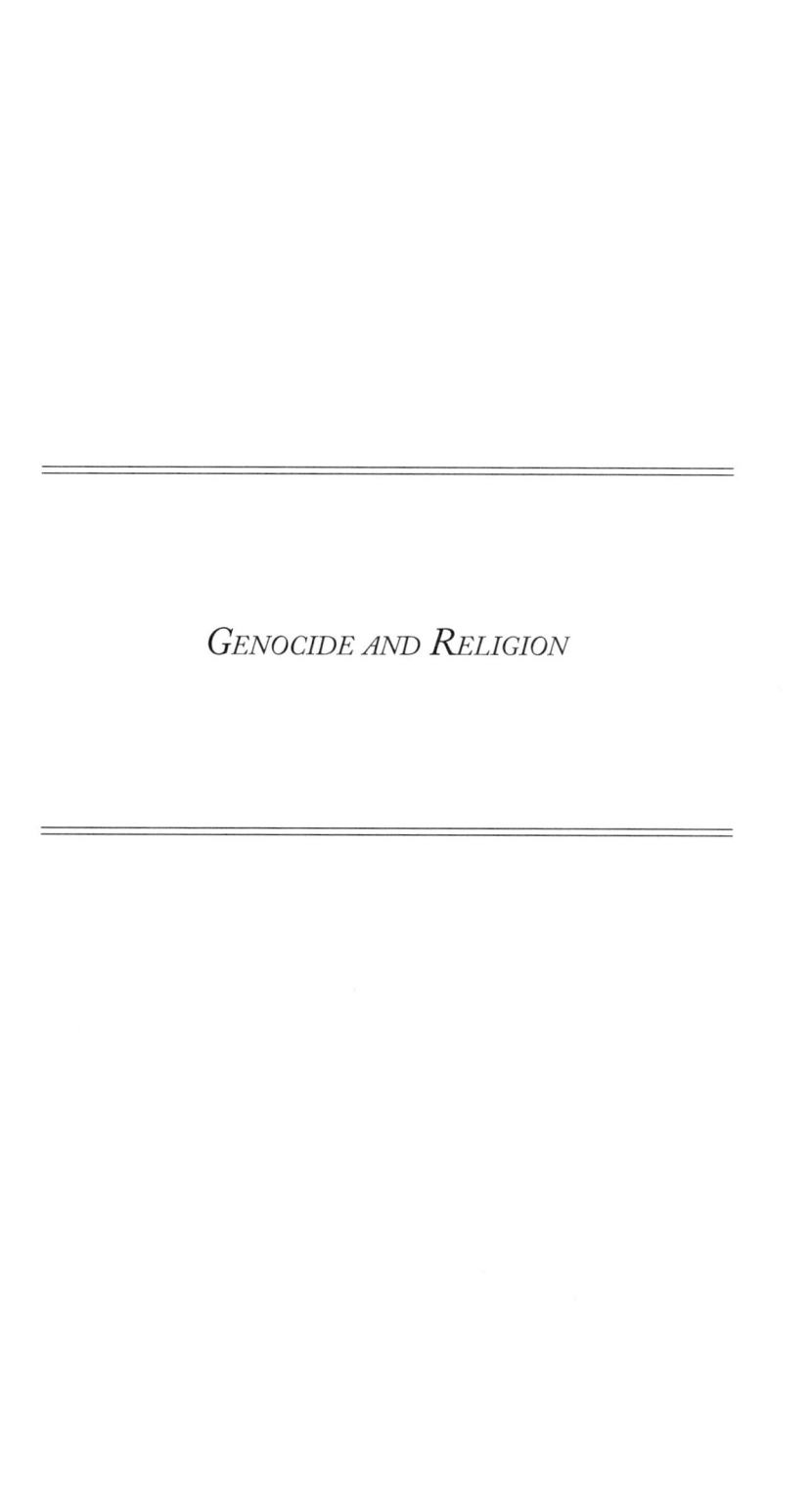

CHAPTER 8

Elite Catholic Isolationism in the United States: Impediment or Failure in the Fight Against Nazi Genocide?

Patrick J. Hayes

Present day assessments of a Catholic contribution to the war against Nazism tend to focus more on whether the Church's pontiffs did or did not do enough. Unfortunately, the historical record that emerges is too often obscured by polemic. In this paper, I hope to clear away some of the stumbling blocks to understanding Catholic positions on the war. First, I have some preliminary remarks on Catholic elites and isolationism, and then I will briefly survey their role in shaping attitudes and policies relative to Catholic participation in the war. Second, I concentrate on one individual whose opinion carried considerable authority on the question of whether the United States should engage in armed conflict in Europe for the sake of the Jews. His name is J. Elliot Ross, a Paulist priest with extensive background in Christian-Jewish relations in 1930s America. By studying Ross' positions, some conclusions may be drawn, clarifying present assessments of the Church's effectiveness in combating National Socialism.

I take *isolationism* to mean a political posture that seeks to preserve national security while forcing other states to address their own internal struggles. As a tactic for diplomacy, it is the opposite of *internationalism*, the positive theory that a state ought to become involved in the affairs of other states, whether through diplomatic efforts, economic policies, or direct military assistance. Isolationists focus on the internal well being of the nation and want to maintain a clear economic or political advantage for their home country by withholding military or other support from potentially belligerent parties. As foreign policy, it is far more passive, though not in an absolute sense. Isolationism places a strain on antagonistic countries, forcing them to resolve their difficulties for the sake of their own national security or the stability of entire regions.

Before its entrance into the war, this was the tacit approach to statecraft the United States pursued with respect to the German National Socialist government under Adolf Hitler.[1] In fact, the nation was loath to enter any European conflict. It did not offer substantial material assistance to governments in order to topple or otherwise inhibit National Socialism, nor did it break economic or political commitments it held with the Hitler regime until after the expiration of the Neutrality Act on April 1, 1939. Couple this with a global embargo against allowing refugees to immigrate and this spelled disaster for Jews throughout Europe.

Attempts have been made to carve out Catholic opinion on isolationist policy from the rest of the population.[2] The range of this opinion included both an opposition to military participation in any foreign conflict as well as a negative view of an arms embargo and a slightly less enthusiastic boycott of German and Japanese goods. Among Catholics, there was overt support for all these forms of isolationist policy. Into these political concerns was added a peculiar fervor for Catholic well being at home and abroad. In the complex culture of inter-war Catholicism in America—one which continually sought both integration into American society and the legitimation and preservation of those ethnic religious loyalties that often pitted Catholics against the wider culture—their isolationism was motivated by an ethos of self-interest.

Perhaps no other group helped shape this perspective more than Catholic elites—a small group of individuals who consciously and publicly contributed to the advance of causes and resolution of problems that concerned Catholics. Their influence on the rest of the

Church in America is difficult to gauge, but Catholic elites were courted by those in power in order to persuade the larger public, Catholic and otherwise, that the government was taking the best approach to foreign policy. Catholic isolationism tended to blend with the national anxiety over participation in a European war. I want to suggest that within a general understanding of American isolationism, there exists a substratum shaped by factors peculiar to Catholic interests. As we shall see, this substratum was an impediment to what could have been earlier interventions on behalf of European Jewry.

Surveying Catholic Isolationism

Turning now to those Catholic isolationists who urged President Roosevelt to keep the United States out of European affairs, it is clear that their individual efforts amounted to a kind of collective campaign. However, there was no organization among these elites. They were simply acting as individuals, using the authority of their good offices to bring about policy measures sympathetic to isolationism.

One of the most public Catholics in Franklin Roosevelt's administration was Joseph P. Kennedy of Boston, a dynastic multimillionaire and former head of the Securities and Exchange Commission. Kennedy was a longtime Roosevelt patron, rewarded for his work with his appointment as United States Ambassador to Great Britain in 1938, a post he held until 1940. Kennedy's isolationism is well known and if communications from February, 1938, are any indication, Roosevelt and Kennedy were of like mind.[3] On numerous occasions he cabled both the State Department and the president himself, indicating that the position of the United States with respect to the European situation ought to remain neutral. These cables usually advised that the administration give no indication of American involvement in the impending European conflict. Throughout 1939, Kennedy made it known to his contacts in Great Britain and France that if war ensued with Germany, Berlin would surely triumph. Appeasement seemed the only acceptable policy, given America's isolationism. Because of Kennedy's recommendations, Great Britain felt continually compelled to sue for peace.

At home, Catholic isolationism was promoted mainly through the Catholic media. Two principle outlets beat the drums for isolationism: Father Charles Coughlin and America magazine. Admittedly, these are strange bedfellows. Coughlin was heard by millions on a weekly radio show, while a much smaller percentage read America, the Jesuit weekly. Their two audiences were often separated by educational and class differences, but they were each articulating the same message.

In the early years of the Roosevelt administration, Coughlin was a popularizer of Catholic social teaching and at first a real friend to Roosevelt's social policies.[4] This alliance was short-lived, however, and Coughlin used his broadcasts to berate the administration at every opportunity, particularly when it sought to become involved in European conflicts. Consequently, Coughlin helped develop the canard that Roosevelt was surrounded by communists. The priest's own popularity eventually suffered as his comments became more and more shrill, and his anti-Semitic rhetoric more pronounced, but it was only in late 1939, when the National Association of Broadcasters set new policies for controversial announcers, that Father Coughlin was silenced. The White House welcomed the hiatus, mainly because it created the space to take up the possibility of American intervention in Europe's war, which formally began in the first week of September, 1939. Meanwhile, Coughlin convinced Archbishop Francis J. Beckman of Dubuque, Iowa, to join with him in lobbying for retention of the Neutrality Act then up for debate in the Senate. Beckman would remain an intransigent, albeit a silent one, especially after the National Catholic Welfare Conference gave its approval, after considerable deliberation, to the Roosevelt administration's decision to aid the Allies in late December, 1939.

These actions were not the remonstrances of isolated clerics. They were joined by several Jesuits on the editorial board of America and notably John LaFarge, SJ, the Harvard-trained promoter of interracial harmony. LaFarge was also one of the founding members of the Catholic Association for International Peace, a group formed in 1927 to discuss and report on various policies affecting international organization. After the war, LaFarge would write in his biography that the CAIP was "not in favor of neutrality where the defense of an invaded country was involved."[5] Whatever the CAIP attitude toward neutrality, the unsigned commentary generated in America left an opposite impression.

In one editorial, the review stated flatly "our first interest is neither Great Britain, nor the Axis Powers, but the United States."[6] Editorialists like Paul Blakely, SJ, were highly critical of Washington, even well into the war, lamenting in the spring of 1942 that "the Senate not only permits the Administration to send our boys to fight and die on foreign lands and waters, but even encourages the administration to use the army and navy wherever a conflict or the danger of a conflict may arise, or be caused to arise."[7] Not incidentally, there was a large chorus of Catholic writers, mainly among the membership of the Catholic Press Association, who gave support to the President under the proviso that he would not lead the United States into the European crisis. By coupling with the Coughlinites on keeping America out of Europe's affairs, America prompted a diverse and large number of Catholics to favor neutrality. For example, a poll taken on November 11, 1939, revealed that almost ninety-seven percent of Catholic college students opposed the United States' entry into the war.[8]

What distinguishes the Coughlinites from the pages of America is that the magazine gave considerable attention to the plight of Jews and Catholics under Hitler's government. "It certainly cannot be maintained," the editors wrote, "that the German people, as a whole, or even a majority of them, are one with Hitler in his attacks upon religion."[9] While Coughlin too readily linked the fate of European Jews with the advance of communism, the Jesuits felt more could be done for Jews as Jews, not as victims of a perceived Bolshevism. They were more careful to attack specific policies, such as Selective Service and certain provisions of the Lend-Lease Act. That they contributed to an overall negative view of American military participation in Europe is attested by polling data collected by the American Institute of Public Opinion and Fortune magazine.[10] It is thanks in part to their collective voice that the president moved slowly and incrementally in bringing the nation into the European fray. Even by November 1941, the United States was at once fully involved overseas, but had not officially declared itself to be at war.

The lay counterpart to America, The Commonweal offered similar sentiments. It did not favor strict neutrality, but neither did it endorse America's entrance into the war. The editors took a decidedly middle-of-the-road approach: "We strongly believe that the best course lies in positive action between appeasement and armed intervention."[11] Together with the Administrative Board of the National Catholic Welfare Conference and the editors of America, Commonweal also went on record opposing conscription. The only intervention that was advocated was war relief for victims. Catholics believed that a dose of prudential reserve was tantamount to patriotic isolationism. It also preserved the moral superiority of the nation over against the barbarity of uncivilized Europeans.

Three further points must be added to this survey. The first pertains to the American hierarchy from 1933-1940. The vast majority of Catholic bishops in the United States was of Irish stock and looked at their own family histories in formulating their political opinions. For many, the thought of assisting the British in a military campaign that would cost American lives was to rub salt in old wounds. Moreover, because the Church was supranational, it could not endorse a particular government's attack on another, particularly one with a large Catholic population. Following Pope Pius XII's proposals for peace issued in January 1940, the American bishops sought to remind the public that the United States was "set on peace not war."[12]

Second, some saw isolationist policies as a means to advance a more pacifist society. The Catholic Worker movement stands in this corner. In and out of the pages of the *Catholic Worker*, Dorothy Day continuously protested against American involvement in war of any kind. In advocating this view, the movement used arguments from the Catholic just war tradition, tightly and comprehensively packaged by Father Paul Hanley Furfey, the noted sociologist at the Catholic University of America. Furfey stands in contradistinction to his colleague and mentor, Monsignor John A. Ryan—the nation's foremost authority on Catholic social thought and one of the few high placed Catholics to advocate for a more engaged foreign policy.[13] Nevertheless, the Catholic Worker Movement maintained its attitude throughout the whole of the Second World War, and worked tirelessly to create a forum for conscientious objection.[14]

Third, and finally, it should be noted that not all Catholic elites were of the same mind on isolationism. Some chose to fan flames in the opposite direction, as in the case of Cardinal George Mundelein of Chicago, a prelate of German extraction with friendly ties to the Roosevelt White House. In May 1937, *The New York Times* reported that Mundelein called Hitler "an inept paper hanger." The statement prompted the Germans to withdraw their ambassador from the Holy See. The heat was turned up on the administration, too, for now several American bishops were coming forward to plead for some kind of intervention on behalf of Europe's Jews.[15] The White House heard them, but with the legal limitations of the Neutrality Act and public opinion favoring continued isolation, the administration felt compelled to delay American involvement in Europe until the last possible moment.

Catholic Isolation: The Case of J. Elliot Ross, C.S.P.

J. Elliot Ross (1884-1946), a Paulist priest, was one of the leading Catholic voices on Christian-Jewish tolerance in America during this period.[16] A sometime contributor to *Commonweal* magazine and other publications, he was an active participant in the work of the National Conference for Christians and Jews, which originated in 1927. His involvement in a still nascent rapprochement with Protestants and Jews was undertaken with some risk, given the opposition to such activities by certain members of the Catholic hierarchy. Yet, the bonds he solidified at the NCCJ helped to move

Christian-Jewish relations forward in America.

Ross gave the fight for religious tolerance respectability and clarity. His main contribution was a highly publicized "pilgrimage" with the NCCJ director, the Rev. Everett Clinchy, and a Baltimore Rabbi, Morris Lazaron in 1933. In their joint venture, the first ever of its kind, these men visited thirty-five cities in twenty-four states, logging over nine thousand miles, with the trio speaking before one hundred and six audiences and making twenty-three broadcasts.[17]

Indeed, when the pilgrimage ended, Clinchy wrote to Ross saying that "I am convinced you belong on the 'faculty' of the National Conference, and there is no better 'student body' in the world for you to teach than the 100 million Americans."[18] Later in 1934, Clinchy, Lazaron, and Ross were chosen as the recipients of the Gottheil Medal by the Zeta Beta Tau fraternity for "the American who has done the most for Jewry."[19] Some members of local press organizations extended the accolades to all three pilgrims. A Denver journal reported that:

> The splendid work of these three men will receive the solid support of all Jews and Christians in Denver. It will be the spearhead that will help eradicate race and religious prejudice, intolerance, and misunderstandings. In a time when Hitlerism appears to be spreading over the world, a movement such as this is a godsend to peace loving and religious people.[20]

It is important to note that this hope of fighting Nazism was an extrapolation from the actual intent of the NCCJ. Before the pilgrimage, Clinchy forwarded a letter to Ross written by a certain John Lynch, who had inquired whether the goals of the trip were perhaps used to front for Jewish opposition to the German government. Ross replied by explaining the aims of the NCCJ. As he saw it, the reason for the organization lay in fostering better relations between Christians and Jews in America. It had no designs for political influence on foreign matters. Ross indicated that he did not think that the tour "should be made into an opportunity for stirring up resentment against Hitler. Any reference to Hitlerism should be merely as an illustration of what may happen if religious prejudices and hatreds are fanned."[21] Ross noted how difficult it could be for "fellow religionists" in another country to help those currently undergoing persecution. He cited how American Catholics would have been adversely affected if other Catholics in Italy or Germany would have come to their assistance in combating the Ku Klux Klan. Foreign aid would have played into the hands of the Klan. "In any activities of mine in connection with [the NCCJ] I wish to steer clear of foreign entanglements," Ross wrote.[22]

This position relies on Ross' own reading of Catholicism in international affairs. In his letter to Lynch, he makes a point of mentioning the difficulties incurred by Catholics coming to the defense of their brethren in foreign lands, as in the case of Mexico. That nation's laws had been severely restrictive toward Catholic culture, to the point where many Mexican bishops were exiled in the United States and scores of churches closed. Only in 1929, on the order of the pope, did the churches in Mexico attempt re-opening. While the Catholic press in the United States deplored the whole situation, it did not advocate for American diplomatic pressure to reverse the Mexican legislation, nor did President Roosevelt volunteer to do so.[23]

Similarly, Ross brought up the bloody revolution in Spain. Spanish liberals hastened both the collapse of the monarchy and the suppression of religion in the elections of 1930. The following year, Republicans and Socialists deconfessionalized Spain, permitting divorce, introducing civil marriage, secularizing education, banning Jesuits, and ending state subvention of the clergy. Catholics across Europe and in the United States watched dumb founded, shocked at once by the actions of the new Spanish government, but also paralyzed by an isolationist grip that did not seem to shake loose until German aid was lent to the fascists under Franco in 1936.[24]

Ross also showed a peculiar distaste for the fame that the tour brought him. Shortly afterward, he began a steady stream of refusals for speaking engagements. His letters reveal a man deeply concerned over the situation in Europe, but from a decidedly isolationist standpoint.[25] He gives no evidence that his position has changed from the earlier communication with Lynch. In fact, he remains strangely quiet about publicly opposing the Hitler regime and consistently resists involvement in efforts to bring about public repudiation of it in the United States and abroad.

One example of this may be found in an exchange Ross had with Samuel Untermyer of New York, a prominent Jewish attorney and an organizer of a global conference in London calling for an "economic boycott of Hitlerism." Untermyer asked Everett Clinchy to invite Ross as a delegate. Ross had been nominated to attend by Salmon O. Levinson, the peace advocate based in Chicago. The plan was to join eight or ten other Americans of various faiths at this conference, including Paul Hutchinson, the editor of *The Christian Century*.

As was his habit, Ross declined. In his reply to Untermyer, he suggested another priest, T. Lawrason Riggs, the Catholic chaplain at Yale University and heir to the Riggs banking fortune. He also mentioned George N. Schuster as a worthwhile invitee. At the time, Schuster was an editor at *The Commonweal* and would later become president of Hunter College. With these suggestions, Ross seemed genuinely interested in bringing about a successful conference, even going so far as to suggest that the organizers contact Cardinal William Bourne in England to solicit his support.

Still, the courtesy of dealing with the invitation also occasioned continued isolationist rhetoric. Ross replied in benign terms.

> It is not necessary for me to say that I think it a calamity for Germany and for the whole world that Hitler ever came into power. I should like to see his downfall hastened. My only doubt is as to the effectiveness of a boycott under the circumstances. My hope is that the Lutherans and Catholics in Germany will soon be able to handle him.[26]

Ross concluded, "I believe that I could not contribute enough to a conference to warrant the expenses of the trip."[27]

Untermyer's reply is equally telling, for just as Ross felt constrained by his isolationism, Untermyer was convinced that international action was needed, especially from the United States. "The boycott is the only weapon in the hands of civilization," he wrote to Ross. Further, he hoped to win supporters who would trumpet the cause of the Anti-Nazi League, the lead agent in the boycott. While he welcomed the suggestion to make contact with Cardinal Bourne in London, Untermyer was less sanguine on the nomination of George Schuster. According to Untermyer, Schuster was "not a sufficiently outspoken advocate of the boycott."[28]

Untermyer knew the situation well. He appealed to Ross' religious sensitivities, explaining to him that Hitler was at that very moment "soft-pedaling" on the relationship between the Reich and the churches until after the Saar plebescite.

> I expect a revival of that bitter religious controversy as soon as the plebiscite is over. Hitler, Moeller, Rosenberg, and the rest of that crowd are atheists at heart. They would like to introduce into Germany their pagan religion which scraps the Old Testament and parts of the New Testament and which exalts the State above the Church. Their purpose is to put all religion under the iron heel of the State, and if they remain in power they will not stop short of that objective.[29]

In his letter, Untermyer told Ross that all financial expenses for the trip would be assumed by the conference organizers, but it was not enough to make Ross a "convinced boycotter." As the conference date approached, Ross wrote again to Untermyer declining the offer. This time, however, Ross sought to assure him that the urgency of the situation was not so dire that it could not be handled by the Germans themselves. "My own reading of history," he wrote, "inclines me to believe that outside interference usually defeats its own purpose."[30] He went on to suggest that Untermyer's program was bound to be ineffectual:

... Suppose that organizations in England and Germany undertook to boycott southern cotton until the South revised its attitude towards the Negro. Would this help the Negro? I don't think so. It would effectively tie the hands of those Southerners who are working for better relations between the races.[31]

After this refusal, Ross' correspondence breaks off considerably. On March 27, 1936, he published his most urgent appeal to forego entering into war. "Of a piece with the foolishness of war," he wrote, "is the foolishness of imagining that preparedness for war is the best guarantee of peace."[32] Days later, on Easter Tuesday of that year, he was afflicted by the first of three strokes. Between illness and pastoral commitments at the University of Virginia, Ross' celebrity dwindled as a national spokesperson on behalf of Christian-Jewish relations. Nevertheless, he continued occasional contact with Rabbi Lazaron and Everett Clinchy of the NCCJ. Gradually, however, even his involvement with the NCCJ showed signs of disengagement.

Perhaps because the volume of correspondence is so limited in the last ten years of his life, one letter from the period stands out. It demonstrates how Ross' own views on isolationism took a decisive turn. Moreover, it bears upon current questions over Eugenio Pacelli's role as the Vatican Secretary of State, prior to his election as Pope Pius XII. In March, 1938, Clinchy wrote to Ross that he was going to Europe "to make some observations about trends in intellectual and religious freedom in the territory stretching from Budapest to Oxford."[33] Ross wrote back suggesting that Clinchy obtain "an audience with the pope or the cardinal secretary of state, and ask quite frankly if anything has been done by the Vatican in regard to anti-Semitism in Poland."[34] He suggested that Clinchy say "this question has often come to you, and that many Jews assert that nothing has been done, although the Poles are such loyal Catholics that a word from the Pope would be sufficient." With Pacelli, Clinchy would be in a position to inquire as to the extent of the Vatican's activities relative to anti-Semitism and that in meeting with him it "would be about as good for your purpose as the Pope."

While Clinchy was on his voyage, Ross suffered his second

stroke, and so was not able to give the NCCJ any more of his attention. Doubtless Clinchy returned to New York dismayed by the events of the German invasion of Poland where both Catholics and Jews would suffer interminable anguish and loss.

Concluding Analysis

From these brief glances into the thought of Father Ross, a complex picture of the Catholic elite emerges. On the one hand, there is clear hesitation over public advocacy for internationalist action. On the other hand, there is a willingness to work privately toward a political resolution of the religious question in Germany and the territories it eventually annexed. His method is an intellectual one, based on a subjective reading of historical trends.

This is not true of other Catholic elites, especially those who saw that what was happening to German Jews could be dangerous to Catholic interests as well. For instance, Hillaire Belloc, writing in *America* in the summer of 1933, declared:

> I confess I cannot myself see how any Catholic can support or condone what has happened to the Jews…. Men who have passed their lives earning their living by their professions in a particular trade have been reduced, through no fault of their own and merely by accident of birth, to penury at a moment's notice. How can that possibly be excused?[35]

In the same way, a 1934 editorial in *The Commonweal* praised a statement of the American Committee on Religious Rights and Minorities decrying Germany's "persecution of Jewish citizens," noting that

> The treatment of the Jews—or of the loyal Protestant and Catholic Germans who will not submit to the full demands of the controlling element—is a question of justice and humanity, of concern to all civilized people.[36]

In both journals, there were Catholics who demonstrated unabashed sentiments over the plight of German Jews.

We simply cannot know whether, had Catholics been more eager to assist England and France against German aggression at earlier stages of the conflict, the Roosevelt administration would have shifted away from its isolationist diplomacy any sooner. What is plain is that the delay in America's involvement in the European war cost lives on a mass scale—both Catholic and Jewish.

Endnotes

1. On isolationism in the Roosevelt administration see Wayne S. Cole, *Roosevelt and the Isolationists, 1932-1945* (Lincoln, NE: University of Nebraska Press, 1983); Robert Dallek, *Franklin D. Roosevelt and American Foreign Policy, 1932-1945* (New York: Oxford University Press, 1979); Jay Pierrepont Moffat, *The Moffat Papers: Selections from the Diplomatic Journals of Jay Pierrepont Moffat, 1919-1943*, ed., Nancy Harrison Hooker (Cambridge, MA: Harvard University Press, 1956).

2. Cf., Alfred O. Hero, *American Religious Groups View Foreign Policy: Trends in Rank-and-File Opinion, 1937-1969* (Durham, NC: Duke University Press, 1973).

3. Kennedy recorded in his diary the instructions Roosevelt had given him prior to his departure for Great Britain:

He indicated his firm intention of keeping our country out of any and all involvements or commitments abroad. He considered the situation too uncertain for the United States to do anything but mark time until things have settled down. He did not seem to resent the position Chamberlain has taken of trying to make deals with Germany or Italy in order to fend off a crisis.

Cf., Amanda Smith, ed., *Hostage to Fortune: The Letters of Joseph P. Kennedy* (New York: Viking, 2001), 236.

4. On the following, see especially Mary Christine Athans, *The Coughlin-Fahey Connection: Father Charles E. Coughlin, Father Dennis Fahey, C.S.Sp., and Religious Anti-Semitism in the United States, 1938-1954* (New York: Peter Lang, 1991); Charles Tull, *Father Coughlin and the New Deal* (Syracuse, NY: Syracuse University Press, 1965).

5. John LaFarge, *The Manner is Ordinary* (New York: Harcourt, Brace, 1954), 250.

6. *America* 64 (October 19, 1940): 42.

7. *America* 64 (March 15, 1941): 618.

8. Cited in George Q. Flynn, *Roosevelt and Romanism: Catholics and American Diplomacy, 1937-1945* (Westport, CT: Greenwood Press, 1976), 64.

9. *America* 64 (November 23, 1940): 183.

10. See Philip E. Jacob, "Influences of World Events on U.S. 'Neutrality' Opinion," *Public Opinion Quarterly* 4 (1940): 48-65. The results of these polls are given in the same issue at 83 and following.

11. "Peace is the Object," *Commonweal* 33 (November 22, 1940): 117.

12. Cf., *Catholic Action* 22:1 (January 1940): 4. For discussion, Thomas McAvoy, "American Catholics and the Second World War," *Review of Politics* 6 (1944): 131-150.

13. Ryan was not alone. One of the most prominent Catholics of the time, Carlton J.H. Hayes, the Columbia University historian and wartime ambassador to Spain, denounced isolationism masquerading as nationalism and saw the Nazi and Fascist movements as the logical outcome of extreme nationalism. Both men, however, were part of a tiny minority of Catholic intellectuals advocating these positions.

14. See, e.g., "Conscientious Objection Duty of Christians," *Catholic Worker* (November 1935): 3, where it states "Catholics should and must refuse to take part in any modern war."

15. This is especially true after *Kristallnacht*, November 9-13, 1938. The *Catholic Worker*, for instance, printed articles by Archbishop Joseph Rummel of New Orleans and Bishop John Gannon of Erie, Pennsylvania, in the December, 1938, issue denouncing the Nazi government and urging prayer and action on behalf of German Jews.

16. Ross was a slice of Americana: a descendent of Betsy Ross and George Ross, one of the signers of the Declaration of Independence. He was an intellectual, did his doctoral work in sociology, and went on to become the Catholic chaplain at Columbia University, the University of Texas at Austin, and the University of Virginia. He would remain in Charlottesville from 1932 to 1943, retiring to the Paulist community at St. Paul's Church in Manhattan where he died on September 18, 1946, at the age of sixty-two. For biographical information, cf., Paul Robichaud, "J. Elliot Ross," *Paulist History*, v. 1:4 (1991): 4-15; Patrick J. Hayes, "J. Elliot Ross and the National Conference of Christians and Jews: A Catholic Contribution to Tolerance in America," *Journal of Ecumenical Studies* 37:3-4 (Summer-Fall 2000): 321-332.

17. A summary of Ross' participation is given by him in "An Ounce of Prevention," *The Commonweal* 19 (1934): 399-401.

18. Clinchy to Ross, December 15, 1933, in Ross Papers, Archives of the Congregation of St. Paul, St. Paul's College, Washington, D.C. (hereafter Ross Papers).

19. See the letter of James Katzman to Ross, March 22, 1939, referring to the previous award in 1934 in Ross Papers. In 1939, the trio received the Gottheil Medal a second time.

20. See "Jews and Christians Join Hands: Meetings in Denver Nov. 19-21, to Fight Bigotry," *The Western Jewish Advocate* 5: 3 (November, 1933): 5. The editorial page of this paper, which was based in Denver, reads in part: "*The Western Jewish Advocate*, dedicated to further better understanding between men of all creeds, is happy to welcome them with open arms."

21. Ross to Lynch, October 6, 1933, in Ross Papers.

22. *Ibid.*

23. It was not until after the Mexico situation had become so egregious, 1934-1935, that Catholics began to exert pressure on the Roosevelt administration. In response, Roosevelt wrote to the head of the Knights of Columbus in November, 1935: "I decline to permit this Government to undertake a policy of interference in the domestic concerns of foreign governments and thereby jeopardize the maintenance of peaceful relations." Cited in Robert Dallek, *Franklin D. Roosevelt and American Foreign Policy, 1932-1945* (New York: Oxford University Press, 1979) 123. Cf., E. David Cronon, "American Catholics and Mexican Anti-Clericalism," *Mississippi Valley Historical Review* 45 (1958) 201-230.

24. See Gabriel Jackson, *The Spanish Republic and the Civil War, 1931-1939* (Princeton, NJ: Princeton University Press, 1965); Frances Lannon, *Privilege, Persecution, and Prophecy: The Catholic Church in Spain, 1875-1975* (New York: Oxford University Press, 1987) 170-223; idem., "The Church's Crusade Against the Republic," in P. Preston, ed., *Revolution and War in Spain, 1931-1939* (London, 1984); A. Montero Moreno, *Historia de la persecucíon religiosa en España 1936-1939* (Madrid: 1961). For American responses to the crisis, cf., Donald Crosby, "Boston's Catholics and the Spanish Civil War," *New England Quarterly* 44 (1971) 82-100; J. David Valaik, "American Catholic Dissenters and the Spanish Civil War," *Catholic Historical Review* 53 (1968) 537-555; and idem, "Catholics, Neutrality, and the Spanish Embargo, 1937-1939," *Journal of American History* 54 (1967) 73-85.

25. Ross' isolationism was common among clergymen of the day. See further Gerald Sittser, *A Cautious Patriotism: The American Churches and the Second World War* (Chapel Hill, NC: University of North Carolina Press, 1997).

26. Ross to Untermyer, November 4, 1934, in Ross Papers.

27. *Ibid.*

28. Ross to Untermyer, November 10, 1934, in Ross Papers.

29. Ross to Untermyer, November 4, 1934, in Ross Papers.

30. *Ibid.*

31. *Ibid.*

32. Ross, "America and War," *The Commonweal* 23 (March 27, 1936): 593-595, here at 595.

33. Clinchy to Ross, March 18, 1938, in Ross Papers.

34. Ross to Clinchy, March 25, 1938, in Ross Papers.

35. See Belloc, "The Persecution of the Jews," *America* 49 (1933): 367-369, here at 368.

36. See "Friends of Germany," *The Commonweal* 19 (February 2, 1934): 365-366.

CHAPTER 9

Christian Hope as a Factor in How Protestants Followed Hitler

Drew A. Parsons

The Protestant Christians in Germany during the pre-Nazi and Nazi era were faced with a decision to ally themselves with the growing Nazi movement or to work against it. Many chose to take their stand with Hitler and the Nazi party, aiding his ascent through their support and encouragement. It is my assertion that a key factor informing their decision to follow Hitler was the harmonic resonance they felt between the dynamics of Christian hope and the nationalistic hope presented by the charismatic leadership of the Nazis. This resonance allowed some to make an almost seamless transition from church life in the Weimar years to ecclesiastical expression under the swastika.

This study will help to inform current Christian expression to be vigilant in the way in which basic doctrines of the faith, like Christian hope, can be a driving force for good or evil in other spheres of social, political, and cultural life. While much criticism is rightly leveled at the radical exclusionary expressions of religious groups on the fringes of Protestant contemporary life, we often overlook the power of similar feelings and expressions of exclusion within the mainstream of Protestant religious institutions and their constituents. It would be easy for us to evaluate the Protestant movements like the German Christians as merely popular radical groups caught up in the fervor of the moment as Hitler came to power. Many of the changes in doctrine and thought proposed by the German Christians were extremely radical, revisionist, and in some cases anti-Christian. Though some Protestant leaders among the clergy and laity fought against what the Nazis and German Christians proposed, too many Protestants actively or passively gave assent to Hitler and his racial program for a renewed Germany to explain it away as the work of a relatively few misguided radicals. Something at the core of Protestant Christian beliefs, teachings, and expression was tapped which provided a broad supportive response to what became the most proficient expression of evil in history. Christian hope in the Protestant tradition will be the core belief explored in this study. Perhaps there is room in future studies to look critically at other basic tenets of the Christian faith in this same fashion to see if such core beliefs can be usurped for evil as was Christian hope.

Christian hope centers around a Christian's understanding that God has acted on behalf of all people to bring them fulfillment of "abundant life" (John 10:10) through the person and personality of Jesus Christ. Through the life, death, and resurrection of Jesus Christ, God has provided a means for persons to, once again, re-enter the abundant life as it is metaphorically portrayed in the Garden of Eden. Through the sacrifice of Jesus Christ, himself a persona of God made flesh, the sin which humans committed that broke the relationship between God and humanity is forgiven and erased. In the words of theologian Rudolf Bultmann, "We are what we are in hope."[1] Our relationship to Christ in this hope is not just ecclesiastical but personal.

The dynamics of hope as they derive from these acts of God have several facets as they are experienced and expressed by Protestant Christians. Hope, as it is realized by the person, has a quality that looks toward a brighter future and it also informs how the person lives in the present. Christian hope is often referred to as an experience of the "now already—not yet."[2] It is "now already" because the act of God in Jesus Christ has been done once and for all and can be experienced to some degree in the present, but it will never have it's more glorious fulfillment in this world tainted by the ongoing sin of humanity. Christian hope assumes that "all have sinned and fall short of the glory of God" (Romans 3:23). In this sense, Christian hope is always critical of the past, yet it is optimistic of the present because the saving Christ lives and works in the present and that saving work is revealed to us in the present life in which we live. The "not yet" anticipates and expects a more glorious fulfillment through an ultimate righteous judgment of all people by God. Those who choose to believe in God's forgiveness through the act of Jesus Christ will be spared that judgment and be restored to an abundant eternal life. Brunner adds, "The Christian hope... is itself the goal to which the Christian faith reaches forward."(346)[3] When Protestant Christians say, "I am saved," they are expressing their Christian hope "now already" because they can feel a joy over against the burden of their sin and they are expressing the "not yet" in that they anticipate a greater joy to come when this life is over.

These dynamics of Christian hope have a role in the everyday life of a Protestant Christian. Since they accept and understand these saving acts of God's forgiveness in Jesus Christ by faith, they live more abundant lives out of thankfulness to God in anticipation of the fulfillment of God's promise to forgive. This thankful response normally takes the path of love toward God and neighbor in expressions of kindness and mercy. These acts of mutuality often provide a foretaste of that glorious future hope promised by God. Some of the "not yet" of hope is experienced as "now already" or realized hope. It is from this experience that the, so-called, "Protestant work ethic" is derived. Basically, it means that if a Protestant is thankful to God, then he responds with a sense of diligence about life. If you are thankful you work hard; if you work hard you will be rewarded. It becomes a cyclical and practical way of experiencing God's grace in a temporal way. Likewise, working hard becomes a part of abundant living as opposed to being lazy. It becomes an outward expression of one's Christian hope.

When extreme stress or crisis occur in the lives of Protestants, sometimes the dynamic of hope is transformed into a different thing altogether. If Protestants experience persecution from others, or if the temporal world around them becomes corrupted or depressed in any way, Christian hope begins to emphasize the "not yet" over against the "now already." Abundant life under these circumstances seems to be interrupted and delayed. The focus begins to change, looking for someone or something that is sent by God to intercede in and correct the crisis or stress so that abundant life can be restored. This can be in the form of a prophet or an event or a sign to instill hope once again in a situation that seems to have no hope. I believe this is what occurred in Germany within the lives of faithful Protestants during the Weimar years leading to the Nazi era.

Because of the extreme stressors experienced by Germans in the post-World War I period, they began to take steps down what Ervin Staub calls, "a continuum of destruction" as they sought to find hope out of their despair.[4] German Protestants began to confuse the Nationalistic and racially based message of Hitler and the Nazis with the dynamics of Christian hope as they understood them. Hope became for them a divine selection of Aryan Germany to lead the way toward a better life, fulfilling God's promises.[5] Christian hope, looking forward yet tied to present behavior, became psychologically bound to the Nazi ideology that emphasized that while sacrifices would have to be made now, the reward in the future would be great. Nicolas Railton writes,

> Disappointment with the Weimar democratic system led many, indeed most evangelicals to look for alternative, radical, and quick solutions to social, economic and political problems in their country. The man (Hitler) who seemed to offer those solutions did not smoke or drink alcohol and lived a sexually abstinent life; he was also said to carry a well-read New Testament around with him.[6]

Protestants could continue to live out their lives in thankful response to God with Hitler as His emissary.

According to recent church growth principles there is a phenomenon in which stressful events in the lives of individuals makes them more receptive to "changes in lifestyle during periods of transition."[7] By using an adaptation of the Holmes-Rahe Stress Test, church members can evaluate the degree to which a prospective member will be open to becoming a Christian during the period of transition. The idea is that the greater a person's stress the more receptive one will be for a change. The greater the length of the stress, the receptivity is increased.[8] At its best, this principle honestly seeks to identify the genuine needs of people and minister to those needs through the life of the church. At its worst, it can deteriorate into capitalizing on a person's weaknesses for the purpose of adding to the church rolls. Either way the principle holds true. People under stress are in a vulnerable state and hope is challenged during those liminal stages of life.

While church growth experts identify this principle for the purpose of making new disciples, the principle can function for those already in the church when they are in a vulnerable state of transition as well. The Protestants of post-World War I Germany can be seen as being in such a vulnerable state of transition based partly on the historic relationship of church and state and how it informed their sense of Christian hope. Since the times of the Peace of Westphalia after the Thirty Years War, the principalities that made up what became Germany aligned themselves with Protestant or Catholic traditions depending on the faith of the local prince. The mutual alliance of the church and state strengthened both in the early formation of the Protestant movement. This relationship would persist throughout German history until the Weimar Republic after World War I. With the defeat of Germany in World War I and the establishment of the Weimar Republic, Germans experienced extremely different and difficult conditions than what they were used to prior to the war. Without a political figurehead like the Kaiser and with the threat of growing Communist control, Germans were uneasy with the freedoms and instability. The terms of the Versailles Treaty were very harsh and left most in Germany disheartened and distressed. The depressed economy brought despair. The need for a renewed hope among the people increased. What was it about Hitler's plan for a new Germany through the Nazi program that had such a strong appeal for German Protestants?

When hope is cast in the terms of divine fulfillment and sanctification and given concrete connection to temporal life, especially when it comes in a strongly charismatic program, then people can become vulnerable to new images of hope from other sources which utilize the language and imagery of former hopes. Daniel Goldhagen, examining the church's role in giving assent and guidance for what he calls "eliminationist" anti-Semitism, asserts that,

> The churches welcomed the Nazi's ascendancy to power, for they were deeply conservative institutions which, like most other German conservative bodies and associations, expected the Nazis to deliver Germany from what they deemed to have been the spiritual and political mire that was the Weimar Republic, with its libertine culture, democratic "disorder," its powerful Socialist and Communist parties which preached atheism and which threatened to rob the churches of their power and influence. The churches expected that the Nazis would establish an authoritarian regime that would reclaim the wrongly dishonored virtues of unquestioning obedience and submission to authority, restore the cultivation of traditional moral values, and enforce adherence to them.[9]

This sanctification of the Nazi propaganda and spiritualizing of the social circumstances of the struggling German nation resonated with the themes of Christian hope leading toward divine fulfillment. Doris Bergen provides a thorough examination of the movement called German Christians. This inter-denominational group proved to be the most enduring and powerful of Protestant organizations within the Third Reich. She says of the conditions that led to Protestant support of the Nazi ideology,

> Abdication of the Kaiser and removal of the regional princes who had served as *summi episcopi*—heads of the church—led many Protestants to fear complete separation of church and

state. Such anxiety and their own efforts to distance themselves and their church organization from the democratic state led them to define the people's church in new ways, often emphasizing ties to German culture and ethnicity.[10]

The German Protestant understanding of church and state structure under the Weimar Government was a strong threat to the stability of their hope as they sought to revert to the pre-Weimar relationships with church and state. This element of stress increased their vulnerability to the hope outlined in the Nazi program. To them it appeared that the Nazis would restore not only the nation but the church as a national body as well.

As Hitler began to outline his ideology against the Jews, he proclaimed, "Thus did I now believe that I must act in the sense of the Almighty Creator: by fighting against the Jews, I am doing the Lord's work."[11] The anti-Semitic fervor of Hitler's ideology, in many cases, added to the resonance of Christian hope for many Protestants. The "eliminationist" (Goldhagen) nature of Nazi anti-Semitism solved, in some ways, the Jewish dilemma Christians had faced for centuries. Jewish rejection of the gospel along with accusations that Jews were the murderers of Christ had always been points of anti-semitic feeling among Christians. These feelings were resurrected as the Jews became targets for the cause of the individual German's unfulfilled hope.

The Christian scriptures provide ample material for the formulation of the attitudes of Protestants during the Nazi years as a means to restore and maintain Christian hope as they understood it. The passage cited earlier from John's gospel which introduces the hope of living abundantly is preceded by these words from Chapter 10 beginning at verse 8; Jesus says,

> All who came before me are thieves and bandits, but the sheep did not listen to them. I am the gate. Whoever enters by me will be saved, and will come in and go out and find pasture. The thief comes only to steal and kill and destroy. I came that they may have life, and have it abundantly.

Here the hope of having abundant life is tied to metaphorical thieves and bandits in the motif of sheep stealing. The thieves and bandits are all those who came before Jesus. It is a veiled reference to all Jewish leaders from the past. The thief in the passage comes to steal, kill and destroy. It is not a great leap for Christians when Hitler proposes that Jews are thieves who come to steal, kill and destroy.

According to George Victor's *Hitler: The Pathology of Evil*, Hitler's perception of Jews stemmed from an unsubstantiated understanding that his grandmother had been seduced by the Jewish man for whom she worked as a maid. The resulting pregnancy gave birth to his father.[12] This "secret" would control events in Hitler's life all the way to his death. He felt robbed of his heritage. Jews would always be suspect in his mind and later became viewed in the same terms as the thieves and bandits of John's gospel with devastating results during World War II. In *Mein Kampf*, Hitler would say, "For whatever culture the Jew appears to possess today is in the main the property of other peoples, which has become corrupted under his manipulation."[13] While he never calls them thieves, he clearly characterizes them as one's who steal. It is a theft of culture which defines the Germans. He does call them "parasites" which also implies one who lives off the abundance of others.[14]

Hitler also writes, "The loss of racial purity ruins the fortunes of a race forever; it continues to sink lower and lower and its consequences can never be expelled again from body and mind."[15] He is implying that the "Aryan" race, by becoming diluted with Jewish blood, is killed as a race forever. In a September speech in Munich following the elections of 1930 Hitler says,

> First it (Jews as an alien dominant race) had killed the spirit; through this loss of spirit the German people had been reduced politically to serfdom; this political serfdom had been transformed into economic slavery which entailed the distress of millions of individual Germans. Out of this distress there had come the uprising, i.e., the people now begin to listen, and the spirit of opposition is the necessary consequence of the national collapse.[16]

Jews would later be characterized as a disease or a cancer which would kill if not treated.[17] Hitler writes in *Mein Kampf* of the perceived proliferation of Jews in all walks of life, "When carefully cutting open such a growth, one could find a little Jew, blinded by the sudden light, like a maggot in a rotting corpse."[18] In a speech at Wilhelmhaven on April 1, 1939, Hitler characterizes Jews as a "Jewish bacillus infecting the life of the peoples."[19]

As to the Jew's ability to destroy, Hitler writes, "By means of the trades-union, which might have been the saving of the nation, the Jew actually destroys the bases of the nation's economics."[20] In Hitler's understanding and apparently in the minds of millions of Germans, the Jews were "their misfortune" because they were stealing, killing and destroying all that they had and all that they were.[21] In doing so their hope was being lost. Abundant life promised to the faithful was being taken away under the Weimar Republic and the Jews were characterized as the thieves, a characterization reinforced by the Christian Scriptures related to hope.

It is ironic that the Confessing Church, the opponents to the Nazi threat to establish a State church under Nazi control, uses the same verses in John 10 as the scriptural basis for opposing Article 24 of the Nazi program.[22] In their interpretation, they imply the Nazi leaders are the thieves in the allegory.

According to J.C.R. Wright, sixty percent of Germany's population was Protestant. About one fourth of those listed as Protestant were considered active members. The majority of the inactive members were from the working classes. The leadership of the churches guided much of the direction the churches would take in the years leading up to the Third Reich. Their choices would have long-term consequences for the success of the Hitler regime.[23] What of the three-fourths of the remaining Protestants who made up the inactive members? I propose that their participation in the Hitler regime was not inconsequential as persons raised in the Protestant tradition. In fact, they may have made up the larger portion of the brown shirts of the early years leading up to the Third Reich. They were from the working class that suffered greatly by being out of work due to the depressed economy. They felt the effects of the depression the most. They were not active in the church because the hope they once knew was being challenged by their life experiences under the difficult life conditions present in Weimar Germany. Wright later adds, "Church leaders also knew that there was strong support for the NSDAP among their parishioners."[24]

In one testimony from Theodore Abel's collection of Nazi autobiographies, the respondent tells how, though he and his brothers and sisters were all baptized, his father would have nothing to do with the church. When the respondent's sister was on her deathbed at age nineteen, his mother pleaded with the pastor to come give her the sacrament. The pastor refused to come to the house because the father was a social democrat.[25] This kind of experience does not necessarily destroy one's hope, it does encourage one to look for the same hope in other ways. In this case the respondent turned to Hitler's movement after his experience as a soldier and as a member of other nationalistic groups in order to fulfill that hope. The three-fourths of Protestants who were inactive, regardless of their class had lost hope in the church as an institution but still longed for those same values within Christian hope of abundant life to which the church introduced them. In the troubled and confusing years from the end of World War I through the years of the Weimar Republic and the Third Reich, many of these found that hope in the nationalistic claims asserted by Hitler.

The elements introduced and discussed above rely on the visions of hope that people have for their present life and for their future existence. Bergen summarizes the behavior of German Protestants this way,

> Few were pious, many were not observant, and some opted to abandon the Christian churches in favor of neopagan groups. But all of them were born into a predominantly Christian society and participated in its culture. Viewed in this light, German Christian efforts represent an explicit attempt to accomplish what most Germans did implicitly: reconcile their Christian tradition with National Socialist ideology.[26]

This is a concise representation of what occurred in the lives of German Protestants and it points to the way in which basic tenets of the faith were transmuted from instruments for good and growth and abundant life into instruments of destruction, both spiritually and physically.

I offer a concluding model related to Ervin Staub's continuums of destruction and benevolence which might help bring these elements into further perspective and provide some guidance for Protestant Christians in particular and all persons in general. Staub's understanding of good and evil lies along a continuum with two extreme ends. This model is helpful for analysis of the cultures of caring and destruction. In this analysis it may be helpful to view good and evil falling on two halves of a circle meeting at two points, good being on the left and evil on the right. Bisecting the circle again from left to right, the top of the circle would represent passionate expressions of good and evil and mediocre expressions at the bottom of the circle. As we live life passionately along the perimeter of this model, we run the risk of slipping back and forth at the top and bottom of that circle between good and evil, most poignantly at the point where passionate good meets passionate evil. Our passion for doing good can easily drift over into what is evil even when the original intent was toward a good goal. When we are in a passionate mode to do good, we may be at a greater risk to compromise our methods and actions in order to bring about the desired hope. The stories of Jesus' temptation in the wilderness (Matthew 4:1-11) may be a prime example of this for Christians. Our greatest temptation comes when we are tempted to do something evil to bring about a good result.

A recent example of this tendency is illustrated by the revelation of Rev. Billy Graham's remarks to President Richard Nixon in early 1972, the year of Nixon's re-election and of the Watergate break-in. In tapes released by the National Archives, Rev. Graham expresses deeply disturbing attitudes towards Jews and his understanding of Jewish influence in relation to how he perceives the state of America at that time. In the conversation following a prayer breakfast,

Graham speaks of the "total Jewish domination of the media" and that the Jewish "stranglehold has got to be broken or the country's going down the drain." When speaking of his relationship to Jews, he states, "They don't know how I really feel about what they are doing to this country. And I have no power, no way to handle them, but I would stand up if under proper circumstances."[27] These remarks are clearly anti-Semitic even as many have tried to defend Graham's remarks as being said in the context of the time. Some suggest that he was speaking more against liberals than Jews.

What is germane to this example in the context which I present it is that I believe Graham was speaking out of a sense of hope for the improvement of the society in which he lived and had spiritual influence. Wanting to see one's society not go "down the drain" is a good attitude in our culture. In 1972, many across America would describe the country going down the drain. Think of all the turmoil we were experiencing then, politically, economically, militarily, socially. It was a time of mixed hope and despair. When given the chance to address the problem of the country going down the drain with the President of the United States, Graham did not offer a plethora of options that I am sure he was aware of in his wide knowledge of American culture. Instead, in his passionate hope to improve the life of the nation, which would always be grounded first in his understanding of Christian Protestant hope, he chose to scapegoat the Jews as the source of the problem. He would add his spiritual blessing on Nixon's re-election as a possibility that change might take place to eliminate the Jewish influence.

In his passion to make America better and using that passion to influence and endorse the nation's leader, Billy Graham, Protestantism's most visible figure of the time, drifted over the top of the circle from passionate good to passionate evil without being able to recall why he did it or, initially, that he had done it at all. If someone as learned and traveled, and who kept the company of "Jewish friends" as Rev. Dr. Billy Graham, can drift back and forth from passionate good to passionate evil so easily given this evidence, one can begin to see how Aryan German Protestants wanting to improve their nation and their churches could passionately drift into the negative stereotypes of Jews which had long been a part of their culture and doctrine as a means to bring about change for bettering their lives, without being aware they were drifting into the evil that would mire them in war and the Holocaust.

Those who fit the Aryan template attest that life in Hitler's Germany was better than during the Weimar years. In the film, *Good Morning, Mr. Hitler*, several people looking back at themselves during a festival filmed during the Third Reich speak of being happy and fulfilled under Hitler's rule. They also attest that they didn't think much about where the Jews were during those times.[28] They seemed to have blocked out the atrocities dictated by the government in order to enjoy what Hitler had done for them. In their passion for the pageantry of German life as it was being re-established, their hope was being fulfilled in a way that they had not experienced during the Weimar years. Their transition from doing what they saw as good for Germany and themselves was not a long drawn out transition from one end of a continuum to another but a short skip across the top of a circle. What is ominous about the circular model is that under these circumstances passionate good can become indistinguishable from passionate evil. Reinhold Niebuhr, speaking of the morality of nations, writes, "There is an ethical paradox in patriotism which defies every but the most astute and sophisticated analysis. The paradox is that patriotism transmutes individual unselfishness into national egoism."[29] Similarly, Christian hope was transmuted, given the circumstances of life in Weimar Germany and the way that the churches related to their governing bodies. I am not advocating that we squelch passionate living. What I assert is that when life gets passionate, we must proceed with caution lest we fall easily into doing what is evil while thinking we are doing what is good.

The Christian faith in the Protestant tradition is one that is grounded in passionate expressions by its very nature. It was passionate love that gave birth to the Christian movement and in the Protestant Reformation that passion emerged again. Each Protestant's call to discipleship is grounded in the passion of Jesus Christ and calls for bold passionate self-giving service in the world. To repeat Bultmann, "We are what we are in hope."[30] That hope is also grounded in passion. Protestant expression in Germany in the years leading up to and including the Third Reich became vulnerable to the stresses of life in the Weimar Republic. The vulnerability to these stresses allowed Protestants to make the transition to comply with the hopes of Nazi ideology in order to achieve the abundant life promised in Christian hope. We must be willing to evaluate continually our passionate hope to be sure that it does not drift into doing evil in order to attain that hope.

Endnotes

1. Bultmann, Rudolf, *Theology of the New Testament*, 101.

2. Brunner, Emil, *The Christian Doctrine of the Church, Faith, and the Consummation Dogmatics: Vol. III*, 341-343.

3. *Ibid.*, 346.

4. Staub, Ervin, *The Roots of Evil, The Origins of Genocide and other Group Violence*, 20-23.

5. Bergen, Doris, *Twisted Cross, The German Christian Movement in the Third Reich*, 11.

6. Railton, Nicholas, *The German Evangelical Alliance and the Third Reich*, 10-11.

7. Arn, Win, Ed. *The Pastor's Church Growth Handbook*, 142.

8. *Ibid.*, 143.

9. Goldhagen, Daniel Jonah, *Hitler's Willing Executioners: Ordinary Germans and the Holocaust*, 435.

10. Bergen, *op. cit.*, 10.

11. Hitler, Adolf, *Mein Kampf,* 1933, 25.

12. Victor, George, *Hitler, The Pathology of Evil*, 13-20.

13. Hitler, *op. cit.*, 126.

14. *Ibid.*, 127.

15. *Ibid.*, 133.

16. Baynes, Norman H. ed., *The Speeches of Adolf Hitler, April 1922–August 1939*, 187.

17. Proctor, Robert, *Racial Hygiene, Medicine Under the Nazis*, 195.
18. Hitler, Adolf, *Mein Kampf,* 1939, 75.
19. Baynes, *op. cit.*, 743.
20. Hitler, 1933, *op. cit.*, 131.
21. Meltzer, Milton, *Never to Forget, The Jews of the Holocaust*, 36.
22. Matheson, Peter, *The Third Reich and the Christian Churches*, 46.
23. Wright, J.R.C., *Above Parties: The Political Attitudes of the German Protestant Church Leadership 1918-1933*, vi.
24. *Ibid.*, 90.
25. Abel, Theodore, *Why Hitler Came into Power*, 246-247.
26. Bergen, Doris, *op. cit.*, 10.
27. "Billy Graham Responds to Lingering Anger Over 1972 Remarks on Jews," *New York Times, (Sunday, March 17, 2002)*, 29.
28. *Good Morning Mr. Hitler.*
29. Niebuhr, Reinhold, *Moral Man and Immoral Man, A Study in Ethics and Politics,* 91.
30. Bultmann, *op. cit.*, 101.

Bibliography

Abel, Theodore, *Why Hitler Came into Power*, Cambridge: Harvard University Press, 1986.

Arn, Win, Ed. *The Pastor's Church Growth Handbook*, Pasadena: Church Growth Press, 1979.

Baynes, Norman H. ed., *The Speeches of Adolf Hitler, April 1922-August 1939*, H. New York: Fertig, 1969.

Bergen, Doris, *Twisted Cross, The German Christian Movement in the Third Reich*, Chapel Hill: The University Of North Carolina Press, 1996.

Brunner, Emil, *The Christian Doctrine of the Church, Faith and the Consummation Dogmatics: Vol. III*, Philadelphia: Westminster Press, 1962.

Bultmann, Rudolf, *Theology of the New Testament*, New York: Charles Scribner's Sons, 1955.

Firestone, David, "Billy Graham Responds to Lingering Anger Over 1972 Remarks on Jews," *The New York Times* (Sunday, March 17, 2002), Sec. 1, p. 29.

Goldhagen, Daniel Jonah, *Hitler's Willing Executioners: Ordinary Germans and the Holocaust*, New York: Alfred A. Knopf, 1996.

Hitler, Adolf, *Mein Kampf*, Boston and New York: Houghton Mifflin Company, 1933.

Hitler, Adolf, *Mein Kampf*, New York: Reynal and Hitchcock, 1939.

Holland, Luke and Paul Yule, *Good Morning, Mister Hitler*, (video recording) Chicago: International Historic Films, 1994.

Matheson, Peter, *The Third Reich and the Christian Churches*, William B. Grand Rapids: Eerdmans, 1981.

Meltzer, Milton, *Never to Forget, The Jews of the Holocaust*, New York: Harper Collins: 1976.

Niebuhr, Reinhold, *Moral Man and Immoral Man, A Study in Ethics and Politics*, New York: Charles Scribner's Sons, 1960.

Proctor, Robert, *Racial Hygiene, Medicine under the Nazis*, Cambridge: Harvard University Press: 1988.

Railton, Nicholas, *The German Evangelical Alliance and the Third Reich*, Bern: Lang, 1998.

Staub, Ervin, *The Roots of Evil, The Origins of Genocide and other Group Violence*, Cambridge: Cambridge University Press, 1989.

Victor, George, *Hitler, The Pathology of Evil*. Washington: Brassey's, 1998.

Wright, J.R.C., *Above Parties: The Political Attitudes of the German Protestant Church Leadership 1918-1933*, Glasgow: Oxford University Press, 1974.

All Biblical References from the *New Revised Standard Version Bible*, Nashville: Thomas Nelson, 1989.

CHAPTER 10

Jewish-Christian Dialogue in Light of Dietrich Bonhoeffer's Understanding of Jews and Judaism

Renate Wind

I

"Only those who cry out for the Jews may sing Gregorian chants!" With these words in 1938, Dietrich Bonhoeffer called his church to task for being "silent where she should have cried out." Dietrich Bonhoeffer is known as one of the very few representatives of the German churches who joined the resistance movement against the Nazi regime. For him this decision was an act of solidarity with the victims of the Nazi terror, mainly with the Jews, "the weakest and most defenseless brothers of Jesus Christ." But it was also the final consequence of a development in his theological thinking. As a German Lutheran theologian he had to free himself from the traditional anti-Judaism of the Lutheran church. I want to focus on some steps of this development towards a Jewish-Christian dialogue.

II

While at the beginning of the church struggle in 1933 Bonhoeffer held a position of theological anti-Judaism—as even many baptized Jews did—at no point did he share the position of anti-semitism. But although we have to distinguish anti-Judaism from antisemitism, it is important to focus on the fact that anti-Judaism produces or at least nourishes antisemitism. Therefore I intend to deal with anti-Judaistic positions within the Confessing Church as well as with Bonhoeffer's efforts to overcome them.

During the year of 1933 the different positions within the German Protestant church became more and more clear. The origin of the Confessing Church was the foundation of the "Pastors Emergency League" against the adoption of the Aryan paragraph in the Church. Within a short period some one thousand pastors had signed the pledge of the Emergency League against the violation of the Christian confession by the Aryan paragraph in the Church. Most of them approved of the Aryan paragraph directed against Jewish officials in the institutions of the state. The struggle of the Confessing Church against the Aryan paragraph was limited to a commitment for the rights of baptized Jews within the church. But of course even this resistance was suppressed by the Nazi government as well as by the National Socialist German Christians, who, after their success in the church elections in July 1933, had occupied all the key church positions. In 1933 the question whether "Aryans" and "Jews" could form a communion in one church was of utmost importance for all members of the new founded Confessing Church. For Bonhoeffer the decision was clear—a church which excludes a particular group of baptized is no longer the "communion of saints," because she has cut a piece out of the body of Christ. "The excluding Church is erecting a racial law as a prerequisite of Christian communion. But in doing so, she loses Christ himself.... The Aryan paragraph is a 'Status confessionis' for the Church."[1]

Many of the Bonhoeffer quotations about Israel and the Jews at that time must be seen in the historical context of the church struggle. Focusing on the point that a racial law must not separate "Jews" and "Aryans" in the Christian community, the difference between Christian and Jewish religion was maintained. This was partly a concession to the conservative Lutherans within the Confessing Church, but also an expression of a theological anti-Judaism, that Bonhoeffer shared with most Lutheran theologians of his generation, for example with his close friend Franz Hildebrandt, a Lutheran pastor of Jewish descent, who already was a victim of the Aryan paragraph. In Bonhoeffer's famous essay "The Church and the Jewish Question," as well as in many early documents of the Confessing Church, of which Bonhoeffer was a co-author, Israel is seen as God's chosen people that rejected the Messiah and that, at the end of its history, will be brought back to him. Therefore Israel is seen as an object of Christian Mission. Although this attitude towards Israel and the Jews was not hostile, it was far away from Bonhoeffer's later willingness to accept the Jews as partners in a Jewish-Christian dialogue.

III

Let me now outline Bonhoeffer's efforts at first to overcome the limitation of commitment for the baptized Jews. Despite his Lutheran background, Bonhoeffer transcended traditional Lutheran ethics, when he urged the church to resist the government when human rights are violated. The church must not fight only for herself; the church is the church only when she exists for others. In his essay "The Church and the Jewish Question," which was given as a lecture to a group of Berlin pastors in April 1933, Bonhoeffer mentioned three possibilities of church action towards the state:

> In the first place she can ask the state whether its actions are legitimate and in accordance with its character as state, i.e. she can throw the state back to its responsibilities. Secondly, she can aid the victims of the state action. The church has an unconditional obligation to the victims of any ordering of society, EVEN IF THEY DO NOT BELONG TO THE CHRISTIAN COMMUNITY.... The third possibility is not just to bandage the victims under the wheel, but to put a spoke in the wheel itself.[2]

It is important to note that this was said in April 1933—as reaction to the boycott of Jewish shops and the introduction of the

Aryan paragraph regarding Jewish officials in the institutions of the state. At that time no one had the slightest idea that this could be the beginning of a development that would lead to the organization of the Holocaust, but it was an attack on human dignity and civil rights, and Bonhoeffer was the single voice speaking for the victims. The influence of positions and efforts of the American Civil Liberties Union, which engages on behalf of politically and ethnically excluded citizens, here should not be ignored. Already on February 6, 1933 Bonhoeffer wrote to Reinhold Niebuhr, his most important mentor during his studies at the Union Theological Seminary in New York, "that a horrible cultural barbarity is threatening, so that we too here must immediately form a Civil Liberties Union." And he added, "The way of the church is darker than ever before."[3]

In April 1933, Bonhoeffer pledged a radical resistance against political decisions that suspend the civil rights of a particular group within society, mainly the Jews, but for socialists and communists, who were victims of the law on the "Reconstruction of the Civil Service" as well. But with this attitude Bonhoeffer remained alone. His demand that the church must be prepared for political resistance isolated him even within the Confessing Church. The only ones who would agree with him, the Religious Socialists, were themselves already among the persecuted. Paul Tillich, for example, was the first "Aryan" professor to be dismissed from office. He immigrated to the United States in 1933.

Another example of an extended commitment for all Jewish citizens is the so-called "Memorandum" of the "Provisional Leadership of the Confessing Church," the most progressive wing within the Confessing Church. In this Memorandum of 1936, for the first time, the government is accused of violating human rights. It attacked not only the de-Christianization of public life, but also the uncertainty of justice, state arbitrariness and antisemitism. "If an antisemitism is forced on Christians within the framework of Nationalsocialist world-view which obliges them to hate Jews, they have to oppose to it the Christian command to love one's neighbour."[4]

The handwriting of Dietrich Bonhoeffer who, at that time, was the director of the preachers seminary of the Confessing Church in Finkenwalde, can clearly be recognized in that statement. Two of his seminarians carried the document abroad, where it was published in the Basler Nachrichten on July 23, 1936. Three month later, the two seminarians and the legal adviser of the Provisional Leadership of the Confessing Church, Friedrich Weissler, a Protestant Christian of Jewish descent, were arrested and put in Sachsenhausen concentration camp. One week later, Friedrich Weissler was dead. As "Jewish," he was separated from the others and exposed to the sadism of the SS-leaders. The first martyr of the Confessing Church was a baptized Jew.

More and more Bonhoeffer declared his solidarity with the whole Jewish people. After the pogrom of the so-called "Crystal Night," he underlined in his Bible two sentences of Psalm 74: "They are burning all the houses of God in the land. We do not see our signs; no prophet speaks any longer and there is none among us who knows how long." Beside them he put the date: 9 November 1938.

At that time the Finkenwalde seminary was closed by the Gestapo, the leading organs of the Confessing Church were destroyed, and many pastors and seminarians were in prison. No one was there to protest against the pogrom. Bonhoeffer wrote in the circular addressed to his former Finkenwalder students: "During the last days I thought a lot about Psalm 74, Zechariah 2:12 and Romans 9:4. That led me into prayer...." They would read these words: "For thus said the Lord—he who touches Israel touches the apple of his eye," and "They are Israelites, and to them belong the sonship, the glory, the covenants, the giving of the law, the worship and the promises." Two years later, Bonhoeffer wrote in a draft for a church confession of guilt (which was made by the German churches only a half century later):

> The church was silent where she had to cry out.... The church confesses that she has witnessed the lawless application of brutal force, the physical and spiritual suffering of countless innocent people, oppression, hatred and murder, and that she had

not raised her voice on behalf of the victims and has not found a way to hasten to their aid. She is guilty of the death of the weakest and most defenseless brothers of Jesus Christ.[5]

These words show that Bonhoeffer was now clearly aware of his own isolation as a "preacher in the desert" and that he began to recognize the connection between anti-Judaism and antisemitism. For him, at that time, the weakest and most defenseless brothers (and sisters) were ALL Jews, not only the baptized ones. For Bonhoeffer the category of "brother" and "brotherhood" had always been of high importance in his vision of the communion of saints. In his draft for a church confession of guilt and later, in the "Letters and Papers from Prison," "brother" also means the non-Christian, the Jewish, the atheist, the socialist brother. This conception of brotherhood transcends the border of nation, class, race and also of religion. This border crossing was connected with a change in Bonhoeffer's theological thinking, mainly as far as Christology was concerned.

IV

"Who are you, Christ?" Bonhoeffer asked this question at the beginning of his Christology lectures in 1933 at the Theological Faculty at the University of Berlin. The question accompanied Bonhoeffer in the last and decisive years of his life. He would pose it anew and more precisely in a letter to Eberhard Bethge from his prison cell in Tegel on April 30, 1944: "Who is Christ for us today?" In reply he would offer no simple, generalized answers, but instead raise liberating and disquieting questions, opening horizons and empowering a praxis that was inspired by the thought that Christ is "the man for others" and "church is only the church when it is there for others." In this vision I see developments which open the way towards an overcoming of anti-Judaism and which open the horizon for a Jewish-Christian dialogue. (Certainly Bonhoeffer's reflections could only be a beginning of that way, which was continued by his friend Eberhard Bethge, to whom this essay is dedicated.)

First, there is a new understanding of Christ. Assuming that Israel is and remains God's own people, Bonhoeffer came to the conviction that Jesus the Messiah can solely be understood within his Jewish context. He recognizes that the idea of the hidden and humiliated Messiah, the crucified Christ, had its true origins in the tradition of the Jewish prophets:

> History seeks to be glorified in the Messiah. History agonizes in the direction of the impossible fulfillment of a distorted promise. History knows about its messianic destiny, but it is frustrated by it. Only at one place does the thought gain a foothold against the stream of the messianic promise, that the Messiah could not be the visible and perceptible centre of historical existence, but that the Messiah must be and will be the centre of history that has been established, yet hidden by God. Thus Israel with its prophetic hope stands alone among the peoples. Thus Israel becomes the location where God fulfils this promise.[6]

In Bonhoeffer's later writings Jesus the Messiah is not primarily "son of God" and "redeemer" as in the view of traditional Christology, but "the man for others," "the man who was as God wanted him to be," who cannot be separated from the traditions of the Old Testament.

> The faith of the Old Testament isn't a religion of redemption. It is true that Christianity has always been regarded as a religion of redemption. But isn't this a cardinal error, which separates Christ from the Old Testament and interprets him on the lines of the myths about redemption...? Christians, unlike the devotees of the redemption myths, have no last line of escape available from earthly tasks and difficulties into the eternal but, as Christ himself, must drink the earthly cup to the dregs.... This world must be prematurely written off, in this Old and New Testament are at one.[7]

This was the first step towards an understanding of Jesus the Messiah as a Jew in a Jewish tradition and of the "Old Testament" as the "First Testament."

Second, there is a new understanding of the Jewish law, the Torah. During the church struggle in 1936, Bonhoeffer wrote his most famous book, "The Cost of Discipleship," an exegesis of the "Sermon on the Mount." In opposition to the Lutheran tradition he demands obedience to God's commands without compromise as they were taught by Jesus, the teacher of Torah. For Bonhoeffer, this obedience was the basic program for an opposition church, which does not allow the world to do what it wants. The book begins with a rejection of the Lutheran position which assigns to the church the proclamation of the "pure" gospel of the grace of God and leaves the world its "autonomy:" "Cheap grace is the deadly enemy of our church.... In such a church the world finds a cheap covering for its sin; no contrition is required, still less any real desire to be delivered from sin."[8] By taking Jesus' teaching of the "better justice" seriously, Bonhoeffer began to discover the importance of the Jewish law, the Torah. He rejected the Lutheran tradition which opposed the Christian "gospel" to the Jewish "law."

Third, there is a new understanding of worldliness.

> God is beyond in the midst of our life. The church stands, not at the boundaries, where human power gives up, but in the middle of the village. That is how it is in the Old Testament, and in this sense we still read the New Testament far too little in the light of the Old.[9]

At the end of his life, Bonhoeffer's understanding of Christian faith is secular, religionless, committed to solidarity. It exists from the "prayer and action of the righteous" and through a border-crossing ecumenical movement from below.[10] The place where Christ now can be found is the midst of the world where he exists as the brother of all people, Christians and non-Christians. For Bonhoeffer, Christ will be present in the political conspiracy, in the perilous praxis of piety that voluntarily assumed guilt, in the encounter with fellow human beings who had been forsaken by the world in the prison at

Tegel and in the hell of the extermination camps. As Christ's disciple, Bonhoeffer was prepared to share Christ's humiliation as well as the fate of the victims. On April 9, 1945, he was hanged in the Flossenberg concentration camp.

V

The "Letters and Papers from Prison" show that, in his last months, Bonhoeffer was increasingly interested in traditions and figures from the Hebrew Bible. He wrote, among others, a poem about Jonah and one about Moses. In these poems he also spoke about himself. Jonah, the prophet, offers to sacrifice himself to avert a disaster because he felt guilty. In another way, this is also true of Moses who, as a just man, brings about reconciliation between God and the people that had failed. It seems that Bonhoeffer had regarded the sacrifice of his life as an expiation in the place of his people and as a last act of solidarity with the victims of German fascism.

The Bible tells us, that there exists no grave of Moses. For Dietrich Bonhoeffer, too, there exists no grave. His body was burned, together with thousands of others whose traces were lost in the Holocaust.

Endnotes

1. Memorandum, "The Jewish-Christian Question as Status Confessionis" in Dietrich Bonhoeffer, Werke, Band 12, Gütersloh 1997, p. 360.

2. Dietrich Bonhoeffer, Die Kirche vor der Judenfrage, ibid, p. 353f.

3. Dietrich Bonhoeffer, Letter to Reinhold Niebuhr, ibid, p. 50.

4. Renate Wind, Dietrich Bonhoeffer, *A Spoke in the Wheel*, Eerdmans Grand Rapids MI, USA 1992, p. 119.

5. Dietrich Bonhoeffer, *Ethics*, SCM Press London 1955, p. 92f.

6. Dietrich Bonhoeffer, Christology Lectures in Dietrich Bonhoeffer Werke, Band 12, p. 308f.

7. Dietrich Bonhoeffer, Letters and Papers from Prison in *The Wisdom and Witness of Dietrich Bonhoeffer*, Fortress Press Minneapolis 2000, p. 32.

8. Dietrich Bonhoeffer, *The Cost of Discipleship*, SCM Press, London 1959, p. 35f.

9. Dietrich Bonhoeffer, Letters and Papers from Prison in *The Wisdom and Witness of Dietrich Bonhoeffer*, p. 68.

10. Renate Wind, *Kirchenkampf und Kontemplation*, in Renate Wind / Craig L. Nessan, Wer bist du, Christus? Ein ökumenisches Lesebuch zur Christologie Dietrich Bonhoeffers, Gütersloh 1998, p. 28.

CHAPTER 11

Resisting or Defending the Faith? Clerical Responses to the National Socialist State

Kevin Spicer

During the Third Reich, seventy-nine of the three hundred seventy-five priests of the diocese of Berlin, Germany, ran afoul of the Gestapo. These priests were either interrogated, warned, fined, arrested, thrown in prison, transported to a concentration camp or executed by guillotine for their opposition to the state. Of this number, the majority did not identify themselves as political opponents of the state. Most of them considered themselves good, patriotic Germans who never compromised the authority of the state and only challenged state practice and/or ideology when the latter directly undermined the authority and teachings of the Roman Catholic church. As a result, these priests often found themselves bewildered by the charges laid against them by the Gestapo. To refute these accusations, they argued that their statements and actions should not be viewed as a form of political resistance against the state, but rather as a defense of their faith tradition against unwarranted attacks and encroachments upon the church's exercise of freedom.

These seventy-nine priests, who in some way questioned or challenged the rights of the state to limit the freedom of the church and her ministers, acted in such a manner for specifically pastoral reasons. Following the tenets of their seminary education, they believed they were merely upholding their faith tradition against slander and attack. However, in the midst of their confrontation with state officials, they quickly learned that the state labeled their pastoral actions treasonous. This led them to respond to state authority in various ways. For example, upon receiving a warning or fine from the state police, many of these priests made the conscious decision never again to question the authority of the state. A number of these priests refused to adhere to the warnings of state police to desist from certain activities or modes of behavior and continued to question state actions against their church. Despite interrogations and punishment, the majority refused to acknowledge their actions as political and therefore as a threat to the state. Others, awakened by threats of the Gestapo argued in defense of pastoral freedom. These individuals boldly took responsibility for their actions and accepted often severe punishments.

In this paper, the choices of Father Albert Willimsky (1890-1940)—pastor of Holy Rosary Parish in Freisack, Brandenburg and his actions in response to state encroachment against religion will be examined. Confrontational by nature, Willimsky was willing to challenge both parishioners and acquaintances in order to let the church's moral truth, as he understood it, prevail. Similarly, he was not afraid to challenge statements by state officials that infringed on the rights and teachings of the church. Although his challenges against the government were based upon statements made by the German bishops in pastoral letters, chancery officials counseled Willimsky to avoid confrontation. Their main concern was to have the pastoral needs of the parish met, which for the most part would prove impossible if the pastor were in jail. Despite the lack of support, Willimsky was not deterred from protesting against what he considered an injustice against the church and his priesthood.

In 1935, the Potsdam Gestapo imposed against Fr. Willimsky a prohibition of residency in the district of Westhavelland.[1] Willimsky was denounced for expressing his sympathy with those who had supported the status quo in the January 1935 Saar referendum. He was also accused of making "disparaging remarks" against Alfred Rosenberg and Reich Youth Leader Baldur von Schirach and was taken to task for questioning the honorableness of the Winter Relief collections.[2] In a separate incident, Willimsky was also cited for not having flown the national flag on the church on a designated day.[3] Having gathered enough evidence against Willimsky, the Potsdam Gestapo introduced criminal proceedings against him through the district attorney's office in Potsdam. He was accused of violating the law of December 20, 1934 against treacherous attacks upon state and party and for disregarding the decree of March 21, 1933, promulgated by the Reich president.[4] On April 4, 1935, yielding to the residency prohibition and in order to avoid further conflict, the chancery office moved Willimsky to Gransee, just northeast of Freisack, and made him pastor of Assumption Parish.

Unfortunately for Willimsky, his troubles did not end there. That is, the priest did not do anything to alleviate his problems with the state. Indeed, he continued to provoke local police and Gestapo with his comments. As a result, in August 1935, the director of the Landjahr (Rural Year) for the Province of Brandenburg denounced Willimsky for reading, during Sunday Mass in May, a prohibited pastoral letter that challenged the curriculum of the Landjahr, for making derogatory statements against the state's racial teaching in his sermon, and, on another Sunday in July, for reading another letter that included challenges to the sterilization law. In addition, he was attacked for his negative statements made against Minister of the Interior Frick and Rosenberg.[5] In the same month, before Willimsky could be questioned by the Gestapo, he also criticized neo-paganism and accused Rosenberg of plagiarism, stealing from other anti-Christian works. A week later, Willimsky then read from articles taken from Catholic newspapers that promoted fidelity and courage among Catholics in their attempt to defend the faith against attacks. These incidents were enough for the Potsdam Gestapo to request prohibition of residency for Willimsky throughout the entire Potsdam region governed by the Gestapo.[6]

Before Potsdam's request was acted upon, the Berlin diocese's Vicar General Paul Steinmann intervened on Willimsky's behalf to contest the decision at the District Governor's office in Potsdam.

Steinmann assured them that Willimsky had been "informed adequately" and that his "official activity as a priest and minister would no longer offer reason for complaints."[7] Through this action, Steinmann appeared to divert or silence Willimsky from continuing to challenge the state. However, Willimsky apparently did not view his actions in any way as an affront to the state. In his reply to Steinmann, Willimsky himself admitted that in May he had read the prescribed pastoral letter without any knowledge of prohibition and only after gaining the permission of a local police officer. In July, he also avowed reading the second pastoral letter, which, according to his knowledge, was ordered by church authorities to be read and was never prohibited by state authorities. He added that, as an "old veteran" (Willimsky had served in the First World War), he had always said to his parishioners that a good Catholic always also had to be a "true servant of the state."[8] However, in the eyes of the Gestapo, Willimsky was far from being an obedient citizen.

For a brief period of time, Willimsky heeded Steinmann's warnings and avoided further confrontation. Even the mayor of Gransee acknowledged that Willimsky had, for the better, recently changed his attitude toward the state and for that reason the former could support the priest's attempt to gain permission to teach religion in the public school.[9] In September 1935, the Gestapo also appeared to have agreed as they lifted Willimsky's residency prohibition for the area of Westhavelland.[10] A few months later, in January 1936, Willimsky optimistically reported to his brother Heinrich that he had also been acquitted of all charges in relation to his comments on the Saar referendum, Winter Relief, and the slander of Rosenberg and Schirach. He was further delighted to report that the judge acknowledged that it was his duty as a Catholic priest "to defend the faith."[11]

Willimsky's confrontational nature, however, soon brought him into conflict again, not only with the state but also with some of his parishioners. The events in police records that sparked his reappearance occurred when Martha S. accused him of boxing a person's ears in the confessional and discussing the content of a confession from the pulpit. The Gransee pastor did not accept these charges lightly and immediately wrote her a letter in which he threatened Frau S. with a lawsuit if she did not retract her statements.[12] A few days later, upon learning of a more malicious attack upon his character, he sent a second letter with similar wording.[13] Thereafter, Gustav S., the husband of Martha, wrote the priest and reminded him to be careful of what he said because they "lived in the Third Reich." Willimsky accepted Gustav's challenge and acknowledged that indeed he recognized that they were living in the Third Reich—a Reich where allegiance was "one of the highest virtues." Then he demanded that Gustav have his wife retract her statements against him. Willimsky's reply also revealed the core of his complaint against Frau S.—that she had willingly chosen to leave her parish in Gransee, in which boundaries she lived, to attend services at another Catholic parish. This infuriated the pastor who saw her action as a direct challenge to his priestly authority. Willimsky told Gustav that his wife acted just like a Protestant and chose which church to attend according to the charisma of the minister who was holding the service. For him, this behavior was entirely unacceptable and undermined the whole structure of parish boundaries and the authority of pastors.[14] After that, there was no further correspondence between Willimsky and Martha and Gustav S. to reveal what became of the charges. However, the extant correspondence showed that Willimsky also went after another parishioner, Frau L., who dared to mock him and the sacrament of penance publicly. He also threatened to report her to the police if she did not withdraw her comments.[15]

The interesting point in both the case of Frau S. and of Frau L. is not that Willimsky was willing to go to great extremes to protect his honor; but rather that, and more importantly, he was still willing to trust the police and justice system to uphold his rights in Nazi Germany, even after he had tangled with the law. Clearly, his trust had to come from the previous court decision in his favor where the judge supported him in his defense of the faith. In April 1936, however, Willimsky soon learned that the courts would not always support his claims. This happened when he was found guilty of violation of the Reich Flag Law of October 24, 1935 (Willimsky had failed to flag the church with the national Swastika flag on November 9, 1935, the anniversary of the Munich 1923 Putsch) and consequently was fined 50 RM plus 2.50 RM for the cost of the proceeding.[16] At the time, Willimsky denied any malicious intent for not following the provisions of the law and requested that the sentence be overturned.[17] Though the court refused to accept his objection, the Chief Public Prosecutor's office (Generalstaatsanwalt) in Berlin discontinued the proceeding and repealed the fine on the basis of an April 23, 1936 amnesty law (which repealed fines and prison sentences of less than seven months).[18] Once again Willimsky had escaped punishment.

In July 1936, Willimsky challenged the state's suppression of Catholicism when he wrote to Bernhard Rust, Minister of Science, Education and Popular Culture, and complained against the practices of the director of the Landjahr home in Alt-Lüdersdorf. The director had refused to allow the girls, who were Catholic and under her care, to attend Mass after learning that Willimsky had recently read a pastoral letter that was critical of the Hitler Youth and had preached against neo-paganism. Instead, she held a service herself in lieu of the Mass. When he challenged her about this, the director told Willimsky that she wished "her girls only to be educated in the National Socialist spirit." In his letter, Willimsky called the director an "instrument of Satan" who used "real Russian and Bolshevist methods" to run the home. He demanded that the government punish and dismiss her.[19] Nothing came of his protest. Nor was Willimsky punished for his harsh accusations against the Landjahr director. On another occasion, in September 1936, Willimsky ran afoul of the director of a different Landjahr home in Löwenberg, where he regularly went to the local school to hear confessions and offer Mass for the boys in the camp. During a regular visit there, Willimsky made statements to two children against the SS newspaper *Das Schwarze Korps* and the *Völkischer Beobachter* for their exaggerated coverage of the morality trials. He also allegedly declared that church persecution in Germany was much worse than the attacks of Bolshevism on the church in Spain. When questioned by the Gestapo, Willimsky readily admitted to making statements against the negative press coverage of the morality trials, but he denied comparing church persecution in Germany with the practices of Bolshevism in Spain. He explained that all he had stated was that the "struggle against religion and priests" everywhere was a "harbinger and a side effect of the Bolshevist world revolution." Once again, Willimsky escaped punishment when the Berlin Chief Public Prosecutor accepted Willimsky's testimony and decided not to pursue the charges.[20] A local administrator, however, did take revenge and barred Willimsky from using the school building for any pastoral activity.[21]

Within less than a year, Willimsky was again denounced for allegedly expressing, during a religious instruction class in Rauenhendorf, his disenchantment and his distaste with the press and for the radio's treatment of the morality trials against Catholic priests and religious.[22] When questioned, Willimsky again admitted to making the statement about the newspapers, but denied uttering any comment about the radio. According to him, he had only followed the argument of his bishop as expressed in a pastoral letter on the morality trials and, therefore, was "totally innocent" of any criminal wrongdoing.[23] Again, Willimsky escaped prosecution when the court dropped the charges against him based upon the stipulations of the April 30, 1938 amnesty law in honor of the Austrian annexation.[24] But this would be the last time.

On October 3, 1938, Willimsky's luck came to an end when the Gestapo arrested him for criticizing the government and its leaders for their treatment of the Catholic church. The month previous, Willimsky had made these comments during a conversation with twenty-four year old Christel S., a Protestant and member of the Nazi party. The two first met when Christel S. approached Willimsky to inquire as to whether the S-Bahn they shared was heading toward Oranienburg.[25] Despite Willimsky's bewilderment of the situation or perhaps because he felt flattered that Christel S. had chosen to ignore the women present in the train car and instead, against the customary norm of German society, approached him, he responded accordingly. When they both later boarded the commuter train at Oranienburg to Gransee and sat near each other, Willimsky engaged the young woman in conversation as they passed the concentration camp Sachsenhausen. After finding out that the young woman was Protestant and had many misconceptions about the Catholic faith, he used the opportunity to clarify the actual nature of the morality trials against priests and also criticized the work of Rosenberg. In a sworn statement, Willimsky testified that he had spoken purely in defense of his religion and in self-defense of his own priesthood and that Christel S. had interpreted his words as a political attack on the state. In this regard, he believed that if Christianity and National Socialism were not able to bridge the existing gap between them, "religious battles" lay ahead, which, he felt, "must be avoided under all circumstances."[26] In this statement, Willimsky revealed that he was not fundamentally opposed to National Socialism, but only opposed to those elements within the movement that opposed Christianity. Despite his own imprisonment, Willimsky was unable to discern the radical differences between the two.

Despite Bishop Preysing's efforts to procure his release from prison, Willimsky remained in protective custody for almost seven months.[27] On May 3, 1939, he was released from jail only by promising to sign a statement "to abstain from any political activity or propaganda hostile to the state in the future."[28] Upon his release, Bishop Preysing immediately transferred him from Gransee to Saint Peter and Paul Parish in Podejuch near Stettin. No correspondence between the chancery and Willimsky exists, but the quick transfer clearly was meant to remove the priest from further controversy. In August 1939, the Special Court of the District Court Berlin found Willimsky guilty of violation of the law of December 20, 1934 and sentenced him to six months in jail. The court then credited him with time served in protective custody.[29]

Willimsky did not last long in his new assignment. He refused to keep his comments about the situation of the Catholic church in Germany to himself. In addition, he did not seem to understand the seriousness of the state's actions against him. Nor was he able to view his actions and statements as, in the eyes of Nazis, ideological assertions with political overtones. In October 1939, Otto H., a salesman in the Stettin Karstadt department store, denounced Willimsky for making derogatory comments about the war with Poland, Minister of Propaganda Goebbels, and the press coverage of the morality trials. During a shopping trip, Willimsky, believing he was addressing a fellow Catholic, had confided in the salesman. When questioned, Willimsky admitted to calling into question the press coverage about the war with Poland. He said he found it hard to believe that "tiny Poland" first attacked Germany. However, he denied making any statements against Goebbels. In his defense, he argued that as a Catholic priest he was "obligated to carry out pastoral care wherever he considered it proper" and insisted that he spoke only as "a Catholic and in a purely ministerial manner."[30]

This time the Gestapo refused to listen to his line of argumentation, especially now that war had broken out. The Gestapo was fervent in its desire to erase any hint of defeatism or doubt in the activities of the government and its leaders. Therefore, on October 10, 1939, Willimsky was arrested by the Stettin Gestapo.[31] By the end of the month, the Stettin Gestapo recommended that Willimsky, on account of his continued hostile stance, be placed in a concentration camp for an indefinite period.[32] The office of the Minister of Church Affairs and the Stettin Gestapo put the decision in the hands of Reinhard Heydrich (1904-1942), Director of the RSHA.[33] On January 9, 1940, Heydrich ordered Willimsky's incarceration in Sachsenhausen and on January 29, 1940, he was transported there with other new prisoners.[34] The harsh conditions and the bitter winter were too much for Willimsky who, on February 22, 1940, succumbed to pneumonia in the camp's infirmary.[35]

The case of Albert Willimsky raises many points for defining and understanding the relationship between the church and state. Primarily, Willimsky protested in defense of his faith tradition and his own priesthood. Whether contesting a critical remark from a parishioner or from the state, he braved any challenge to his priestly authority. Through his own living out of the priesthood, he thought himself invincible when combating any attack on the faith. His early successes in the court system perhaps reinforced this invincibility in his own mind, if not in the minds of others. His scorn of the Nazi press, especially for their editors' exaggerations in their coverage of the morality trials, instilled in him a desire to rectify the situation by informing people of the party's lies. Confrontational by nature, Willimsky was willing to challenge both parishioners and acquaintances in order to let the church's moral truth, as he understood it, prevail. In this process, he apparently exhibited a tendency to talk too liberally about issues that he wished to rectify and seemed to pay no attention to political expediency, especially while awaiting trial after his incarceration. Willimsky will be remembered for his fidelity to his faith while living amidst a world determined to attack it. Everything outside the Catholic faith was beyond his sphere of concern. Willimsky also had to deal as well with centuries-old animosity between Catholics and Protestants. Many accusations against him, including two of the more serious denunciations, came from individuals who belonged to a Protestant denomination and who also supported National Socialism. Living within this kind of confessional tension, Willimsky was often very alone. Although his challenges against the government were based upon statements made by the bishops in pastoral letters, chancery officials encouraged the priest to avoid confrontation. Their main concern was to have the pastoral needs of the parish met, which proved impossible if the pastor was in jail. In three cases, the chancery's answer to Willimsky's difficult situation was to transfer the priest to a new parish. Despite these moves, Willimsky was not deterred from protesting against what he considered an injustice against the church and the priesthood.

Endnotes

1. On the background of Willimsky's life and a brief summary of his activities in the Third Reich see Ursula Pruß, "Pfarrer Albert Willimsky," in Zeugen für Christus. Das deutsche Martyrologium des 20. Jahrhunderts, I, Helmut Moll, ed. (Paderborn: Ferdinand Schöningh, 1999), pp. 117-121. See also, Heinz Kühn, Blutzeugen des Bistums Berlin (Berlin: Morus, 1950), pp. 160-164.

Resistance or Defending the Faith: 195
Clerical Responses to the National Socialist State

2. Record of telephone conversation between District Governor Potsdam and Lichtenberg, March 20, 1935, BLHA Pr. Br. Rep. 2a Pol. 3034, f. 237.

3. Gestapo Potsdam to Gestapo Berlin, March 29, 1935, BLHA Pr. Br. Rep. 2a I Pol. 3034, f. 236R.

4. Gestapo Potsdam to Gestapo Berlin, August 23, 1935, BLHA Pr. Br. Rep. 2a I Pol. 3034, n.f.

5. Landjahr Director Province Brandenburg to the District Governor Potsdam, August 7, 1935, BLHA Pr. Br. Rep. 2a II Gen. 287, n.f.

6. Gestapo Potsdam to Gestapo Berlin, August 23, 1935, BLHA Pr. Br. Rep. 2a I Pol. 3034, n.f.

7. Steinmann to District Governor Potsdam, August 26, 1935, BLHA Pr. Br. Rep. 2a Gen. 287, n.f.

8. Willimsky to Berlin Chancery, August 26, 1935, BLHA Pr. Br. Rep. 2a Gen. 87, n.f.

9. District Administrator to Gestapo Potsdam, January 16, 1936, BLHA Pr. Br. Rep. 2a II Gen. 287, n.f.

10. Gestapo Potsdam to County Administrators (Landräte), n.d., BLHA Pr. Br. Rep. 2a I Pol. 3034, f. 278.

11. Willimsky to Heinrich Willimsky, January 1, 1936, BArch Berlin R 58 2522, f. 181.

12. Willimsky to Martha S., January 25, 1936, BArch B R58 2522, f. 178.

13. Willimsky to Martha S., January 28, 1936, BArch B R58 2522, f. 179.

14. Willimsky to Gustav S., February 2, 1936, BArch B R58 2522, f. 183.

15. Willimsky to Frau L., April 29, 1937, BArch B R58 2522, f. 182.

16. District Court Gransee, Summary of Punishment, April 24, 1936, BArch B R58 2522, f. 187. Willimsky later testified that he was fined 100.00 RM for not flagging the church with the Swastika. However, the former document contains the actual amount of the verdict and fine directly from the court. For Willimsky's testimony see Protocol of Inquiry, November 15, 1937, BLHA Pr. Br. Rep. 2a I. Pol. 3034, ff. 317-318.

17. Willimsky to District Court Gransee, April 27, 1936, f. 188.

18. Chief Public Prosecutor Berlin to Minister of Justice, December 20, 1934, BArch B R5101 22247, n.f.

19. Willimsky to Rust, July 7, 1936, BArch B R58 2522, f. 172.

20. Chief Public prosecutor Berlin to Minister of Justice, December 17, 1936, BArch B R5101 22247, ff. 12-13.

21. County Administrator to Willimsky, September 26, 1936, BArch B R58 2522, f. 193.

22. District Governor Potsdam to Kerrl, December 22, 1937 with attached letter from Walter D. to Goebbels, June 21, 1937, f. 50, BArch B R5101 22247, f. 50.

23. Protocol of Inquiry, Gransee, November 15, 1937, BLHA Pr. Br. Rep. 2a I Pol. 3032, ff. 317-318. In passing, I wish to interject that these trials were initiated by the Nazi state against allegedly derelict priests. Although intended to root out immoral offences committed by priests, these trials were used to discredit the church and its clergy at large. On the morality trials see Hans Günther Hockerts, Die Sittlichekeits Prozesse gegen katholische Ordens angehörige und Priester 1936/37. Eine Studie zur nationalsozialischen Herrschaftstechnik und zum Kirchenkampf, VKZ B6 (Mainz: Matthias-Grünwald, 1971). See also Preysing to Lammers, May 27, 1937, Barch B R43 II/155, ff. 88-105.

24. District Governor Potsdam to Kerrl, BArch B R5101 22247, f. 52.

25. Chief Public Prosecutor Potsdam to Minister of Justice, October 17, 1938, BArch B R5101 22247, f. 137.

26. Willimsky to Examining Magistrate of the District Court Potsdam, October 27, 1938, BArch B R58 2522, f. 170.

27. Preysing to Chief Public Prosecutor Berlin, December 21, 1938, BArch B R58 2522, f. 152.

28. On May 11, 1939, Willimsky signed the statement. Gestapo Concluding Report on Willimsky, October 31, 1939, BArch B R58 2522, f. 116.

29. Special Court Berlin Decision, August 3, 1939, BArch B R58 2522, f. 153.

30. Interrogation of Willimsky by Gestapo Stettin, October 20, 1939, BArch B R58 2522, ff. 111, 113 R.

31. Gestapo Stettin Remarks, November 3, 1939, BArch B R58 2522, f. 118.

32. Stapo Concluding Report on Willimsky, October 31, 1939, BArch B R58 2522, f. 116 R.

33. Roth to RSHA, Telegram, November 21, 1939 and Roth to RSHA, Telegram, December 12, 1939, BArch B R58, ff. 128, 130.

34. Heydrich to Gestapo Stettin, January 9, 1940 and Gestapo Stettin to Commandant of Sachsenhausen, January 27, 1940, BArch B R58 2522, ff. 204, 207.

35. Gestapo Stettin to Stapo Stettin, Telegram, February 20, 1940, BArch B R58 2522, f. 211.

GENOCIDE AND CULTURE

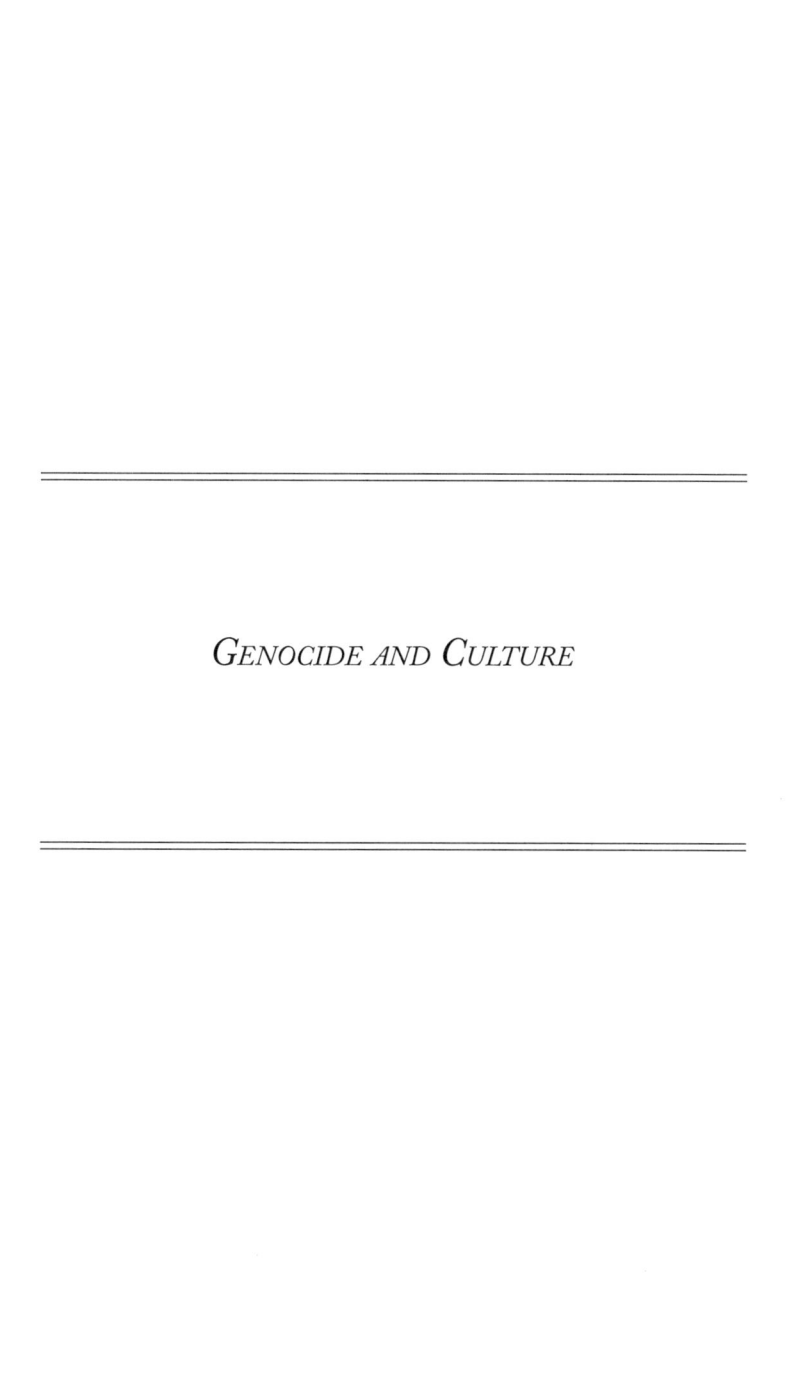

CHAPTER 12

Re-Reading Bernhard Schlink's *The Reader* as a Mirror of Germany's Holocaust Memory

Karin Doerr

The 1995 novel *Der Vorleser, The Reader* in English,[1] by the German judge and writer, Bernhard Schlink, soared to fame both inside and outside of Germany, particularly after the phenomenal exposure it received by the popular U.S. talk show host Oprah Winfrey in 1999. The book was on the New York Times bestseller list for many months and became a hot item for literary circles; Schlink was much in demand for interviews and readings. Even before the work was translated into twenty-five languages, including Hebrew,[2] the Hollywood company Miramax had bought the film rights. The reviews of *The Reader* were generally favorable,[3] and German and North American professors swiftly adopted it into their curricula. Schlink received several coveted literary awards for this novel.[4]

Its plot is that of a postwar German youth sexually and emotionally involved with an older woman who turns out to be a putative Nazi perpetrator. This combination of love story and Holocaust crime includes her trial, her crucial illiteracy and subsequent suicide in prison. In addition, there is, for a German novel, a rare description of a face-to-face encounter with a Holocaust survivor. There are as well recurring questions about Germany's guilt for the genocide, and thoughts on how second generation Germans face their country's Nazi past. The following essay is concerned with Schlink's fictional rendition of Germany's war and post-war history and how his characters cope with their nation's legacy.[5]

Hence, the following questions need to be addressed: How does *The Reader* fit into literature whose palette is the Holocaust? How does Schlink, as a contemporary German author deal with the genocide, its victims and perpetrators? What does his choice of a female Nazi culprit signify? What does the work convey about Germany's collective memory in terms of past involvement and present responsibility? Finally, what are the moral issues raised by Schlink's novel?

First, we shall situate this work in the genre of Holocaust fiction that is, by its very nature, embedded in history. Often authors of that fiction borrow style and form from actual accounts, diaries, or memoirs in order to enhance credibility. They sometimes add authenticating devices such as appended bibliographies, biographical statements, and/or references to actual events, Nazi perpetrators or survivors. These works usually focus on (predominantly Jewish) women victimized by (male) German Nazi perpetrators and thus portray an extreme power imbalance.[6] This perspective underlies Marlene Heinemann's definition of this new, post-war genre as "a body of writings unified by its historical subject, namely the persecution and annihilation of Jews and others [during the Shoah]."[7] For certain authors and readers, the inclusion of violent sex or rape occurring predominantly in concentration camp settings may pose a perverse attraction to the Shoah. Such works then fall into the category of voyeuristic or titillating Auschwitz eroticism.

In Holocaust fiction, the narrational voice is either in the third person or from the vantage point of victims. A Nazi perspective is unusual. A rare example is Martin Amis' 1991 novel, *Time's Arrow*, which is told by a German SS camp doctor modelled after Mengele.[8] Alexander Tisma's 1993 book, *Kapo*, presents the point of view of a male concentration camp guard with a dual role as culprit and victim. The 1993 American novel, *The Kommandant's Mistress*, by Sherri Szeman,[9] contains contrasting narrational positions in two fictive memoirs, one from the perspective of a concentration camp commandant modelled after Rudolf Hess, and the other from a female Jewish inmate.[10] Critics have termed such alternate "takes" on Holocaust events "post-modern" because their equal validity circumvents moral judgement. Such equivalence diminishes the distinctions between the psychological processes and blurs the lines between victim and victimiser.[11]

Over the decades, scholars have expressed different levels of concern with all types of literary dramatizations of the Shoah. They seem to generally agree that their authors ought to adhere to basic historical facts. Barbara Foley explains that "the specific link with history carries the burden not merely of ensuring verisimilitude but also of guaranteeing credibility."[12] Sidra DeKoven Ezrahi, one of the earliest critics of Holocaust fiction, finds that "[t]he tension between internal accountability to the imagination and external accountability to the victims expresses the heart of the dilemma of Holocaust literature in America."[13] One of the more recent voices is that of Sara E. Horowitz who crystallizes two critical poles reflecting this literature: "Holocaust fiction [is] seen by many readers as—at best—a weaker, softer kind of testimony when compared to the rigors of history, or—at worst—a misleading, dangerous confusion of verisimilitude with reality."[14] Berel Lang adds a philosophical dimension to the discourse: "In all writing about the Nazi genocide ... it is not only that subject which has morally distinctive features; the writing itself is distinctive in its conceptual, literary, and, finally, in its moral features."[15]

These representational views express in one form or other that "certain limitations, literary and moral, are intrinsic to 'imaginative' literature—novels, drama, poetry—about the Nazi genocide" (*Act and Idea* 122). They all echo Theodor Adorno's admonitions about the potentialities of art after the caesura of the Holocaust.[16] This critical preoccupation helps propel the ongoing discussion about fictionalising this event and particularly about the connection between imagination and reality. Checking literary representation against historical veracity is not to prove errors in detail, but rather to establish the equilibrium of truth and fantasy. Discrepancies or omissions may reveal the position of authors either as subjective individuals or as representatives of a nation. The work may then reflect how they view the past and how collective memory operates.

Holocaust scholars usually look with a more critical eye upon those texts that originate in Germany, the matrix of the Nazi crimes. Over the decades, a few North American academics in the field of German (some of them survivors) have written specifically on German Shoah representation.[17] The most recent study is that of American *Germanist* Ernestine Schlant, *The Language of Silence: West German Literature and the Holocaust*.[18] Her 1999 assessment of the country's mainstream literature is already discernable from her title. She calls it "a literature of absence and silence contoured by language" (1). Omer Bartov, in "German Soldiers and the Holocaust," concretizes this image:

> ... we rarely encounter victims; when victims are mentioned, they appear only as represented by the perpetrators, as threatening imaginary figures or as dry statistics, as administrative abstractions or as ideological constructs. They rarely make an appearance as normal, ordinary human beings.[19]

In *Mirrors of Destruction*, he places his critical emphasis on *The Reader*, and discerns in Schlink's work an underlying notion of victimized Germans and a failure to portray the historical veracity of Holocaust events and victims.[20]

The Reader, now part of the international body of Holocaust literature, differs from other such works because of its unusual male/female, perpetrator/victim depiction. Through the eyes of its first person narrator and main character, the German lawyer Michael Berg, we see the Nazi perpetrator Hanna Schmitz, Jewish survivors, and most importantly, himself. His involvement and emotional entanglement with Hanna is always in the foreground of the story. At the same time, *The Reader* offers us a unique glimpse into the mind of an educated German, one generation removed from the Third Reich era, and his post-Holocaust contemplations. Further, Schlink employs fantasy in crucial episodes of his novel and consequently digresses from and distorts history.

As this peculiar story unfolds, the two Germans emerge as victims of their country's Nazi past. This is evident in the way the author presents Hanna's war crimes. The mystery around her cruel outbreaks against her young lover in the beginning of the story and her precipitous disappearance is lifted at her trial, taking place decades later. She and a few other German female SS guards are held responsible for the death of a large group of Jewish women on a tortuous "death march" near war's end. One night, these concentration camp inmates were contained in a church, which was then bombed by the Allies. During the ensuing fire, the door was kept locked and the women burned to death. The male guards had left and Hanna's crime was her alleged failure to open the church door. The accusation against her rests on a report of this incident, which she admits to having written. This is the incriminating factor that makes her responsible for the deaths. Schlink presents her testimony at the trial as follows:

> It all happened so fast ... suddenly we were alone with the women in the church. They [the male guards] left behind some weapons, but we didn't know how to use them, and even if we had, what good would it have done, since we were only a handful of women? How could we have guarded all those women? ... We could not just let them escape! (*The Reader* 127-128)

At this point of the interrogation, a confused and helpless Hanna turns to the judge with a personal question: "What would you have done?" (128).

Schlink portrays her (and the other female guards) as abandoned by the men in command, and, at the trial, defenseless in the face of the judge's questions. Hanna is here stereotyped as a vulnerable woman in two traditionally male dominated areas, war and the court. The author thus changes the image of the typical Nazi perpetrator from a leading and influential agent in the genocide to a hapless female bystander. The narrator guides the reader to view Hanna in the same manner as he does, namely with understanding and commiseration for her helpless entanglement in an intimidating situation. Both he and the story line block the perception of her as a Nazi perpetrator at the time of the church fire and, earlier, her being a concentration camp guard.

We do remember (mainly male) Nazi officials charged with crimes against humanity who usually pleaded "not guilty" because they claimed to have only "followed orders" or, worse, "could not remember."[21] Some women culprits were charged with war crimes.[22] One such trial took place in Düsseldorf, in 1975, involving six female guards and nine SS men, all at the Majdanek death camp. They remained tough and obdurate, and stubbornly silent about their criminal acts.[23] A life sentence was given to Hermine Ryan, née Braunsteiner, for her extreme brutality against female inmates at Majdanek as she helped to send Jewish women to their deaths. Witnesses testified that she would also kick them with her iron-shoed boots, hence was given the nickname "the mare."[24] Schlink, a judge himself (but not at this trial), was aware of this and other cases and of the demeanor of these women before the court.[25] We may surmise that he wove one particular detail into his novel: the testifying survivor recalls a female guard called "the mare" (*The Reader* 119). Consequently, when Michael once likens Hanna to a "horse," she reacts strongly: "'A horse?' She disentangled herself, sat up and stared at me in shock" (*The Reader* 71). Although no more is mentioned in Schlink's work, the suspicion that she was that vicious guard is intimated but not confirmed.

Nevertheless, the circumstances around Hanna's case solicit the readers' compassion for her. We are privy to a fateful twist in her story, namely, that she takes responsibility for the death of the prisoners because she is ashamed to admit her illiteracy. In other words, she could not have written the damning report. This particular problem of hers diverts us further from considering her criminal responsibility and the true victims of this incident. Schlink in turn does not stress the ordeals and the fate of the Jewish women who, after having suffered persecution, incarceration, starvation, sicknesses, and near death in the concentration camps, were burned alive in the locked church. There are only two survivors from that fire, whom he leaves at the margin of his story and of history. His albeit fictional account therefore comes close to being a "representation of the Jewish fate *in absentia* (Parry 257)."

Schlink calls the two survivors simply "mother and daughter" (*The Reader* 120). This expressionistic portrayal turns them into anonymous figures—ironically a term used by the Nazis for Jews— and survivor "types," rather than actual people.[26] Those familiar with Ruth Klüger's popular German account *weiter leben—eine Jugend*, will form the connection to the perhaps best-known mother-daughter survivor pair within the German Holocaust context. This possible link to actual survivors remains unnoticed by and unexplained to the English reader. Klüger's book was written in German for Germans and, as she states, specifically for her friends in Göttingen.[27] But in Schlink's novel, the daughter's account is in English, which is treated, in part, as a confusing linguistic distancing device or barrier for the narrator: "… the alien language … created a strange concatenation of distance and immediacy" (*The Reader* 118). He goes further in his almost outrageous criticism of her written account: "She writes about herself and her pubescent, precocious, and, when necessary, cunning behavior with the same sobriety she uses to describe everything else" (*The Reader* 119).

The survivor/daughter appears briefly during the trial and towards the end of the novel as a sketchy, one-dimensional character. If the author does concede her suffering it "remains abstract and evokes no emotion in the reader," to use Bartov's words (*Mirrors of Destruction* 223). Worse, she functions as witness and accuser in Hanna's trial. The narrator sums up the negative perception of the "daughter's" court testimony: "… it makes no one sympathetic, neither the mother nor the daughter, nor those who shared their fate in various camps and finally in Auschwitz…" (*The Reader* 118). Michael Berg's cold observation renders the victim and her fate secondary and understated, if not unimportant. The author extends this lack of sympathetic reception to the other second generation Germans viewing the trial, i.e., the law students, by remarking on their distraction: "they could smile and whisper to one another or even show traces of impatience" (*The Reader* 100). Hanna too displays no awareness of the fact that she experienced the Holocaust on the other side of history, i.e. on the side of the German killers and seems to convey neither compassion nor remorse for the survivor. She *does* focus on Michael: "Hanna turned around and looked at me" (116).

The fact that the two survivors in *The Reader* are marginal, nameless characters, allows us to speculate about the significance of the names of the two German protagonists Michael and Hanna as popular biblical names (the Hebrew spelling of Hannah has an h at the end, and the German Hanna is often the abbreviation of Hannelore). Although we do not know Schlink's reasoning, we could suggest a desire to establish an affinity with Jews. This would include the family name Berg, which is a common Jewish name. But the two names could also signify a minimization of the importance and distinction of German and "Jewish," especially as viewed and practiced during the Nazi period.[28] Schmitz in turn is a very typical, perhaps stereotypical and common, German family name (a pun on *Schmutz*, "dirt?"). It may allude to Hanna being very ordinary, like "you and me" so to speak, as many sympathetic readers of this work have suggested.[29] She seems indeed very common if judged by her humble background and lack of education. She works as a tramway conductor in post-war Germany. However, her past and present illiteracy and her sadism make her extraordinary. Illiteracy was not a typical trademark for a German during the Nazi era, female or not, even less so for a member of the SS (most SS men were highly educated). As for sadism, we encounter it in the treatment of Jews and others during the Holocaust, but one cannot generalize that all Germans were sadists. Besides, Hanna's violent, sadistic outbreaks, as presented in the novel, are also directed towards her young German lover and, most importantly, they are linked to her illiteracy, or rather her fear or shame of its discovery.

Berg realizes this fact during the trial. Therefore, his exclusive compassion for her is as a person, not a perpetrator.[30] In lengthy expositions he confesses his attraction and repulsion and thus remains the principal character in the novel, as its title, *The Reader*, suggests. The work's first and last sentences both contain his "I."

Hence, he exposes his inward gaze on his emotional conflict as well as questions about Germany's genocidal past. His contemplations reveal that Hanna, as the Nazi perpetrator, and he as second-generation German lover, gradually emerge as victims of their country's history. By contrast, "the true victims of the period, those who died and those who survived, have no face" (*Mirrors of Destruction* 223) and no soul. In German, *der Vorleser* alludes to a person or persons who read aloud to one or more who listen. In Schlink's work they are the storyteller, Berg, and Hanna, the listener, as the two individuals engaged in an intergenerational relationship. They are tightly connected through this act of reading, at first, as part of their sexual ritual. Later, he sends her tapes with his readings to prison.

But there is another type of *Vorleser* in Schlink's work: Young Jewish women have to read to Hanna in the concentration camp before she sends them to their deaths. Reading to someone is, in a civilized world, a refined, innocent, and caring activity and is presented as such in the novel, which even includes the concentrationary universe. Therefore, the "selections" of the girls to be killed are minimized by the focus on their temporary role as Hanna's readers. It remains unclear whether there is sex involved. The story suggests Hanna's benevolence in delaying rather than implicating her in their murder. Ironically (in fact incredibly), and for this short time, the girls hold a superior position over her, which signifies a role reversal within the realm of death and destruction. This disturbing twist in Schlink's text clashes not only with the known "selections" for "private purposes," i.e., sexual use and abuse in the Nazi camps, but also the consistent power relationship between perpetrator and victim. "Selections" of those who were to die or who were to live a bit longer have remained among the most horrible facts of the Holocaust.

More bizarre still is this delay of the Jews' gassing or admitting to let a group of women burn to death, all to conceal illiteracy. Schlink's narrow and persistent focus on the accused being caught in the web of her own dilemma obfuscates the fact of the Nazis' monstrous and far-reaching decision that all Jews were to die. Only in a country that respects human rights, would the refusal to open the church door during the fire be considered a crime of negligence causing death; but not so during the Holocaust where law was blind to the persecution and destruction of Jews. During the "death march," as portrayed by Schlink, the Jewish women are guarded, but not to keep them from harm's way. Figuratively and literally, the church's sanctuary is a most likely unintended ironic comment on Christianity's failure to protect Jews. In the novel, too, it serves as an easy way to contain the prisoners at night. This is expressed clearly in Hanna's interchange with the court judge. He asks, "Were you afraid the prisoners would overpower you?" Her answer is indirect and begins and ends with more questions: "... how could we have restored order? There would have been chaos, and we had no way to handle that. And if they'd tried to escape ...?" To the judge's subsequent inquiry, "Where you afraid that if they escaped, you would be arrested, convicted, shot?" she reiterates, "We couldn't just let them escape!" (*The Reader* 127). Although the author raises an important issue with the last question, the focus remains on Hanna's helpless state, the need to do her duty and not free the prisoners, even to the point of letting them burn to death.

Schlink, almost in passing, assigns blame for the burning church onto Allied bombs and thus makes *them* liable for a variation of "crimes against humanity." For contemporary German readers this scenario may trigger memories of enemy bombings of German cities, facts that Germans prefer to remember. Omer Bartov takes issue with Schlink's reason for the church fire and tries to set the record straight:

> The crime of which Hanna is accused is indeed not comparable to what we know of the Holocaust.... Of course, SS guards had in fact frequently locked Jews in buildings (usually synagogues) and set them on fire themselves, without the assistance of enemy bombers... (*Mirrors of Destruction* 220).

There is a parallel example, the horrific event during World War II at Oradour-sur-Glane in France comes closer to history. There,

[t]he women and young children were separated from the others and made to wait in the church.... The church was set on fire, and the women and children were either shot or burned to death. In all, six hundred and fifty-two people—mainly women and children—had been killed.[31]

But even this incident is an exception because the victims were not Jewish, and the massacre was a German collective reprisal against this French village for resistance activity.

If we compare real events with Schlink's fiction we have to wonder whether this was the same war. Take another incident recorded about the first weeks of the war, when a special German task force, upon entering Poland, had orders to murder and burn Jews "under the pretext of combating insurgents:" "Murder was only one of the methods used by von Woyrsch's police to terrorize the Jews of Bedzin. Another was arson:"

> [R]ampaging Order Police razed the synagogue and a number of other buildings in the Jewish community.... *Einsatzgruppe* and German army personnel using flamethrowers razed the buildings and shot people as they fled from the burning structures.... In Dynów ... Order Police from Woyrsch's Operational Group found at least a dozen Jews in the synagogue and set it afire, killing all inside before the eyes of horrified local residents. [32]

These atrocities were part of the activities of this particular German military group within a short period of days in September 1939, not to mention the murderous activities of the *Einsatzgruppen* throughout the war. Schlink, although himself a judge, also ignores the fact that German perpetrators of such atrocities largely escaped justice or received light sentences in war-crimes trials of the 1960s.[33] Yet, in *The Reader*, he has his female concentration camp guard face life imprisonment for her crimes. *She* is the single victim while in the real world there was little or no justice on behalf of countless victims.

His narrator, Michael Berg, is not sure whether to understand or condemn her (*The Reader* 157). He talks about the "… pain I went through because of my love for Hanna …" (*The Reader* 171), and is "tormented by the old question of whether I had denied or betrayed her (*The Reader* 216)." He sees himself as "not guilty because one cannot be guilty of betraying a criminal," and yet also as guilty of having loved that criminal. The question of guilt about loving a criminal, and not necessarily a Nazi perpetrator, takes many turns and gets twisted up with the notion of shame for Germany's past.

We observe that all of Hanna's actions during the Holocaust and beyond are based on her inability to read. She does not admit in court that she is unlettered, and the judge finds her guilty without knowing the true and therefore "justifiable" motivations behind her behavior. A certain burden falls upon the narrator, and with him the reader of the novel. Both are aware of Hanna's Achilles' heel, which serves as the key mitigating factor in judging her to be not guilty in human terms even if she is guilty before the law. Seen in this light, we too, are convinced that her life sentence is inappropriately harsh. We as readers also feel addressed by her question to the judge, "What would you have done?" (128). When there is no answer, the author reinforces a typical German response to the Holocaust, namely, that, at worst the Germans were reluctant perpetrators and at best, had no choice. Hanna's handicap and apparent lack of options therefore elicit compassion and understanding. Schlink's portrayal of Hanna's ordinariness echoes Daniel Jonah Goldhagen's controversial book, *Hitler's Willing Executioners* (1996). But whereas Goldhagen generalizes the guilt of all ordinary Germans, Schlink suggests its opposite, i.e., the innocence and victimization of Germans, even when they were culpable. In addition, he equates innocence with ordinariness in legal and moral terms. Thus he takes the ordinary German off the hook when it comes to ultimate responsibility.

Michael Berg may represent typical confusing and conflicting feelings of shame and guilt about the Holocaust: "What should our second generation have done, what should it do with the knowledge of the horrors of the extermination of the Jews?" (*The Reader* 104)

Schlant criticizes this lack of a "clear position" in Schlink's novel (*The Reader* 215). Indeed, his words sound almost as helpless as Hanna's before the court, and the question begs for the obvious answer, namely, to face the facts. But this important question remains rhetorical as well. Moreover, it is posed in the language of the Third Reich, Nazi German, rather than in contemporary and thus more compassionate words (e.g., rather "murder or genocide of the Jewish people").[34] This linguistic practice of using Nazi speech mirrors the way Schlink deals with the survivors in his novel, namely, in an impersonal, detached manner.

More finite statements and unanswered questions by the protagonist show his inability to come to grips with the Nazi genocide:

> We should not believe we can comprehend the incomprehensible, we may not compare the incomparable, we may not inquire because to inquire is to make the horrors an object of discussion instead of accepting them as something in the face of which we can only fall silent in revulsion, shame and guilt.... (*The Reader* 102)

And then there is unanswerable banality, "To what purpose?" (*The Reader* 104). The logical answer to these clichéd questions then would be silence. The key words here are shame and guilt, together with revulsion. Grammatically, the first two German verbs *sich schämen* (to feel ashamed) and *sich schuldig fühlen* (to feel guilty) are reflexive. They reflect the stance of the entire novel by referring to the subject, the self, rather than focusing on the Other, in this case, the Holocaust victims.[35] "Revulsion" expresses a sense of loathing. All three terms suggest an individual turning away from fact and can be equated with German social behavior regarding the Holocaust. By contrast, the verb *trauern um* (to mourn someone) would concentrate on those murdered, instead of the self, and involves empathetic remembering of the dead. Germans call this active process of mourning *Trauerarbeit*. They also coined the special and well-known term, *Vergangenheitsbewältigung*, for coming to terms with the Nazi past. But, as the German psychologist Mitscherlich and others have concluded, due to complex psychological ramifications, it is exactly this working through that has not been achieved after the Holocaust, and this extends into the present.[36] Martin Walser, the Frankfurt Peace Prize recipient, captured this fact in October 1998, when he spoke of the "historic burden, the eternal shame" of Germans and the inner resistance against continued representation of this shame or disgrace in the German media.[37] Inga Clendinnen, in *Reading the Holocaust*, formulates a moral obligation that escapes Schlink's narrator: "We must do more than register guilt, or grief, or anger, or disgust, because neither reverence for those who suffer nor revulsion from those who inflict the suffering will help us overcome its power to paralyze, and to see it clearly."[38] *The Reader* fails to achieve this clarity of vision.

Nevertheless, Schlink, as a celebrated German writer, functions as "the seismograph of a people's moral positions" and approaches the Holocaust from a nation's "privileged position of literature" (3). Ernestine Schlant summarizes succinctly the attitude of the postwar generations of Germans:

> ... in subsequent years it has become obvious that the successor generations are equally burdened with their elders' legacy, and that they, too, may be unable to recoup the affective dimension required for genuine mourning—not remorse for deeds they did not commit or mourning for a Hitler who to them is at most a historical figure, but a mourning for the parents' generation, the deeds committed by them, and for the victims (13-14).

This often voiced criticism of Germans not being able to mourn the Holocaust victims needs elaboration. First, it is difficult to genuinely engage in an act of mourning when one does not know the dead. In the case of the Jews, it would have been nearly impossible for the perpetrator generation to bring forth such feelings, since they had first declared the Jews subhuman and then condemned them to be killed. To be sure, not every individual German wanted their deaths but, as it has been proven in many studies, antisemitism of varying degrees was widespread and disseminated by the Nazi state. And if it was not strong prejudice that turned so many Germans into bystanders, then it was simply a lack of concern for their neighbor's fate. For Germans to mourn Jews, what is needed is to recognize passive complicity as one factor of what went so terribly wrong in Germany. Also, they have to perceive its victims as people. Usually, when dealing with Jews in German life and literature, there is no sufficient societal and historical context within which they can emerge as real individuals; rather they always seem to be a monolithic group.

The Reader conveys a blurred image of Germans and Jews by what Donahue calls the "'numbness' plea" (70). It disables Michael Berg's feelings for the victims:

> Even then, when I was preoccupied by this general numbness, and by the fact that it had taken hold not only of the perpetrators and victims, but of all of us, judges and lay members of the court, prosecutors and recorders, who had to deal with these events now… (*The Reader* 98)

Schlant explains such serious shortcomings, as well as the inadequate historical treatment by Germans as

> a desire for and tendency toward continuity. This desire for continuity can be seen as an attempt to deny the radical break constituted by the Holocaust. The desire for the connection with a historical past in which the Holocaust would be a horrifying anomaly negates its shattering impact in favor of the fantasy of a totalizing and "normalizing" worldview (15).

At the same time, Schlant credits Schlink with depicting, at the end of *The Reader*, the beginning of a dialogue between Germans and Jews when Michael visits the survivor/"daughter" in New York on behalf of the dead Hanna. If such an encounter is rare in German literature, the scene, which has met with little critical attention, warrants closer examination. First, the meeting occupies a short space in the novel's conclusion. Berg, in his capacity as a German "legal historian," meets with the "daughter" and presents her with "a bank check plus a tea tin with the cash," as stipulated in Hanna's "instructions" (*The Reader* 210). This melodramatic gesture trivializes and sentimentalizes the moral weight of the genocide. Hanna's belated contrition, doubtlessly genuine, seems childlike and naïve. We know that few Nazis showed remorse or admitted wrongdoing. Is this turn of events perhaps meant to be a "female response" that speaks to the reader's heart? The survivor raises the subject of absolution and swiftly rejects this post-mortem gift. This again casts a negative light on her, this time for a more serious reason, which could be called her inability to forgive (on behalf of the dead).

Christianity preaches forgiveness, especially if a criminal expresses contrition before dying. Instead, we observe this surviving Jew, the only one who could actually grant it, refusing this very last wish. The notion of forgiveness has been amply debated after Simon Wiesenthal's *Sunflower* story. Berel Lang states that,

> ... at times the refusal to grant forgiveness may itself become a moral wrong—if indeed the request for forgiveness has been made in good faith about a forgivable act of injustice. ... the person who has been wronged initially becomes himself guilty of a wrong, which might be characterized in conventional terms as being "unforgiving."[39]

But the Nazi genocide can hardly be called "a forgivable act." However, Schlink's portrayal of Hanna's action during the church fire is turned into a deed that should somehow be forgiven. It could be argued that the narrator/author does not consider the moral weight of "To forgive all is not only not to understand all, it is—by itself, at any rate—to understand very little: about justice and the good, on the one hand, and about wrongdoing and evil, on the other."[40]

In this scene, Schlink gives the survivor the upper hand as she rejects Hanna's money as a personal recompense. This leaves the responsibility for its distribution solely in the hands of Michael.

Ironically, it is to be contributed to a fund for "illiterate Jews," itself an oxymoron for the People of the Book. Would a fund for poverty stricken Jews be so impossible to conjure? The German narrator describes the survivor as follows: "Everything about her was matter-of-fact: her manner, her gestures, her dress. Her face was oddly ageless; the way faces look after being lifted. But perhaps it had set because of her early sufferings." Possible suffering is mentioned here but again, not in a clear manner. In fact, one is not quite sure whether she has had a facelift. Schlink's narrator often puts forth two contrary possibilities, and the reader of his novel may chose either. The survivor lives "in New York in a street near Central Park," which may allude to her financial well-being and the fact that she has made it in the "new world." The way she is described suggests an economic advantage and cosmopolitan remoteness that come too close to antisemitic stereotyping. No specific mention is made about her destroyed life, her loss of family, her uprootedness and new beginning in a strange land with a foreign tongue, not to mention her traumatic memories, her Holocaust experiences, the burning church, the post-war trial, etc. Instead, Berg blocks any such questions by mentioning that Hanna "knew what she had done to people in the camp and on the march.... She dealt with it intensively during her last years in prison" (*The Reader* 213-14). The use of "people," "camp" and "march" neutralizes the extreme Holocaust situation and minimizes it linguistically.

Here would have been an opportunity for a German to ask questions, even in fiction, and, more importantly, to listen to one individual who miraculously survived Nazi persecution and planned murder. As Clendinnen says with much insight, "we, to whom such things have not been done, have an obligation to be attentive" (54). Instead, the topic of discussion between Berg and the Jewish survivor is on his involvement with and possible victimization by Hanna, the German perpetrator. This important episode in Schlink's novel reduces the genocide to a personal, German-oriented problem. Hence, Germans maintain hegemony of that memory as well. This echoes German social discourse that leaves unstated the multiple layers and facts of the Holocaust reality. To the generally better informed North American readers of such works, the author must seem unfamiliar with the discourse and extensive scholarship on the subject of the Holocaust. One of the aspects relevant to the encounter with a survivor would have been the psychological ramification of survival.

Hence, Schlink's omissions and inaccuracies invite criticism of his fictive anomalies and question their historical legitimacy. Cynthia Ozick, Holocaust scholar and Holocaust fiction writer herself, in "The Rights of History and the Rights of Imagination," speaks forcefully against the notion of such (mis)representation:

> In the name of the autonomous rights of fiction, in the name of the sublime rights of the imagination, anomaly sweeps away memory; anomaly displaces history. In the beginning was not the word, but the camera—and at that time, in that place, the camera did not mislead. It saw what was there to see. The word came later, and in some instances it came not to illuminate but to corrupt.[41]

This is a harsh verdict on some Shoah literarture. Barbara Foley's words are equally strong when she mentions "a distinctly postmodernist merging of subjective fantasy with objective reality" (354). In Schlink's text, illiteracy of an SS woman may be considered such a "fantasy." The author explains it as an intended metaphor for "the moral illiterates whom [Hanna] represents."[42] But even as a possible metaphor it does not work. According to the story, she develops contrition for the genocide victims only after learning to read in prison. How do we then explain the moral bankruptcy of those Germans who were not illiterate? If Hanna represents the German perpetrator whose mitigating circumstances and suicide absolve her and free her morally of wrongdoing, then the same would hold true for other war criminals. (This in fact held true for someone like Albert Speer who now is seen as "decent" by most historians.) Schlink uses illiteracy like a literary metaphor for blindness. It may be interesting to note that the reading tapes that Michael provides her in prison, do not contain any Holocaust material but rather classical works of German and world literature. These belong to the canon of High German culture and were the same texts that the Nazi elite once read (as did all educated Germans before, during, and after the Third Reich). Yet the humanistic and ethical values of these masterpieces provided no moral basis for those Germans during the Nazi period who embraced an immoral ideology and acted to fulfill a barbarous utopia.

If we take Hanna's newly found literacy at face value, it is implausible she could have reached a state of such enlightenment and contrition with the ability not only to read very demanding texts by Holocaust writers like Primo Levi, Elie Wiesel and others but also to fully comprehend them in their intricate philosophical nuances. Only in prison, and with her newly acquired skill of reading, does she see the light, so to speak but her response is purely emotional. Knowledge crushes her and literally kills her, and thus, *she* then becomes a victim of the Holocaust. Seen in this light, the novel functions as an apologia, not only for post-war German generations, but actually for the perpetrators of mass murder and for the rest of bystanding Germans. Finally then, the perpetrator is compared with any "ordinary" person caught in a situation of "no choice" (but to murder), and is absolved of individual moral responsibility.

Schlink's protagonist claims that, "the world of the camps is part of our collective imagination and completes our ordinary everyday [world]" (148), which echoes Walser's statement about the "constant presentation of Auschwitz" in German public life. Yet, Schlink's depiction of fictive Holocaust related events is flawed if viewed within the larger context of the genocide. Also absent are explicit references and knowledge of Jewish life, tradition, and history. Rather, the Jews are still an enigma, strangers, and sometimes a taboo subject. This lack of adumbration for the experiences of the Holocaust survivors is noticeable throughout his novel. One reason for such limitations in German writing can be seen in the fact that the Holocaust left a void in German society where there had been Jews before. Thus, Germans have had next to no chance to encounter Jewish survivors or interact with them, whether or not there was a desire on either side to do so. In that sense, Schlink's portrayal mirrors Germany's reality, both physically and psychologically. But this situation is not mentioned as such in his work. Instead, we observe a cultivated innocence that his characters (and many Germans) display when they are confronted with issues of Germany's Nazi past. They speak the words "Concentration Camps" or "Final Solutions," but they do not feel their devastating meaning. Instead, Germans now compete with Jews to assert Nazi victimhood.

This kind of German self-victimhood displayed in *The Reader* echoes a generally held position that Germans either verbalize or repress. Many recall and recount their own stories while remaining mute on the events of Nazi persecution of Jews and their genocide. The findings of a recent study may serve as a representative example of this attitude:

> ...after reading more than 1,000 Gestapo and Special Court case files and speaking with scores of people who spent their younger years in Nazi Germany, it is not clear to me whether that older generation feels compassion even now for the victims of the crimes perpetrated by their former country. Most older Germans do regret that these crimes were committed, if only because they placed a heavy and lasting burden on Germans. Many ageing Germans, as they now face their own death, look back at their past not remembering that they were once perpetrators or bystanders but with the sense that they have been the real victims of Nazi terror.[43]

In this rationalization, the "specificity of Jewish suffering is obliterated and the role played by perpetrators in their fate is transcoded" (Parry 262). In this light, Omar Bartov's critical judgment underscores the disingenuous-ness of this recent literary work from Germany:

> *The Reader*, then is about Germany as victim. It is a victim of its history of murder, to be sure, but then, even the murderers them-

selves are victims, and those they ultimately victimize are the next generation of Germans. It is a German fate (*Mirrors* 224).

Although Schlink poses valid rhetorical questions, he provides no answers and places the responsibility of interpretation entirely upon his readers. As a German, one can attempt to respond to them—or not. As general readers, we may bring in our own historical knowledge and test it against the author's representation—or not. There is no suggested moral obligation to come to terms with the past. Instead, Bartov concludes, "numbness and obsession are a means to avoid responsibility and reject all ethical categories" (*Mirrors* 224). Donahue's verdict is as severe: "Though it has been hailed as a significant advance in the literature of *Vergangenheitsbewältigung*, this book is in fact remarkably shy about historical, legal and ethical detail" (67). He also rightfully rejects the possibility of Schlink's intended "ingeniously 'encoded'" criticism of his narrator (73). In fact Schlink's novel does not criticize the German perpetrators' having operated on the "secondary level of virtue," i.e. "to do one's duty," for which the Nazis certainly created the situation.[44] Thus, the culpable individuals can justify immoral behavior rather than to recognize that such behavior was unethical in its indifference to humanistic values. If these distinctions were not clear at the time of the crime, they should be made evident with the aid of hindsight.

One fact remains: the Holocaust will not disappear from the historical map even if it is suppressed or misrepresented. Berel Lang states that the "most radical alternative" to its representation is not to have written about it at all (*Act and Idea in the Nazi Genocide* 160). But Schlink did not decide on silence. We may thus want to consider the merits of his oblique artifact based on James E. Young's belief, as expressed in *Writing and Re-Writing the Holocaust*: "the *memory* of the Holocaust—even if it is 'inauthentic' or second-hand—lives on and even begins to replace the event itself."[45] Taking into consideration that *The Reader* has now worldwide renown, its moral ambiguity and critical deficiency need to be exposed. We can thus perceive this literary work from Germany as a mirror of how a perpetrator nation rationalizes or obfuscates their forefathers' crimes against humanity and how it transforms and transmits them. For this reason it is perhaps our obligation to discuss *The Reader's* flaws and show how collective memory can function in the face of genocide.

Endnotes

1. Trans. Carol Brown Janeway (New York: Random House, 1998).

2. It appeared in 1998 under the title *Naar Hakriya* ("The Reading Youth"). I thank Ed Klein for this reference.

3. Ian Sansom gives a good review overview in his short analysis, "Doubts About the Reader," in *Salmagundi*, no. 124/125 (Fall 1999) 3-16, as well as William Collins Donahue in his very critical reading, "Illusions of Subtlety: Bernhard Schlink's *Der Vorleser* and The Moral Limits of Holocaust Fiction," in *German Life and Letters* (54:1 January 2001). See also the blurbs on the dust jacket of the English hardcover edition.

4. Donahue mentions the Hans Fallada and the prestigious Heine prizes (62).

5. A shorter version of this article was first presented at the 32nd Annual Scholars' Conference on the Holocaust and the Churches, Union, NJ: Kean University, 2-5 March, 2002. I wish to thank Gary Evans for his editorial help.

6. Two American examples of such fiction are *The Shawl*, by Cynthia Ozick (New York: Knopf, 1990) and *Anya*, by Susan F. Schaeffer (New York: Macmillan, 1974).

7. Marlene Heinemann, *Women Prose Writers of the Nazi Holocaust* (Ann Arbor, MI: U Microfilms International, 1986) 1.

8. Martin Amis, *Time's Arrow or The Nature of the Offense* (New York: Hamony, 1991). For an excellent analysis of this work see Ann Parry, *Journal of European Studies*, vol. 29 (Sept. 1999) 249-67.

9. Sherri Szeman, *The Kommandant's Mistress* (New York: Harper Collins, 1993).

10. Aleksandar Tisma, *Kapo*, trans. Richard Williams (New York: Harcourt Brace, 1993).

11. See Karin Doerr, "The Depiction of Auschwitz in an American Novel: Sherri Szeman's *The Kommandant's Mistress*," in *Rendezvous: Journal of Arts and Letters*, vol. 34, no. 1 (Idaho State U: Fall 2000) 37-46.

12. Barbara Foley, "Fact, Fiction, Fascism: Testimony and Mimesis in Holocaust Narratives," in *Comparative Literature* 34 (Fall 1982) 330, 346.

13. *By Words Alone: The Holocaust in Literature* (Chicago: U of Chicago P, 1980) 216.

14. *Voicing the Void: Muteness and Memory in Holocaust Fiction* (Albany, NY: State U of New York P, 1997) 1.

15. *Act and Idea in the Nazi Genocide* (University of Chicago Press, 1990) 118. See also his latest work on the subject, *Holocaust Representation: Art Within The Limits Of History And Ethics* (Baltimore: Johns Hopkins UP, 2000).

16. Ann Parry, in "The Caesura Of The Holocaust In Marin Amis' *Times Arrow* and Bernhard Schlink's *The Reader*," uses the notion of the caesura of the Holocaust in her interpretation of these two works in the *Journal of European Studies*, vol. 29 (Sept. 1999) 249-67. She explains that caesura is generally "defined as a radical break that necessitates a re-thinking of the relation between past, present and future, as well as completely reconstituting ideas about evil and what it is to be human" (249).

17. Ruth Klueger (formerly Angress), *Germanist* and Auschwitz survivor, is an early critic with articles such as "A 'Jewish Problem' in German Postwar Fiction" in *Modern Judaica*, 5 (1985) and "Discussing Holocaust Literature" in *Simon Wiesenthal Center Annual*, 2 (1985) 179-92. There is also the work of Susan E. Cernyak-Spatz entitled *German Holocaust Literature* (New York: Peter Lang, 1985). See also Helga Druxes "Remembering as Revision: Fictionalizing Nazism in Postwar Germany" in *Modern Languages Studies: Holocaust Literature*, xxiv, 4 (Fall 1994) 54-62.

18. (New York: Routledge, 1999). See also Bosmajian, Hamida, *Metaphors of Evil: The Shadow of Nazism in Contemporary German Literature* (Iowa City: U of Iowa P, 1979).

19. Omer Bartov "German Soldiers and the Holocaust," in Omer Bartov, ed. *The Holocaust: Origins, Implementation, Aftermath* (New York: Routledge, 2000) 177.

20. Omer Bartov, *Mirrors of Destruction: War, Genocide, and Modern Identity* (Oxford: Oxford UP, 2000).

21. Richard Overy. *Interrogations: The Nazi Elite in Allied Hands, 1945* (New York: Penguin B, 2001).

22. But celebrated cases, such as the one of the notorious Irma Grise were not the norm.

23. Ingrid Müller-Münch, *Die Frauen von Majdanek: Vom zerstörten Leben der Opfer und der Mörderinnen* (Reinbek bei Hamburg: Rowohlt,1982).

24. ("Daß auch ihr Spitzname—Kobyla, die Stute—den sie ihrer Angewohnheit verdankte, Häftlinge mit ihren eisenbeschlagenen Stiefeln zu treten, immerhin 46 Zeuginnen gut im Gedächtnis geblieben war.... aktiv Hand anlegte, um die dort Inhaftierten zu quälen und zu töten.") See Müller-Münch 93.

25. See Interview with Eleanor Wachtel, *Queen's Quarterly*, vol. 106, 4 (Winter 1999) 544-55.

26. "Figuren. Figures. Corpses dug up and burned by members of the Sonderkommando 1005. Also, derogatory for Jews and other people chosen for deadly medical experiments." Robert Michael and Karin Doerr, *Nazi Deutsch/Nazi German: An English Lexicon of the Third Reich Language* (Westport, CT: Greenwood P, 2002).

27. (Göttingen: Wallstein, 1992). The dedication reads: "Den Göttinger Freunden—ein deutsches Buch" (A German book to my Göttinger friends). The English version is now available as *Still Alive: A Holocaust Girlhood Remembered* (New York: Feminist Press, 2001).

28. If the name of a Jewish German did not reflect their Jewish background, he/she, by law, had to add "Israel" or "Sara" as a middle name on all documents.

29. As one among many German professors remarked:

> Schlink's book is very different from most other literature or film on the Holocaust, since it presents the perpetrator as a human being like us; we might even find her attractive and loveable as the narrator does—which complicates our view of the perpetrators and our own position.

E-mail exchange on WIG List, April 1999.

30. For an analysis of the subject of compassion in Schlink's novel, see Jerimah P. Conway, "Compassion and Moral Condemnation," in *Philosophy and Literature*, vol. 23 no. 2 (October 1999) 284-301.

31. Eric Carlton, *Massacres: An Historical Perspective* (Hants, England: Scholar P, 1994) 127.

32. See Alexander B. Rossino, "Nazi Anti-Jewish Policy During the Polish Campaign: The Case of the Einsatzgruppe von Woyrsch," in *German Studies Review*, vol. xxiv, no. 1 (Feb. 2001) 39 and 41.

33. "Although the Zentralstelle in Ludwigsburg investigated well over 100,000 cases of former Nazi perpetrators, as of 1993 only 6,487 Nazi criminals were tried and 6,197 convicted by various German courts on charges of murder or accomplice to murder. Only 163 received life sentences." Fischer, Klaus P., *The History of an Obsession: German Judeophobia and the Holocaust* (New York: Continuum, 1998) 418. In the case of Lammerding, member of the SS detachment acting at Oradour-sur-Glane, "escaped and was later condemned to death *in absentia*.... He made his way quietly back to Dusseldorf where he built a prosperous engineering concern, and died there in 1971." Quoted from Eric Carlton, 127.

34. Scholars have remarked on this practice and associate the use of the Nazis' language with (albeit unintentional) siding with the perpetrator instead of the victims and survivors of the Holocaust. They find it

> so firmly entrenched in texts and scholarly literature that it will probably never entirely be replaced; but its use is no less objectionable since it

renders harmless the unspeakable reality of the Holocaust and continues to use the terminology of the murderers.... (92)

See Walter F. Renn, "Textbooks: Treatment of the Holocaust and Related Themes," in Randolph L. Braham, ed., *The Treatment of the Holocaust in Textbooks* and "The Crystal of Memory or the Smoke of Remembrance?" in *Confronting the Holocaust: A Mandate for the 21st Century. Studies in the Shoah.* Vol. XIX Eds. G. Jan Colin and Marcia Sachs Littell (New York: UP of America, 1997) 152.

35. See Karin Doerr and Kurt Jonassohn, "Germany's Language of Genocide at the Turn of the Century" to be published in 2002.

36. A. and M. Mitscherlich, "Die Unfähigkeit zur Trauer um den erlittenen Verlust des Führers ist das Ergebnis einer intensiven Abwehr von Schuld, Scham und Angst" in *Die Unfähigkeit zu trauern* (München: Piper, 1983) 34.

37. See acceptance speech of the peace prize "Erfahrungen beim Verfassen einer Sonntagsrede" (1998).

38. (Cambridge: Cambridge UP, 1999) 182.

39. See the chapter "Reliving or Revoking the Past: Two Views of Forgiveness," in Berel Lang, *The Future of the Holocaust: Between History and Memory* (Ithaca, NY: Cornell UP, 1996) 133.

40. See the chapter "Germany Reunified: The Stigma of Normalcy," in Berel Lang, *The Future of the Holocaust*, 140.

41. In *Commentary* (March 1999) 27.

42. Leslie Cohen. Interview with Bernhard Schlink. Books in *Jerusalem Post*, 2 July 1999, 13B.

43. Eric A. Johnson, *Nazi Terror: The Gestapo, Jews, and Ordinary Germans* (New York: Basic B, 1999) 486.

44. This useful definition is from Peter Hayes' lecture, "The Chemistry of Business-State Relations in Nazi Germany," The University of Vermont: The Miller Symposium, 21 April 2002.

45. *Essays on the Nature of Holocaust Literature and its Critical Interpretation* (Ann Arbor, Michigan: U Microfilms International, 1983) 38. See also James E. Young, "Holocaust Documentary Fiction: The Novelist as Eyewitness," in *The Art of Memory: Holocaust Memorials in History*, James E. Young, ed. (Regensburg, Germany: Aumüller, 1994) 200-15.

CHAPTER 13

Literary Representations of the 1915 Genocide of Armenians: An Important Topical Genre Continuing in the New Millennium

Rubina Peroomian

Commensurate with the history of the Armenian persecutions and massacres, Armenian literature has been a repository of responses to these collective experiences, responses shaped and reshaped through time by multiple layers of influences such as Judeo-Christian teachings, cultural determinants, historical archetypes, as well as evolving national ideals and political aspirations.[1] Within this context, literary responses to genocide are the amalgamation, the echo, and the culmination of all these responses, as the Genocide is the culmination of all historical catastrophes in terms of its eschatological nature and impact.

Armenian Diasporan post-genocide literature in its entirety is a response to the Armenian Genocide. It embodies the attempts to conceptualize the catastrophe and in one way or another relates to it:

> Children of massacre,
> children of destruction,
> children of dispersion,
> oh, my Diaspora ...
> someone was calling
> in my dream.[2]

These lines from a poem published in 1987 are a rendering by Armenian American poetess Diana Der Hovanessian of the makeup of the Diaspora and the interrelationship between the Diaspora and the Genocide. Hilda Kalfayan-Panossian, a native of Constantinople residing in France, laments: "Spiurk [Diaspora] is my pain / like an agony that never ends / unable to speak / and yet full of hope." The Diaspora for her is the site of "destruction and disintegration," the outcome of the Genocide that obliterated all rules and regulations, effaced order and value in the life of Armenians thrust in the Diaspora, caught in a prolonged agony.[3] Will this prolonged mental state continue into the new millennium? The Event is sliding into the past century, is there a reason for the continuation of genocide literature? And if there still exists a milieu open to its development, what direction will these responses take?

The Armenian Genocide has generated a plethora of literature across generations of survivors. Each writer, each poet has strived to encapsulate the cataclysm in art, to comprehend it, to render meaning to his/her harrowing experience, to let out the last cries of the dying nation, to vent the pain, the rage, the frustration of the surviving few against the denial of the perpetrators and the indifference of the world's bystanders.

Some argue that one has to live the hell in order to be able to create its representation in art; yet even such representation will be a mimesis, according to Platonic logic, one step removed from the Truth of the unthinkable reality of genocide. Elie Wiesel has said that only one who has been there, has the right to speak, and Alvin Rosenfeld asserts that "the best portrayals of 'life' in Nazi concentration camps are produced by those who themselves experienced the meaninglessness of the two categories of life and death."[4] The generation with first-hand experience of the Armenian Tragedy did not succeed in creating the masterpiece. The most talented writers and poets were massacred at the outset. The attempts of the surviving few did not bear fruit. Is it reasonable to hope that succeeding generations of Armenian writers would be able to reach that pinnacle, the successful conceptualization of the genocide in art?

Literary Representations of the 1915 Genocide of Armenians: An Important Topical Genre Continuing in the New Millennium

My contention is that the coming generations of Armenian literati—some obsessed with the Genocide, others only now discovering the traumatic past, the cause of the unspoken pain in the family, and still others finding the freedom to entertain the topic as they choose—have strong potentials. With the distance of time and space in their favor, with a deeper knowledge of history, and with a talent for grasping the poetics of violence, they have favorable possibilities to be able to confront the Genocide. Their work is likely to encompass the echoes of the nation's collective psyche shaped by the violence, the pain of dispersion, the effects of self-accusation, the search for identity or the struggle to cope with a dual identity, the effects of the past, and present role of the perpetrators and world bystanders.

Fiction is socially conscious, as Melvin J. Vincent suggests, and offers deeper insight into both human character and events and their significance."[5] The fictionalized Armenian Genocide provides that deep insight into the Event with a potential impact that works in two distinct dimensions. The internal dimension accounts for its cathartic quality. It also works as an essential fuel to keep the fire burning in the soul, to keep alive the Armenian consciousness of a colossal injustice awaiting redress. The external dimension deals with the potential impact of such literature on world public awareness.

Anne Frank did just that for the Jewish Holocaust. Published in English in 1952, her diary was the first to penetrate the American consciousness and shape the American, or rather the universal, reception of the Holocaust. Alvin Rosenfeld attributes this to the subtlety of the subject: not too harsh, not too Jewish, not too disturbing.[6] Then came Steven Spielberg's *Schindler's List*, surpassing the impact of Anne Frank's Diary. This was a completely new approach to the Jewish tragedy, one that portrayed not the victimization of the Jews but the confrontation of good and evil, the savior and the executioner, and the conclusion was not a depressing one but a happy reunion of survivors, now mostly affluent people. This is something that the public can readily grasp.

What does the public know about the Armenian Genocide?

The survivors of the Armenian Genocide, scattered throughout the world, in most cases did not speak of their horrible experience. They had an inner compulsion to leave everything behind and live in the New World integrated in society like everyone else; if they told their stories, it would set them apart. The prejudice of mainstream society against newcomers, especially in America, contributed to that conduct. There was also the intent to spare their children, to protect them against the paralyzing memory with which they had to live. Their response to genocide was silence.

For some, this period of silence was never broken. It was only after their death that their children discovered the tremendous burden of memory that weighed so heavily upon their parents' souls and caused their sometimes peculiar behavior. Virginia Haroutounian's Orphan in the Sands (1995) is an example.[7]

David Kherdian speaks of the same experience:

> Why have I waited until your death
> to know the earth you were turning
> was Armenia, the color of the fence
> your homage to Adana, and your other.[8]

Even today, when this generation is almost gone, the memoirs keep appearing in the press. They are being written by the second, even the third generation. In some cases, the author is simply reproducing what was left in writing by the survivor. Hovhannes Mugrditchian's *To Armenians with Love: The Memoirs of a Patriot* (1996) is an example.[9]

In other cases, the raw material, survivor testimonies, is elaborated and embellished to become the response of the new generation to the memory of their parents, to the genocide of their people. Peter Balakian's *Black Dog of Fate* (1998),[10] Stina Katchadourian's *Efronia: An Armenian Love Story* (1994),[11] and Carol Edgarian's *Rise the Euphrates* (1994) are examples of this category.

The success of these works in the United States can be attributed to the fact that they are being produced within the conventions of American culture. They are palatable to the American taste and acceptance of horror stories. The second and third generation poet or writer has mastered the criteria. As Arpiné Konyalian Grenier puts it, the new writer "faces the tragedy, accepts it, mourns it and transcends it." She adds, however: "It is tricky and slippery to face emotion and express it in unadulterated fashion."[12] It is indeed a challenging task, for it is sometimes impossible not to succumb to the waves of irrepressible emotion.

Leonardo Alishan was never able to transcend the tragedy that was his grandmother's, the tragedy that became his fate at the age of nine:

> I try to be a spectator of that tragedy which culminated in a London hospital room in 1978 where Granny saw Turkish horsemen around her bed before she died. But, alas, I am not the spectator. I am a character caught in that play which never, never, never reaches its equilibrium.[13]

It is through his grandmother, as is the case for most second or third generation writers, that Alishan sees the Armenian suffering, the Genocide:

> In the center of my dream
> there is a church of stone in Van
> sealed from outside
> exhaling screams and smoke from the inside,
> its congregation of Armenian folk
> replacing the candles with their flesh.
> There is a church in my dream
> made with the bones of dead gods,
> babies and parrots' prayers;
> always, all night, in flames
> but never burning to the ground.
> And in the church burns a statue of Mary
> With my Granny's face, wax dripping down her eyes
> drop by drop, on the skin of my dreams.[14]

In some cases, the topoi associated with the Genocide appear as fragmented images imposing themselves upon everyday life in the New World. Many of Peter Balakian's poems in *Sad Days of Light* (1983) illustrate this duality.[15]

These responses are definitely different from the immediate reactions of those who attempted to recapture in art the hell through which they themselves had lived. They tried to find the source of the evil in the character of the Turk. They tried to explain the Catastrophe, laud the spirit of self-defense, chastise the cowards and their lowly means of survival. They tried to interpret the calamity as a twist in the relationship between man and God, even defied God, cast doubt on His existence or His oneness.

The next generation, the orphans of the desert who began their adult life in the Diaspora, expressed the pain of orphanhood, took refuge in the world of dreams; they blamed the past generation and the values and traditions they had transmitted to them.

The Armenian Genocide is now sliding into the past, but we still question why it happened. Why did the world let it happen? Why this terrible injustice? These are questions that have no answers and cause frustration. Justice has not been rendered, and the Armenians cannot put their dead to rest. One and a half million souls seem to haunt them. There are two other underlying reasons why Armenians are still so obsessed with the Genocide and why the subject keeps surfacing in their literature. The perpetrator's denial of the crime and the use of intrigue to secure allies and distort history is one reason. And they always find reasons for their denial. Edgar Hilsenrath, the German-Jewish author of *The Story of the Last Thought*, the most impressive novel of the Armenian Genocide, has a long list of reasons he puts forth with his unique sarcasm and playful style. "Where do they find them?" asks the storyteller's shadow in the novel. "In their fears," replies the storyteller.[16] "In their fears!" No explanation could be as expressive as this one word—"fears." Then, there is the vague image of a lost homeland that kindles a sense of yearning and deprivation.

The American culture of the 60s and 70s encouraged the search for one's roots since it became more and more permissive of group affiliation and identification. And the trend continues. In the case of Armenian-Americans, the Armenian past was obviously associated with the massacres and deportations, a captive homeland swept clean of its indigenous people, and a decimated family. The modern responses were thus shaped through looking back to that historical source of self-understanding, and self-identity. And it did not and does not matter whether or not the individual Armenian has lost family members in the death marches. All are survivors of genocide. "We are children of Der Zor," writes Diana Der Hovanessian:

> Even though your mother was a baby
> in Worcester, and safe
> and your father a young soldier
> in Mourad's mountains
> and you a generation from being born,
>
> * * * * *
>
> even without a single
> relative who lived to march,
> lived past the march. We are children of Der Zor.[17]

The commemoration of the 50th anniversary of the Armenian Genocide in 1965 and the heightened political activism of the Diaspora played a pivotal role in sensitizing the new generation, kindling self-consciousness and self-recognition among a stratum of youth, who were now thoroughly immersed in the mainstream culture yet still searching for the source of their own particularity.

The echoes of this search reverberate in literature, both in the works of immigrant writers and of those born in America. Among the second generation survivor-writers in the United States, Peter Najarian stands out with his *Voyages* (1971). Najarian's *Daughters of Memory* (1986) and Peter Balakian's *The Black Dog of Fate* (1998) are also examples in which the Armenian component is gradually pulled out of a nebulous memory hole to become an important dimension in the Diasporan Armenians self-identity.

Vahé Oshagan, an emigrant from the Middle East, portrays the assimilated, alienated generation in America against a backdrop of national traditions, the past, the roots calling the generation back, demanding action, be it in the most unconventional way, as is the case in Odzum (Consecration). Indeed, this well wrought short story reverberates with the effects of collective victimization, dispersion, and alienation, that is, the effects of genocide in Armenian-American community life.[18]

The pain and frustration resulting from the struggle to adjust to one's dual identity as well as the search for an ideal image of the Diasporan Armenian echo in almost the entire literary output of Hakob Karapents. Nubar Agishian and Penyamin Nourigian are two other immigrant writers who develop an array of characters caught in the turmoil of dual identity and intermarriages leading to assimilation.[19]

Then come the newer poets and writers, all emigrants from Middle Eastern countries (Vrej Armen, Boghos Kupelian, Vahé Berberian, Vehanoush Tekian and Ishkhan Jinbashian) who write in Armenian and whose artistic creations portray the painful transition, the make-up of the new Diasporan Armenian. The hardship of dislocation, the memory of the dead family have become a part of the Armenian heritage and are transmitted from generation to generation. How they have responded to their Armenian heritage depends on that linkage, whether they love and cherish it and live stranded within it, or hate it, run away and try to free themselves from it. In all cases, the response is an act of desperation.

The intensity of this struggle for an Armenian identity does not necessarily exist to the same degree in other Diasporan communities. In some cases, this struggle is only that of the intellectual elite, and the wound of the Genocide bleeds through the literary works they produce. Sevda Sevan's novel *Rodosto, Rodosto* (written in Bulgarian, 1981) permeates the Bulgarian Armenian poetess-writer's motivation to capture the impact of genocide on the mental state of its survivors and the perpetrators' perception of the event, as well as their unchanged attitude toward the few remaining Armenians.[20]

Literary Representations of the 1915 Genocide of Armenians: 233
An Important Topical Genre Continuing in the New Millennium

In a most recent poem, "Voghjuin kez nor dar" (*Greetings to You, New Century*, 1999), Iranian-Armenian poet Varand hails the New Century with hope and expectations for the deliverance of the nation. And, significantly, the source of his chagrin and the tears he sheds is the continued captivity of his homeland, symbolized by Mount Ararat. "For the star-reaching captive did not return home yet," he reasons, and the crime against the nation remains unresolved: "For the righteous blood boiling in my veins is the blood I shed on the roads to Deir el-Zor."[21] Azad Matian, another Iranian-Armenian poet, uplifted by a young woman singing the famous song "Krunk" (Crane) during a vigil at the Genocide monument, writes the poem "April 24, 1996 (to Gariné for singing Krunk)." He expresses his bewilderment with unanswered questions and fading memories. He struggles to come out of this hopelessness:

> Where are we
> and bound for where?
>
> * * * * *
>
> Who are we
> and heading for what?
> Hating, hating this endless pain
> and one another
>
> * * * * *
>
> and believe again
> in the eternal life of my stricken race.[22]

For all intents and purposes, the new response has stemmed from the attempt to confront the Genocide in order to grasp its historical and psychological impact, to enhance the fading memory or to construct one with which to relate and identify. The constructed reality can be an imagined one. Hilsenrath's *The Story of the Last Thought* sets a perfect example. It constructs brick by brick the reality of Thovma Khatisian's family history, "from the little idyllic mountain village to the torture chambers of the Turkish rulers."[23] Khatisian's family was wiped out completely during the Genocide. As a young boy, he was raised in a Turkish family. Dagmar Lorenz notes in his review of this novel, Khatisian had a choice of self-identities: Turkish, Swiss or Armenian.

> The last was for him the hardest to attain, since he had to reconstruct or even construct an entire biography and national history. Yet he chooses to become a survivor of the massacres and a witness.[24]

Thovma's inquiries led him to patch together his own story, albeit an imagined reality. And, one day, he says,

> I had a genuine family history. I knew my roots. I had a father and a mother again, and I had many relatives. I also had a name with a tradition, one that I could pass on to my children and grandchildren.[25]

Hilsenrath is truly compelling as he interweaves imagination, dream, and reality in the thoughts of Thovma Khatisian at the end of the long and torturous road that is called "life." His last thoughts, as those of all Armenian survivors, fly back to Mount Ararat, to Hayastan. Perhaps their thoughts never left these places. Perhaps, Armenians never left these places. The dead Armenians whisper, Hilsenrath suggests, and "when Armenians whisper at night, the Turks have nightmares...."[26] because in every Armenian's dream "Anahit, the mother of Armenia," will find Hayk, "her lost son" [toward the end of the novel, the storyteller calls Thovma Hayk to invoke "the first of the Armenians." Incidentally, according to the storyteller, Thovma's mother was called Anahit]. Hayk "will be fruitful and have many descendents. And the children of Hayk and their children's children, will people this land, which was always meant for them." Finally, as with the last thought of Thovma Khatisian, the last thoughts of all Armenian survivors, before they draw their last breath, "will fly back into the gaps in the Turkish history books."[27]

New responses to the Armenian Genocide were generated in the Diaspora, particularly in America. In fact, in recent years the increasing fragmentation and particularization of American culture, the prevailing theory of multiculturism, and the political atmosphere have played as the catalyst and booster of the new Armenian-American response to the past, to history, to genocide. These new responses will certainly influence the literary output of the Republic of Armenia. That is one of the goods, the commodities if you will, that we shall see crossing the Diaspora-Armenia bridge to reach the thinkers and the ordinary citizens of Armenia. Literature will become one of the major footings of mutual awareness and eventual unification. This will come about, as Vahé Oshagan puts it, from "the strong attachment of all poets to the national ethos." One important reason, Oshagan continues,

> is that throughout the past centuries, the Armenian literary elite has always been involved with national ideology i.e., survival of the nation and the preservation of the culture. This in itself is a political ideal, and all poets, Diasporan or Armenia-based, have been and are committed to it.[28]

Sooner or later, the "Armenia-based" literati will rid themselves of the constraints of the Soviet era and its lingering ideologies; the forced detachment from the Armenian past and the Genocide in particular will be lifted off the minds as it is lifted off the political atmosphere; interest to address these issues will increase and Armenia will join the Diaspora in responding to the past, to history, to the Armenian Genocide. These literary responses will continue as an important intellectual endeavor both in Armenia and the Diaspora. They will serve to build and enhance the monument of the Armenian collective memory but, more important, they will serve to find a way to overcome the Catastrophe and make national survival possible.

Before proceeding any further, I would like to make it clear that, despite Soviet restrictions and censorship, the Genocide did not cease to occupy the minds of Soviet Armenians, be it as a painful memory secretly transmitted from generation to generation, be it as a covert leitmotif in literature, or be it as innocent reminiscences of the native village or hometown. Eghishé Charents, Gurgen Mahari, Khachik Dashtents set the example. Silva Kaputikyan speaks of those covert expressions of longing, pain and suppressed tears of the older generation, the Western Armenian survivor-refugees in Soviet Armenia, as the conduits to transfer and to build the collective memory of the unsolved injustice.[29]

The fiftieth anniversary of the Armenian Genocide was a turning point in the evolution of political thought in Soviet Armenia, as it was in the Diaspora. On the morning of April 24, 1965, for the first time in Soviet Armenian history, a huge crowd took to the streets in Erevan and marched in commemoration of the victims of the Genocide, demanding the return of their ancestral lands, and calling for a just solution of the Armenian Question. Silva Kaputikyan reminisces about the event:

> They were going
> To claim their orphaned dead and orphaned tombs,
> To kneel and kiss the orphaned sacraments
> Of Maruta Monastery,
> To bring back the land
> And pull out of it the Lightening Sword,
> To bring back the rock and bring out Kurkik Djalali
> To say that we are able to saddle our father's dragon-slaying horse,
> To say that we are the owners, the lords of the House of Sasun
> And the cause of Sasun.
> The month was April,
> And the day was right.[30]

After that day, nothing was the same. The Khrushchev thaw was succeeded by the Brezhnev restrictions and renewed censorship; yet masterpieces like Paruyr Sevak's "Anlreli zangakatun" (Immutably Tolling Bell Tower), Mushegh Galshoyan's "Tsirani poghe" (The Purple

Horn), and Hrant Matevosyan's "Metsamor" (the name of a district in Armenia), as well as Gevorg Emin's poems of rage and tears for the victims, were produced. The Soviet Armenian dissident literature prepared the ground for the Karabagh movement in 1988, a nationalistic uprising demanding the unification of Karabagh (an Armenian enclave in the Soviet Republic of Azerbaijan) with Soviet Armenia.[31]

Rediscovering the past, writing about the Genocide, and dealing with previously forbidden historical subjects in literature, however, have not gained momentum in today's relatively free atmosphere, while historical research in these areas has come a long way. Rare are the voices like that of the young poet Ludvik Turyan who expresses disillusion and at the same time the aspiration for justice for all of mankind. In his poem "Justice," Turyan begins by treating justice like a toy, when he knew little about the fate of his people and about justice that was denied to them:

> Justice, if you had been given to me
> as a toy when I was a child,
> I am sure I would have broken you
> to bits to find what made you tick.

Shattered at the thought that there is no justice in the world, he continues with a pessimistic note. He sees no light at the end of the tunnel:

> What healer
> you could have been, had you arrived
> centuries ago
>
> * * * * *
>
> But Justice, our globe is aging, aging,
> You are too, and I am afraid you may die
> of old age before you really arrive.[32]

Independence in Armenia since 1991 has provided an incomparable freedom for the literati but paradoxically has brought about, especially in the first years, a socioeconomic atmosphere quite unfavorable for artistic endeavors. Sporadically, we hear voices that sing the song of the orphaned lands of Armenia and the calamity that befell the nation. These creations are mostly in the genre of lamentation. With a heart full "With the grief /and the gloom of Armenians," Gurgen Gabrielyan, a poet of Artsakh (Karabagh), laments the sufferings of his people. Robert Esayan, a younger poet of Artsakh, searches in history, in the destruction of his people in Western Armenia, for the source of the present plight in Karabagh and the carnage that went on for years at the hands of the Azeris.

In a poem dedicated to the sixteen hundredth anniversary of the development of the Armenian alphabet, Ruben Vardanyan paints the landscape of Armenian history and the Armenian Genocide with sullen darkness and morbid metaphors. Silva Kaputikyan, whose mother and grandmother were refugees from Van, remembers their ordeal and that of her people in "Hin karote" (*The Old Yearning*, 1992).[33] The poem captures Kaputikyan's preoccupation with the fate and the unresolved cause of the Armenian people. In her imagination three generations, her grandmother, her mother, and herself, walk together through life as girls of the same age harboring the same yearnings, the same unfulfilled dreams, the same shattered hope for return to the ancestral home. Kaputikyan implies that national pain and aspirations do not diminish with the succession of generations.

The theme of Genocide, if entertained at all in the poetry of Armenia, is within the framework of old responses. Only in a few cases, when the atrocities against the Armenians of Azerbaijan and Karabagh are lamented, is a new accent added: a thread is passed through history to link these pogroms to the Genocide, and the new Azeri perpetrator is identified with the Turk of yesteryear. New voices are rare, and they are heard in the most unexpected contexts and conceptualizations. An expressive example in prose is Aghasi Ayvazyan's "Antun turke" (The Homeless Turk). In this imaginative interaction with the Turk, the nation's hatred and rage pour out. Fate brings the Armenian and the Turkish wanderers together under a freeway overpass in Pasadena, where the homeless hang out. The Armenian blames the Turk for their plight:

Literary Representations of the 1915 Genocide of Armenians:
An Important Topical Genre Continuing in the New Millennium

> You Turks, if you had not invaded Armenia from Central Asia, or wherever you came from ... if you had not driven my grandfather out of his home in Bitlis or Kars or wherever ... if you had not slaughtered the children and the old ... I could welcome you in my house in Bitlis or wherever. We could drink wine together.[34]

Another example, this one in poetry, of such an innovative voice in literary responses to Genocide in Armenia is Henrik Edoyan's call "Hey, Turkish Poets." The author addresses the Turk, and, at the same time, he intimates the importance of the role of literati, in this case the Turkish intellectuals at the time of the Genocide. Edoyan believes that they could make a difference and prevent the atrocities. The first stanza sets the pattern:

> If one of you, just one, had spoken up
> "Why kill this trembling kid,
> his slaughtered parents were enough,"
> We might have raised a glass together
> if not a monument.[35]

I wonder if Edoyan has read Nazim Hikmet's poetry of rage and admonishment, but, on the other hand, he is a voice in the wilderness.[36]

Literary works on the themes of Armenian suffering and especially the inflicted injustice may be few in Armenia due to the lingering effects of the past restrictions. However, taking into consideration the current efforts to elevate and enhance national education in schools and to broaden involvement in the national struggle for the just solution of the Armenian cause and also in view of the fact that the Diaspora literature with these themes at its core is being avidly read, one can presume that the inclination to address these issues will increase and genocide literature will soon form an independent corpus and find new directions.

Based on this presumption, I believe that, although historians will continue their research and new documents will continue to shed light on the issue, it is the literary representations that will shape the understanding of the Armenian Genocide for future generations. It is the power of the artist's imagination that can capture the unthinkable, the genocide, and provide, as Yehuda Bauer would say, the "metaphysical comprehension," of the Armenian Genocide.[37]

Paraphrasing Emil Fackenheim's words, I conclude with this idea: to renew the past for present life has always been an essential obligation of historians, philosophers, and, I may add, the literati as well, and never before has this task been so indispensable.[38] Therefore, I would like to submit that future responses to the Armenian Genocide, be they fragmented and incoherent, as an imposition of the theme itself, will stand as a monument to the Armenian aspiration to become a nation again. They will provide the needed dialogue between history and literature to place the Armenian Genocide within the ongoing saga of a living people, to find a way to resolve the tragedy, and to make national survival and perpetuation possible.

Endnotes

1. For an analysis of paradigms of responses to collective sufferings in national catastrophes through time and multiple layers of constituent elements, see Rubina Peroomian, *Literary Responses to Catastrophe: A Comparison of the Armenian and the Jewish Experiences* (Atlanta, Georgia: Scholars Press, 1993).

2. Diana Der Hovanessian, *About Time* (New York: Ashot Press, 1987), from a poem titled "Diaspora," p. 22 (quotation marks by the author).

3. Hilda Kalfayan-Panossian, "The Wake," trans. Vahé Oshagan, *RAFT* 9 (1995): 15-16.

4. See David Roskies, "The Holocaust According to Literary Critics," *Prooftext* 1 (May 1981): 209-16.

5. See Bernard Cohen, *Sociocultural Changes in American Jewish Life as Reflected in Selected Jewish Literature* (Rutherford, Madison, Teaneck, NJ: Fairleigh Dickinson University Press, 1972), p. 32.

6. See Alvin H. Rosenfeld, "The Americanization of the Holocaust," in Alvin H. Rosenfeld, ed., *Thinking About the Holocaust After Half a Century* (Bloomington and Indianapolis: Indiana University Press, 1997), pp. 141-44.

7. *Orphan in the Sands* is the story of the author's mother, who only in the final days of her life shared with her daughter her terrible ordeal during and after the Genocide. It is the story of the daughter, who resented her mother's strange behavior and strove all her life to adjust to it, only to learn in the end that it was the Genocide and its aftereffects that had ruined her mother's and her own life.

8. David Kherdian, "For My Father," in a collection of poems titled *Homage to Adana* (Fresno, CA: The Giligia Press, 1970), unpaginated. This and the poem quoted next are examples of many which resonate the ineffaceable, tormenting memory of the Genocide indirectly transmitted to the author through his father to whom the collection is dedicated.

9. Hovhannes Mugrditchian, *To Armenians with Love: The Memoirs of a Patriot* (Hobe Sound, FL: Paul Mart, 1996).

10. For a review of this book, see *The Chronicle of Higher Education*, June 12, 1998. In this review the book is presented as one in which "personal discovery and history merge" (p. B7).

11. For a brief analysis of Stina Katchadourian's *Efronia, an Armenian Love Story* (Boston, MA: Northeastern University Press, 1994), see a book review by Rubina Peroomian, *Journal of the Society for Armenian Studies* 7 (1994): 205-08.

12. Arpiné Konyalian Grenier, "The Apprentice in Exile: Toward an Armenian-American Poetics," *Aspora*, 1: 1 (Fall 1993): 17-32 (quotations, pp. 26-27).

13. Alishan, "An Exercise," p. 352.

14. From an unpublished poem, "*ECCE HOMO.*"

15. For an analysis of these images in "The History of Armenia," see Shirinian, *Armenian-North American Literature*, pp. 110-15.

16. *The Story of the Last Thought* was published in German in 1989, (English translation by Hugh Young, London: Scribners, 1990; 2d ed. London: Sphere Books, 1991. Edgar Hilsenrath's *The Story of the Last Thought* was the winner of the 1989 Alfred Döblin Award. The novel is a unique representation of the Armenian experience with a different scope and a different approach. See p. 345 for this quotation.

17. Part 2 of the three-part poem, "Tryptich." The quoted part is titled "Why Sand Scorches Armenians." See *About Time*, p. 14.

18. "Odzum" (Consecration, 1988) and "Telefone" (The Telephone, 1988) are two examples in which Oshagan shows how a shocking event in the life of the Armenian community (an act of sacrilege, deliberately staged in an Armenian church, by three youth belonging to an extremist terrorist group in "Odzum" and the news of the suicide mission of an Armenian youth group against the Turkish embassy in Lisbon in "Telefone") can stir the ashes of oblivion and indifference in assimilated American Armenians and bring to the surface of their conscious the long forgotten sense of Armenianness.

19. For a brief thematic analysis of works by these authors, see Rubina Peroomian, "The Transformation of Armenianness in the Formation of Armenian-American Identity," *Journal of the Society for Armenian Studies* 6 (1992-93): 119-45.

20. A chapter of this novel, translated by M. Terzian into Armenian, is published in *Otaralezu hay groghner* [Armenian Writers Writing in Foreign Languages] (Erevan: Erevan State University Press, 1989), pp. 404-56.

21. Varand, "Voghjuin kez, Nor Dar" (Greetings to You, New Century), *Nor Dar* 2 (1999): 232.

22. Azat Matian, "April 24, 1996 (to Gariné for singing Krunk)," trans. Vahé Oshagan, *RAFT* 10 (1996): 55-57.

23. From the backcover of the book.

24. For Dagmar C.G. Lorenz's book review, "Hilsenrath's Other Genocide," see the *Simon Wiesenthal Center Annual* 7. Quotation, p. 3.

25. Hilsenrath, *The Story of the Last Thought*, p. 16.

26. *Ibid.*, p. 462.

27. *Ibid.*, p. 464-65.

28. Oshagan further explains that "this may seem slightly outdated at a time when Western poetry has abandoned the notion of a mission and has become an expression of total independence and purely personal vision." See *RAFT* 8 (1994): 3-4.

29. Silva Kaputikyan, *Tsave nuinpes tsnum e neruzhutiun* ["Pain Also Generates Strength"], in *Hayatsk Yerevanits*, No. 4 (25), April 15, 2000, p. 5.

30. Silva Kaputikyan, *Ejer pak gzrotsnerits* [Pages from Locked Drawers] (Erevan: Apolon Press, 1997), p. 678. There are a few references here to the Armenian national epic "David of Sasun." David used the ancestral Lightening Sword to fight and slay the enemy. Kurkik Jalali is the legendary horse belonging to this family of Armenian epic heroes. According to an Armenian legend, after fighting against injustice and all the evil in the world, David's son, Pokr Mher, was imprisoned in a cave, and one day this last figure of the epic family will ride his horse back to the world to set the Armenians free. "The House of Sasun" here has a more general sense than the region of Sasun. It is a reference to Armenia.

31. Parenthetically, it should be noted here that dissidence in Soviet Armenia did not have the same meaning as in Moscow or other parts of the Soviet Union. Whereas Soviet dissidents fought against the Communist regime, the Armenian dissident movement was nationalistic, sensitive to the past, to history, to the Genocide, and to the lands lost to Turkey.

32. Ludvik Turyan, "Justice," trans. Dianna Der-Hovanessian, *RAFT* 11 (1997): 45-46.

33. Kaputikyan, *Ejer pak gzrotsnerits*, p. 658.

34. Aghasi Ayvazyan, "Antun turke" [The Homeless Turk], *Nor Dar*, no. 2 (1999): 58-60.

35. Henrik Edoyan, "Hey, Turkish Poets," trans. Diana Der Hovanessian, *RAFT* 6 (1992): 11.

36. Nazim Hikmet (1902-1963), a Turkish Marxist writer-poet, a rebellious soul against oppression, also speaks about the Armenian massacres. In the poem "Evening Walk," written in 1950 (or "Evening Stroll" in a 1954 publication of Hikmet's poems by another translator), he has this to say:

> The grocer Karabet's lights are on. This Armenian citizen has not forgiven the slaughter of his father in Kurdish mountains. But he loves you, because you also won't forgive those who blackened the name of the Turkish people.

As most of Hikmet's writings, this poem is also autobiographical, and he himself is his addressee (the "you" throughout the poem). See Selected Poems of Nazim Hikmet, tr. Randy Blasing and Mutlu Konuk (New York: Persea Books, Inc. 1975), p. 60.

37. James E. Young, *Writing and Rewriting the Holocaust* (Bloomington and Indianapolis: Indiana University Press, 1988), p. 7.

38. See Michael L. Morgan, "To Seize Memory, History and Identity in Post-Holocaust Jewish Thought," in Rosenfeld, *Thinking about the Holocaust*, p. 172.

CHAPTER 14

Testimony from the Ashes: Final Words from Auschwitz-Birkenau Sonderkommado

Susan L. Pentlin

Recently, as I read Jan T. Gross' book, *Neighbors: the Destruction of the Jewish Community in Jedwabne, Poland*, I paused to think about his comments, calling for new approaches to Jewish testimony about the Holocaust. He explained that:

> All we know about the Holocaust—by virtue of the fact that it has been told is not a representative sample of the Jewish fate suffered under the Nazi rule. It is all skewed evidence, biased in one direction: these are all stories with a happy ending. They have all been produced by the few who were lucky enough to survive.[1]

At first, this seemed misleading, if not blatantly wrong to me. While it is obviously true that all postwar memoirs are written by survivors, it seems cynical, at best, to call theirs a "happy ending" after what they endured.

Upon further consideration, I thought that Holocaust diaries and commentaries written before liberation could offer a different perspective. David Patterson suggests that: "Unlike other diaries, the Holocaust diary is not the daily record of life but is the account of a daily struggle against death."[2] Diarists Abel Herzberg, Mary Berg, Avraham Tory and Hillel Seidman, among others, even though they did, in fact,

245

live to see liberation, had only fragile hope, as they faced impossible odds for survival.[3] It is even more apparent that diarists such as Zelig Kalmanovitch, Chaim Kaplan, Etty Hillesum, and Calel Perechodnik foresaw their tragic murder at the hands of the perpetrators.[4]

With further reading, however, I realized that Gross took this argument into account. Nonetheless, he believes that even these testimonies are skewed. He explains that:

> Even statements from witnesses who have not survived ... belong to this category. For what has reached us was written only while the authors were still alive. About the "heart of darkness" that was also the very essence of their experience, about their last betrayal—we will never know.[5]

So, on second thought, I began to understand the import of his argument. Using his criteria, I then began to "deconstruct" his thought-provoking remarks and to consider if this may be, in fact, a failing of all testimony. Clearly, we can only know what happened from what writers were able to record about their lives.

Using his criteria, I began to look for testimony from writers who, expecting their imminent death, may reveal the unknowable. During this process, the diaries and commentaries of six Jewish *Sonderkommando* in Auschwitz-Birkenau—Salmen Lewental, Marcel Nadjary, Chaim Hermann, Salmen Gradowski, Lejb Langfus and an unknown author[6]—works written, in great haste, and buried in the ash pits beside the crematoria—emerged as a category of their own. These writers lived and worked "in the heart of darkness." They lived amidst death. They saw, felt and smelled it all around them and they grew to know it, as they witnessed the murder of thousands of victims from throughout Europe, on an everyday basis.

Wladyslaw Bartoszewski, an Auschwitz survivor and Christian rescuer, points out that the *Kommando's* "only justification of existence was their participation in the process of extermination and in obliterating its trace."[7] They became, unwillingly, a part of the German machinery of death. Over eight hundred men worked as *Sonderkom-*

mando, when gas chambers in the four crematoria at Birkenau were in full operation.[8] In order not to leave witnesses, the Germans executed the crematoria workers every few months.[9] Clearly, there was little, if any illusion or hope that any would be among the spared. They knew the Germans would not leave any eyewitnesses to such a crime. When Birkenau was evacuated in January 1945, in fact, only a few specialists, thirty men in Crematorium V and about seventy men from the last *Abbruchkommando* or demolition crew, were still alive and fewer lived to see liberation.[10]

Only the SS men did the actual killing by bullet, fire or gas. The *Sonderkommando* were special details, mostly Jews, assigned to the crematoria and gas chambers as helpers. Their quarters were isolated from other inmates and they stilled their needs with food and supplies brought to the camp by the victims. They were assigned to stand by as victims arrived on ramp and then were rushed into the undressing chambers and the gas chambers; then they waited until the final screams ceased. They went into the gas chamber and removed valuables from the corpses, including gold teeth, before sending the bodies to the crematoria ovens. Some held victims down as they were shot.

Some stoked the crematoria fires, loaded the corpses, cleaned out the ashes or worked outside, near the fire pits where bodies, the living among them, were thrown onto the pyres. Others were given special assignments to clean the hair of victims for German industry, to forge the gold recovered into bars for the German treasury and to burn personal effects of the victims. A detail of fifty men helped the Germans as they liquidated the gypsy camp.[11] These were tasks never before assigned to men.

Thus, as Gross suggests, it requires new nomenclature and analysis of meaning to understand these accounts which provide new insight into the nature and perspective of memory in Holocaust testimony. For comparison to the six *Sonderkommando* accounts, I also take into account four *Sonderkommando* contributions from after liberation—the Birkenau drawings of David Olère and the published memoirs from Filip Müller, Daniel Bennahmias and Miklos

Nyiszli[12] as well as two postwar depositions by *Sonderkommando* members Henryk Tauber, Szlama Dragon and Alter Feinsilber.[13] These and the testimonies discovered at Birkenau are the only ones we have from victims who saw, with their own eyes, the final stage of the Nazi plan for racial annihilation. Unique among Holocaust testimony, they form the smallest and rarest body of extant writings in Holocaust literature.

Czech believes that the *Sonderkommano* authors had a plan for their writings. They were preparing manuscripts for burial and may, because of the great haste, have "... very likely divided the themes amongst themselves and thus could transmit ... the three stage destruction of the Jewish population which Nazi Germany had planned...."[14] Like other final messages from the Holocaust, the *Sonderkommando* wanted readers to understand not only what they had seen and experienced.[15] They were also seeking forgiveness for what they had been forced to become a part of as prisoners in the crematoria.[16] Each of the manuscripts deals with different events and also gives a different perspective due to the level of education, the age of the writers, the family they lost, and what they had actually seen and been forced to do as crematoria workers.

A Polish resident of Oswiecim located a lengthy diary near Crematorium III in April, 1945. He left the city right away, however, so it was only rediscovered in 1970. Entitled "The Resettlement," its author was clearly a member of the *Sonderkommando* named Lejb, who was on a transport from the Makow Mazowiecki ghetto which arrived in Auschwitz on December 6, 1942. He was accompanied by his wife Deborah and young son Samuel. Further investigation has determined that Lejb was most likely a member of the resistance named Lejb Langfus.[17]

Langfus begins his notes with the peaceful morning on October 31, when the Germans gathered Jewish workers from villages in the vicinity of Makow. They terrorized the crowd by executing twenty young, Jewish men, chosen at random, before announcing their impending deportation from the ghetto to Auschwitz or a transfer camp at Mlawa. He analayzes the actions of the Jewish leadership and of the ghetto Kommissar Steinmetz. He then continues his detailed account, by interspersing the deportation of the ghetto, the trials at Mlawa and journey to Auschwitz with his own personal tragedy.

He describes how people sought to escape their fate by, fruitlessly, turning to Polish friends, running out into the fields and unearthing their valuables. Finally, they came to the tragic realization that not saving themselves was not the worst, the worst was they could do nothing to save their children. With great poignancy, he describes his wife's desperation as she realized this. Their son Samuel, who had already learned the meaning of death, saw his mother and broke out in hysterical crying. In the most tragic words imaginable between father and son, Samuel cried out: "Papa, I want to live, do whatever, you can do, so that I may live ... I would so like to live!" (p. 84).

Husband and wife sat over their sleeping child during that night, agonizing over how to save him, but finally accepting that they neither could save him nor could they abandon him. Langfus tried to imagine the hopelessness of his life without the child. The next afternoon, Steinmetz gathered the ghetto and told them those who were capable of working were going to Auschwitz and could take their spouses and children, clothing and laundry goods along. The ghetto was excited and looked for hope in his words. Although most were suspicious at this sudden change of behavior, few wanted to believe that it was all "a typical bluff, a deceitful trick" (p. 94) and that all was lost.

He describes very realistically how the relationship between children and parents changed:

> When a child left the house for a minute and then came back, his mother ran towards him, remained standing in the door and observed her child with streaming tears. Then she turned her head, so that the child would not suffer from seeing this.... The husbands sat alone in their rooms, deep in thought and silent. Difficult, painful thoughts were going through their heads, to which they had no answer, no solution. (p. 96)

The deportation was not just of a community, but individuals, each of whom confronted his own hopes and sorrows.

The liquation of the ghetto began on November 18. At a breathless pace, Langfus describes gendarmes driving everyone to the street under a deadly barrage of blows. The mob was so large, people were trampled and parents had to hold their children up over their heads to save them. The people were shocked as even Germans they had traded with earlier swung at them "with cynical rawness and dreadful brutality" (p. 105). From there, they were taken to Mlawa and, at first, quartered in Jewish homes recently abandoned and looted. Apparently, from there Langfus and his family were selected and taken to a dark, filthy mill, where they were kept without food or water, until the final trip to Auschwitz.

He remembered how they spent the next days in conversation about what awaited them, trying to reason out the German actions in a situation where reason had no rule. He recalled that:

> We considered, what was awaiting us at the end of the journey: death or life? Is it possible, that the Germans would provide for women and children, at their own cost? Will they leave us in peace and feed us during the war? Our eyes had seen too many crimes for us to be able to believe that. So what was the purpose of all the preparations? Was it only to isolate us, so that we could not betray any state secrets, which our eyes might have seen in the closed Makow ghetto? Or why don't they permit us to take anything along? The living require that. And why don't we receive any sign of life from the Warsaw Jews? (pp. 114-115)

And then they boarded the train to Auschwitz, where they arrived the following evening. Tersely, he recalled the selection process as men watched their wives and children climb into the autos which would take them directly to the gas chambers.

The last section of Langfus's manuscript is, undoubtedly, the most personal, and horrifyingly, detailed eyewitness account of a gassing in Holocaust literature. He recounts how the victims "were pressed in as many as would go. Hard to even imagine, that so many people could find room in such a small place." He described the process and the reaction of the victims:

> Then all the doors were hermetically sealed and gas was poured through a small hole in the ceiling ... the people locked inside could no nothing more. So they cried out in bitter, lamenting voices ... many cried "Schma Israel." All tore out their hair that they had been so naïve and had allowed themselves to be led here, here behind these closed doors. With a single mind, which reached the outside, with voices, which screamed to heaven, they let loose their last cry of protest against this enormous, historical injustice, which was being perpetrated on totally innocent people in order to kill whole generations in this terrible manner with one blow. (pp. 124-125)

The vividness of the description leaves no doubt that Langfus was there when the gas was released and later as the chamber doors were opened. He quietly confesses, to himself and the reader, that he found his wife and child among the corpses.

As in the very pit of hell, when they opened the gas chamber, the workers found "a formless mass of human bodies, lying in five or six layers, up to a meter high. Mothers froze to the ground in a sitting position, hugging their children, and the men died, hugging their wives" (pp. 125-126). Some of the victims were blue in appearance, others looked as if they were sleeping. Next, he outlined the final step in the Nazi death machine—the burning of the bodies and then, full of passion, he ended his manuscript, lamenting the lack of resistance they gave the Nazis before deportation: "how great is our disgrace!" (p. 129).

On March 5, 1945, Soviet investigators found Salmen Gradowski's diary, buried in a canteen, in an ash pit near Crematorium II.[18] He enclosed a letter, dated September 6, 1944, explaining why he was burying it: "I wanted to leave this as also [sic] other numerous notes as memento for the future world of peace, so that it may learn what had happened here." The manuscript itself is a diary which

Gradowski, who came from Luna near Grodno, had completed and buried ten months earlier. This discovery led to others, perhaps in part because of Gradowski's encouragement to investigators.

In the letter, he explained that the *Sonderkommando* had chosen to bury their works near the crematoria. He wrote, explaining "I have buried this under the ashes deeming it the safest place, where people will certainly dig to find the traces of millions of men who were exterminated." But, he added, the Germans had begun to dig up the ashes and take them to the Vistula River, so he had moved his diary, now "saturated with the blood of not always entirely burnt bones and pieces of flesh," to the new location near Crematorium III. He encouraged the finder to "search everywhere, in every inch of soil. Tens of documents are buried under it, mine and those of other persons, which will throw light on everything that was happening here" ([Letter], pp. 76-77).

The manuscript contains no information about the gas chambers, because he broke off the diary with his selection to the *Sonderkommando*. The planned revolt had been postponed by the camp resistance, but the crematoria workers, as he explained in his letter, were growing impatient:

> We ourselves have lost hope of being able to see the moment of liberation ... we, the "*Sonderkommando*," have long since wanted to put a stop to our horrible work which we were forced to do under threat of death ... we wanted to do great things. But people from the camp, a section of the Jews, Russians and Poles, have ... forced us to put off the date of the mutiny. That date is approaching. It may happen today or tomorrow. I am writing these words in a moment of great danger and excitement. May the future judge us on the base [sic] of my notes and may the world see in them if only one drop, the minimum of this tragic world amidst which we had lived. (p. 77)

A last addendum to his diary, written perhaps a few weeks later, shortly before the *Sonderkommando* revolt on October 7, 1944, ends abruptly with the words "but lately [...]" (p. 107) Most likely, he fell during the mutiny.[19]

Gradowski wrote his diary account to a "friend," recalling with penetrating honesty and intensity his experiences in the Kelbasin transfer camp and his community's deportation to Auschwitz by train. He characterized this as the beginning of the Nazi systematic processing for death, the entranceway for the victims to the crematoria of Birkenau. He explained how he visually had recorded these events of the world they had lost to memory, explaining:

> You see, my friend, how people stand at the small window of the carriage as if rooted and look out into the free world. Everyone wants to satiate his eyes, flitting everywhere, as if in premonition that he is seeing everything for the last time. One has the impression of sitting in a fortress, rushing on, before which a film reel is moving with many coloured pictures of the world that is saying good-bye to the people imprisoned in the carriage. It looks as if the world wanted to tell them, "Fill your eyes as long as you can see me, because I appear to you for the last time." ([Diary], p. 78)

He writes in an impersonal tone, not mentioning his family, perhaps to hold back his tears while he is living on their graves. He does not record his farewell to his wife, mother and sister, but he had dedicated the diary to the memory of his family, "burnt alive at Birkenau" (p. 77).

He relates his experience, in the present tense, which emphasizes that it is still happening to him, that he is still in Birkenau. We learn that even on the trains people thought of happy moments and clung to hope. At first, they were overjoyed to see Jews working with yellow patches on their clothes along the track. However, the sight of people along the tracks, drawing their fingers, menacingly, across their throats and pointing to the ground, alarmed them. He explains that: "Everyone tries to dispel black thoughts wakened by those signs, everyone tries to dull one's perceptivity and pay no attention to the picture in front of our eyes…" (p. 88). That is, even though every one had clearly seen them.

He relives the moment of arrival, not as a passenger, but with the insight of the crematoria worker who understands the trip as a passage to death. Emotionally, he seeks to warn his friend so, that unlike him, the friend can gain understanding and know to revolt the next time:

> See, who has come to welcome us. Soldiers in helmets on their heads, with riding-whips in their hands, accompanied by big vicious dogs. Are these the open arms which were to welcome us. Nobody understands what this escort is waiting for, why such a discouraging welcome. Why? What are we that it is necessary to welcome us with weapons and savage dogs? We have come to work, after all, like quiet, peacefully disposed people, what were therefore such precautionary measures for? Wait a little, you will soon understand. (p. 93)

Once he had been tattooed and reached the bunkers, he describes the disbelief each man confronted when learning from "old hands" about the fate of their family; each man's horror is like the next one's, all lost in a sea of bitter hopelessness. In this horrified state, he recalled, the *Kapo* told them to obey the discipline of German order and stay clean, if they wanted to escape torture before they died. The room seniors also told them: "remember that you have to turn into automatons and move in accordance with our will" (p. 103). He held on to these words, apparently, to justify his own compliance.

The unknown author of a manuscript found near Crematorium III, in 1952, was probably an Orthodox Jew from Bedzin or Sosnowiec.[20] In his manuscript "Particulars," he devotes himself to recording events of resistance and betrayal in the gas chambers. His writing seems a catharsis. He chastises himself for holding life too dear and not sharing the fate of the transports. Yet, he found it remarkable that many of the victims still had hope. In the summer of 1944, he was in the crematorium when a transport arrived from Slovakia. The victims knew that their death was imminent. As they were sent from the undressing room into the gas chamber, one woman cried: "Will perhaps a miracle happen after all?" (p. 115).

Attached to this manuscript were several pages of "Notes" dated, November 26, 1944. From these, it is certain that he survived the uprising, and felt liberation was near, but that he would not see it. He notes that the demolition of Crematorium II had just been completed and the motors since "they serve to gas people on a large scale" had been sent to Mauthausen and Gross-Rosen. (Notes, p. 120) He wants to warn the reader not to trust the Germans and not to wait too late before revolting. His final words are: "170 remaining men. We are sure that we are being led to die. They selected thirty persons who will remain in Crematorium V." He requested that his writings, when discovered, be published with the title *Amidst a Nightmare of Crime* (p. 122). It is unknown if he perished soon after writing this message, or if he was selected to work in the demolition squad.

The writings of Salmen Lewental, from Ciechanow, remained in the earth in two locations near Crematorium III until 1961-1962, so, unfortunately, parts were rendered unreadable by dampness. His commentary was written to accompany a diary from the Lodz Ghetto. This was written by an unknown author who must have brought it with him to Auschwitz in August 1944. Lewental had probably discovered it among the victim's effects left outside the gas chamber. The Lodz diary was so moving and full of detail about the torments of the ghetto, he felt it his duty to preserve it. In the commentary, he gave directions which investigators followed and, a year later, they recovered his own diary.[21]

He was apparently part of a plan to bury testimony, to leave a record for scholars and researchers. He feared the manuscripts might never be discovered, because he implores his readers: "… from human ashes—at other places, look well, and you will find much … look for the extensive material which will be of great value to you, the greater world." He wants the postwar world to understand how vast and seemingly unstoppable "this unheard of systematic plan of the extermination" by the Germans was ([Kommentar], p. 193).

He praised the uprising in the Warsaw Ghetto and other revolts because it is "better to fall from bullets and grenades in battle" (p. 194) than as one of "a small group of gray men" (p. 195) in the crematoria. With insight, he dispelled the myth that the Jews would be saved through work, explaining:

> But I cannot bury this, without adding a few words about the great mistake which we have all made, as we have persuaded ourselves that he [i.e. the enemy] needs people for work; it is true that he needs some, but the annihilation of the Jews is his chief goal. (p. 196)

His diary begins with the transit camp Malkinia and his arrival at Auschwitz in December, 1942, where he was assigned to work at the bunkers at Birkenau.[22] He records his struggle with his own guilt and sense of cowardice as a bystander, although he writes as one whose death is certain. He feared only that should any of the *Sonderkommando* survive, they would not relate what had occurred, because he confessed:

> There was a time in this camp, in the years 1941-1942, when each man, really each one, who lived longer than two weeks, lived at the cost of other victims, at the cost of lives of other people or on what he had taken from them [...]. ([Diary], p. 147)

In his narrative, he tries to understand why the *Komando* workers clung to life, some at any cost. With anguish, he recalled the psychological shock the new *Sonderkommando* felt when they first witnessed the victims of their transport driven to their deaths:

> [...] the rest of people were driven [...] (from the barrack?) to the bunker, where they were gassed. The same were heard [...] and shouts, as in the night. How tragic and horrible was the sight, when—as it later transpired—[...] these same men who had to drag out corpses and [burn them].... As it became evident later, after getting to work, each one recognized his fam-

ily. To the Kommando, recently formed on that day, men were namely included who had only just arrived at the camp with the transport and were at once driven to [that work]. In this way all our community had perished, the entire Jewish settlement from our town, our dear parents, wives, children, sisters, brothers. ([Diary], p. 134)

He commented on the injustice their families suffered,

they perish in the gas only because they are Jews, only because they are [supposedly] of a worse [race?]. ... every day trains with transports of people arrive ... whom these bandits [...] lead to the bunker of death and suffocate with gas [...]. (p. 134)

And yet, in time, some of the workers became accustomed to the sight. He explained: "[...] they got so used to it that it was even strange [that one wanted] to weep and to complain" that he and others grew ashamed (p. 139).

Later at the beginning of 1944, he wrote two, detailed and deeply moving descriptions of the arrivals at the crematorium. The first was about three thousand naked women at Crematorium III, dumped from the lorry because most were too weak to stand. He relates tender conversations, among mothers and daughters, as they waited in the undressing room. He also recorded the gassing of six hundred Jewish boys, aged twelve to eighteen, who begged the SS for mercy. "We stood completely aghast and as if paralyzed by this mournful weeping." When he looked at the SS men, he could not help asking himself: "Did they not [have] any children ever?" (p. 178)

Marcel Nadjary, from Greece and a friend of Danny Bennahmias, was the only one of the *Sonderkommando* writers to see liberation. In 1980, his letter was found in a thermos by Polish school children as they planted a tree near Crematorium III.[23] It is a personal letter to his family in Greece. In sections that are legible, he confesses to them: "The dramas, which my eyes have seen are indescribable" (p. 271) and foresees no chance of his own survival. He had been forced to carry bodies to the ovens and then sieve the ashes for bones. At the final selection in the crematoria, he was assigned to the demolition crew. In January 1945, he slipped out of the crematoria yard with a group of *Sonderkommando* and joined the evacuation to Mauthausen, where he was liberated.

In February 1945, Chaim Hermann's letter was found in the ashes.[24] It is a moving, private farewell to his wife and daughter, dated November 6, 1944. His letter informs them of his deportation from Drancy to Auschwitz in 1943 and his assignment to the gas chambers. He wants to reassure them that he has been honorable and his conscience is clear. He writes that: "Ever since I have been here I have never believed in the possibility of returning...." He explained, that "... Dante's hell is incomparably ridiculous in comparison with this real one here..." (p. 185). He does not believe the Germans will leave witnesses, but in spite of that, he admits still holding a bit of irrational hope for a miracle.

In closing, with chilling immediacy and a sense of purpose, he explains to his loved ones that:

> My letter is coming to the end of my hours, so I am sending you my last farewell for ever [sic], these are my last greetings, I embrace you most heartily for the last time and I beg you once more, do believe that I am going away calmly, knowing that you are alive and our enemy is broken. It is even possible that through the history of "Sonder Kommando" you will learn the exact day of my end, and I am in the last group of 204 persons, just now Crematorium II is being liquidated, where I am waiting in tenseness and they are also speaking just now about our liquidation in the course of this week. (p. 190)

Facing his death as a martyr, he calls for revenge.

Postwar depositions and memoir accounts by former *Sonderkommando* are told in quieter voices. Though they do not differ in substance, they focus on the details of the crematoria killings, more than on the systematic process and steps of the "final solution." They record events, but use less description and imagery, as if fearing they will be accused of embellishment or that artistry is a defilement of the victims. In oral history interviews, Daniel Bennahmias does not recall any details of the deportation to Auschwitz, other than how his mother, who had a great fear of death, was tormented when another woman died and fell across her lap. He sits in long silences with the interviewer. When he speaks, his voice can barely be heard, as he fights the emergence of memory.

Both Miklos Nyiszli and Filip Müller begin their accounts with the arrival at Auschwitz and thus do not question how they got there. Their works lack the power and the sense of language found in the buried testimony. As an assistant to Mengele, Nyiszli witnessed the gassings in Crematorium III, but his account is distant and clinical. He does not reflect on his own role in the process and seems to feel some empathy with his tormentors. Müller is testifying, as before a tribunal of law (he was a witness at the Frankfurt Auschwitz trial), and his memoir has the same tone as depositions taken immediately after the war. Both give measurements and descriptions, but, perhaps conscious of how the postwar world may judge their acts, they keep their emotions at bay.

David Olère, a worker in Crematorium III, gives us the most powerful picture of the torture suffered by the victims in the gas chambers. With his return to Paris, he was haunted by his memories. Finding it difficult to convince his wife about what he had witnessed, he began, as if obsessed, to redraw pictures of his experiences at Auschwitz and make detailed sketches of the architecture of Crematorium III. From 1945 to 1947, he drew a series of works titled "Memento." These are a visual memoir of the death factory Auschwitz. Through his art, he tries to understand what had happened to him and to empathize with the victims. He does not hesitate to record the horrors of selections on the ramp, SS men throwing children into the fires, bodies being dragged from the gas chambers and piles of corpses before the ovens.

That victims hope to the last breath to survive is not surprising. That these writers and witnesses to the enormity of German crimes also may have had hope, even to their last minute, must be an indicator that hope is simply a human response. These men had grown to know death and saw it in a way not previously witnessed. They had been in the gas chambers and had looked into the cruel eyes of the perpetrators. They knew "the heart of darkness." They were still alive, as they wrote, but in the shadow of the crematoria, the line between life and death grew blurred. After months in the crematoria, they were more dead than alive. Hermann explained to his wife: "I knew, just like all of us, that all connection with the other world was broken, this is an entirely different world..." (p. 186).

These, their last testaments to the future, reveal these *Sonderkommano* as men of religious convictions and moral depth. As they watched the Jewish population of Europe forced into the gas chambers, young girls raped and children thrown into fire pits, out of racial hatred, they saw the German plan for extermination laid out before them without deception. They were unwitting witnesses to events whose magnitude and horror was without precedent and which is not documented elsewhere. There should be no doubt, that the buried testimony at Birkenau conveys to us the essence of what the *Sonderkommando* experienced, as they confronted "the final betrayal." They *have* told us what they knew.

Endnotes

1. Jan T. Gross, *Neighbors: The Destruction of the Jewish Community in Jedwabne, Poland* (Princeton, N.J.: Princeton University, 2001), pp. 141-142.

2. David Patterson, *Along the Edge of Annihilation: The Collapse and Recovery of Life in the Holocaust Diary* (Seattle: University of Washington Press, 1999), p. 237.

3. Abel J. Herzberg, *Between Two Streams: A Diary from Bergen-Belsen*, tr. Jack Santcross (London: Tauris, 1989); Mary Berg, *Warsaw Ghetto; A Diary*, ed. S.L. Shneiderman, (New York: L.B. Fischer, 1945); Avraham Tory, *Surviving the Holocaust; The Kovno Ghetto*, tr. Jerzy Michalowicz, ed. Martin Gilbert (Cambridge, Mass.: Harvard, 1990); Hillel Seidmann, *The Warsaw Ghetto Diaries*, tr. Yosef Israel (Southfield, MI: Targun, 1997).

4. Zelig Kalmanovitch, "A Diary of the Nazi Ghetto in Vilna," tr. Koppel S. Pinson, Yivo Annual of Jewish Social Sciences, 8 (1953), pp. 9-81; Chaim Kaplan, *Scroll of Agony*, ed. Abraham I. Katsh (New York: McMillan, 1965; rev. ed. New

York: Collier, 1973); Etty Hillesum, *An Interrupted Life*, ed. Arno Pomerans (New York: Pantheon, 1983); Calel Perechodnik, *Am I A Murderer? Testament of a Jewish Ghetto Policeman*, ed. and tr. Frank Fox (Boulder, Colo: Westview, 1996).

5. *Gross*, 142.

6. Salmen Lewental, [Diary], Chaim Hermann [Letter], Salem Gradowski, [Letter] and [Diary] and unknown author, [Particular] and [Notes] in *Amidst a Nightmare of Crime. Manuscripts of Members of Sonderkommando* (State Museum at Oswiecim (State Museum at Auschwitz, 1973; Howard Fertig, 1992); Salemn Lewental, [Kommentar], Nadjary, [Brief] and Lejb [Langfus] "Die Aussiedlung" in *Im Mitten des Grauenvollen Verbrechens. Handschriften von Mitgliedern des Sonderkommando* (State Museum at Oswiecim, 1996). Page numbers referring to the appropriate work appear in the text.

7. Wladyslaw Bartoszewski, "Epilogue," in *Amidst a Nightmare of Crime. Manuscripts of Members of Sonderkommando*, pp. 192.

8. Danuta Czech, *Auschwitz Chronicle* (New York: Henry Holt, 1989), p. 699.

9. Miklos Nyiszli, *Auschwitz: An Eyewitness Account of Mengele's Infamous Death Camp*, tr. Tribere Kremer and Richard Sleaver (New York: Sleaver, 1960), p. 145.

10. *Czech*, p. 754.

11. Franciszek Piper, *Auschwitz 1940-1945, Central Issues in the History of the Camp*, vol. III, tr. William Brand (Auschwitz-Birkenau State Museum, 2000), p. 194.

12. David Olère, *A Painter in the Sonderkommando at Auschwitz* (New York: Beate Klarsfeld, 1989); Fromer, Rebecca Camhi, *Sonderkommando: The Holocaust Odyssey of Daniel Bennahmias* (Tuscaloosa, AL: University of Alabama, 1993). Several of Olère's drawings were introduced as evidence at the trial of David Irving against Deborah Lipstadt and Penguin Books. Filip Müller, *Eyewitness Auschwitz: Three Years in the Gas Chambers* (Chicago: Dee, 1979); Miklos Nyiszli, see n. 9. Nysizli, a physician, was assigned to work in the morgue and dissection room in crematorium III with Josef Mengele.

13. [Depositions] by Sonderkommando Henryk Tauber, May 24, 1945 and Szlama Dragon, May 10, 1945 (selections) in Jean-Claude Pressac, *Auschwitz: Technique and Operation of the Gas Chambers* (New York: Beate Klarsfled Foundation, 1989). [Deposition] by Stanislaw Jankowski [Alter Feinsilber], April 16, 1945 in *Amidst a Nightmare of Crime*, pp. 31-68.

14. Danuta Czech in *Im Mitten des Grauenvollen Verbrechens*, pp. 10-11. This and all other quotes from the German edition are translated by the author of this paper.

15. For comparison see David Graber, "My Last Will," *Warsaw*, 3 August 1942 in "To Live and Honor and Die with Hope: Selected Documents from the Warsaw Ghetto Underground." Archives, ed. Joseph Kermis (Jerusalem: Yard Vashem, 1986), pp. 67.

16. Israel Gutman, "Holocaust Diaries" in *Encyclopedia of the Holocaust*, Israel Gutman, vol. 1 (New York: McMillan), p. 374.

17. Lejb [Langfus], "Aussiedlung," *Im Mitten des Grauenvollen Verbrechens*, pp. 73-129.

18. Salmen Gradowski, *Amidst a Nightmare of Crime*, pp. 74-77; 77-108.

19. Bernard Mark, "Remarks on the Manuscript of Salmen Gradowski" in *Amidst a Nightmare of Crime*, p. 74.

20. Unknown Author, *Amidst a Nightmre of Crime*, pp. 112-122; he indicates that all of his notes were signed J.A.R.A. These letters have not been deciphered. He also writes that his manuscripts are entitled "Displacement" and "Auschwitz." Several sources assume that the former is the same manuscript published as "Die Aussiedling" by Lejb [Langfus] in *Im Mitten des Grauenvollen Verbrechens*. The German edition includes the work of the unknown author and Lejb's [Langfus] manuscript as separate entries.

21. Salmen Lewental, [Kommentar], *Im Mitten des Grauenvollen Verbrechens*, pp. 192-197; [Diary], *Amidst a Nightmare of Crime*, pp. 130-178;

22. These were two farmer's cottages near Birkenau used as early gas chambers.

23. Marcel Nadsari, *Im Mitten des grausamen Verbrechens*, pp. 270-274. Since the original publication, it has been confirmed that his name was originally misread from the manuscript and should be Marcel Nadjari or Nadjary. He died in New York in 1971.

24. Chaim Hermann, *Amidst a Nightmare of Crime*, pp. 181-190.

CHAPTER 15

Imre Kormos: Unknown Hero of the Hungarian Jewish Rescue and Resistance

George S. Pick

Summary

This paper sets forth a hitherto unrecognized chapter in the history of Hungarian Jewish rescue and resistance activities during the Holocaust. It demonstrates the ingenuity and effectiveness of one man in his efforts to save the lives of hundreds of Hungarian Jewish men, women and children in the fall and winter of 1944 in Budapest.

This was the work of a remarkable man using the alias of Imre Kormos, who established a network of hiding places in Budapest, camouflaged as textile factories producing uniforms for the Hungarian Army. He also organized a number of rescue groups as well as an armed resistance unit.

A Man Who Foresaw the Future

Kormos was born Imre Kohn on March 9, 1897 in *Tiszaföldvár*, a small town in central Hungary, and raised in *Törökszentmiklós*, a larger town nearby, where his father owned a haberdashery. During the first year of World War I, Kohn was drafted into the Austro-Hungarian Army, where he served on the Eastern Front.[1]

Kohn sympathized with the communist movement and in 1919

joined the newly formed Hungarian Red Army during the short-lived Republic of Councils (Soviets). The communist dictatorship collapsed in August 1919[2] and he fled from the campaign of massive and brutal reprisals known as the "White Terror."[3] However, by the end of November 1919, it was safe for Kohn to return to *Törökszentmiklós*. There he established himself as a successful businessman in the textile industry.[4] By the mid-1930s, Kohn had accumulated a considerable fortune. At the same time, he maintained his sympathies for and ties to the illegal Hungarian Communist Party. The police suspected that he was a communist agitator. Kohn got married in the late 1920s and had two daughters. One daughter's description gives the impression that Kohn was an independent minded man who had no illusions about the immediate future and the danger of an upcoming war, which he thought was inevitable. Several times in the 1920s and 1930s, Kohn was arrested.

On May 28, 1938, the first major anti-Jewish legislation (Law No. XV of 1938) was enacted into law.[5] That summer Kohn took his family and his considerable wealth and moved to Budapest where it was easier to hide. It was there that he took the *nom de guerre*, "Kormos," and obtained false papers to match his new, non-Jewish identity.[6]

In January 1939, the Hungarian legislature adopted Law No. II: 1939, ("On National Defense"). Article 230 of the statute provided the basis for establishing a labor service system for those who were deemed to be "unreliable," which in the late 1930s included all Jews.[7] Jewish men were going to be placed in segregated *különleges munkásszázadok* ("special labor service companies"). These units were placed under the command of Christian officers and staff. Under a secret decree, those in the twenty five to forty two age group were called up first, to be followed by those between forty three and forty eight, and eventually by those of forty nine to sixty.[8] On May 4, 1939, the second major anti-Jewish law (Law No. IV: 1939) went into effect. This statute mandated a series of crippling political, civil and economic restrictions designed to exclude large segments of the Jewish population from economic life; for example, Jews could not own businesses.

Shortly after he moved to Budapest, Kormos had reestablished his ties with the leadership of the illegal Hungarian Communist Party. At the same time, he became active in business and established several companies between 1939 and 1942. Kormos quickly recognized opportunities in the emerging wartime economy of Hungary and was able to accumulate additional wealth in a short time. This wealth became a crucial means by which he was able to undertake his activities between 1942 and 1944. Kormos also developed an expanding network of new contacts, consisting of businessmen, liberals, army officers and blue-collar workers. He frequently brought home several dinner guests, and among the regular guests was a man named György Gyékis, who was to play an important part in my life.

On June 27, 1941, Hungary joined Nazi Germany in the war against the Soviet Union. The third anti-Jewish law based upon the Nazi Nuremberg laws of 1935 was enacted on August 2, 1941.[9] On August 19, 1941, the Ministry of Defense issued Order No. 27300, eln. 8-1941. This order regulated all aspects of the *kisegitö szolgálat* (auxiliary service, which included the special labor service companies), that affected all Jews of military age.[10] On April 12, 1942, the deployment of the Second Hungarian Army began. The General Staff had decided earlier that up to ten percent of all those mobilized would be Jews. Furthermore, Minister of Defense Order No. 15802, dated March 17, 1942, stipulated that portions of the auxiliary service, involving Jews, would be utilized in military operation zones.[11] The Hungarian use of Jews in war zones was a unique practice among the Nazis or the armies allied with them.

In the spring of 1942, relying on false papers, Kormos avoided the military call-up. It was at this time that he reconnected with Árpád Pauker and László Frisch, two friends from his hometown, who had moved to Budapest. Pauker's and Frisch's social and commercial backgrounds were similar to those of Kormos. During the next three years these three men helped each other and, more importantly, they helped many others.[12]

In April 1942, at the time of the first large scale call up of Jewish laborers for the auxiliary service, Kormos first took advantage of his contacts in the military establishment. Kormos and his friends started a company which they named *Felsöruházati Ipar és Kereskedelmi KFT* (Outer Garments Industry and Commerce Limited) and submitted a proposal to the army to manufacture army uniforms at extremely low prices. As part of his audacious proposal, Kormos requested that he be provided with a textile factory and be allowed to recruit skilled tailors from the Jewish labor force that had already been inducted to the auxiliary service. The army awarded him a contract and provided him with a confiscated textile plant, previously owned by a Jewish manufacturer. This plant, located at Csángó Utca (Street) 6/b, was declared a *I Osztályú Hadiüzem* (an essential war plant).[13] He also received special permission to recruit Jewish laborers designated for the Eastern Front. The raw material came from the Army Logistics Agency, and the Csángó Street "war plant" did the cutting and assembly work. Very few uniforms were made, in accordance with Kormos' orders, but despite this low productivity, as well as complaints and threats from the Defense Ministry, the Csángó Street war plant was allowed to function. Using this subterfuge, Kormos was able to prevent the transfer of hundreds of laborers to the Russian war zone.[14]

During 1943 and early 1944, the Kállay government of Hungary was deep into secret negotiations with the Western Allies in order to extricate Hungary from the war. Hitler decided that only the occupation of Hungary, an important buffer state between Germany and the advancing Soviet Army, could prevent Hungary's defection. German forces occupied the country on March 19, 1944.[15]

On the day of the German occupation of Hungary, Kormos and his family went underground. They moved into a hidden room of Gyékis' apartment. Kormos, with his false papers, moved freely throughout the city. He and his family stayed in Gyékis' apartment until early July.[16]

In June 1944, the 164,000 Jews of Budapest were forced to relocate into specially designated Yellow-Star houses. By early July, Hungary, with the exception of Budapest, was virtually *Judenrein*. The stage was set for their deportation from Hungary.[17] However, on July 7, 1944, on the eve of the beginning of the mass deportations from Budapest, the Regent of Hungary, Admiral Horthy, decided to suspend the deportations.[18] Five days earlier, Allied aircraft had conducted a devastating attack against Budapest.

After the attack Kormos relocated his family outside Budapest with families of Christian acquaintances. Kormos himself stayed in the capital and moved into the apartment of István Alföldy and his wife—an old acquaintance—in downtown Pest. Alföldy was willing to hide Kormos for a large sum of money. Soon Alföldy's apartment became Kormos' headquarters where he met with members of Jewish and Communist resistance cells and planned his actions.[19] While he was hiding Kormos and others, Alföldy was in contact with the agents of the *Budapesti Rendörfökapitányság Politikai Rendészeti Osztálya*[20] (the rough equivalent of the Nazi Gestapo, henceforth, referred to as the "Police Bureau for Political Security") and members of the fascist and collaborationist *Nyilas* (Arrow Cross) Party whom Alföldy entertained frequently. Alföldy was playing a very dangerous and duplicitous game whereby, on the one hand he helped Kormos and the underground and, on the other, maintained friendly ties with the Hungarian Security agents and the fascists.

On October 15, 1944, after the abortive attempt by Horthy to extricate Hungary from the war, Ferenc Szálasi, head of the *Nyilas* party, assumed supreme power. One week after the *Nyilas* takeover of Hungary, Szálasi agreed to the transfer of 25,000 able-bodied Jewish males to the Reich to perform hard labor. On October 26, the Minister of Defense, issued Decree 975/M.42-1944, which authorized the transfer of seventy Jewish units of the auxiliary service (between October 26 and November 11, 1944) to Germany.[21]

Meanwhile, hundreds of Jews who had escaped deportation from the Budapest suburbs and made connections with the growing Kormos organization were sent to the already crowded Csángó Street war plant. Soon the place became too small for such a large group of victims seeking safe haven. In response to this overcrowding, Kormos leased two more buildings, one at *Király Utca* (King Street), thirty-six and another at *Kisdiófa Utca* (Little Walnut Street)

6, both in Pest. In late October 1944, the original tailor company and the new escapees were dispersed to these newly leased buildings, on *Király* and *Kisdiófa* Streets, to make room for yet more escapees in Csángó Street. Armed "guards" were posted in front of these buildings to complete the illusion. The Csángó Street war plant supplied the guard uniforms.[22]

Obtaining provisions for the hidden escapees became a significant problem for Kormos who worked with a number of people to supply food for those in these hiding places. An example of such a supplier was László Erdös, a mechanic and part-time urban guerrilla who, with Kormos' help, obtained transportation papers and equipment enabling him to purchase food in the countryside. Kormos generously rewarded Erdös for his work.[23]

During the month of November 1944, an additional forty thousand Jews—mainly women, children and the elderly were deported from Budapest. They were forced to march toward the Austro-Hungarian border one hundred twenty-five miles away. Among certain groups the mortality rate exceeded fifty percent.[24] Those who survived ended up in German labor camps. Few survived the war. Jews still in the capital suffered atrocities and mass killings on a daily basis. Hundreds of victims were marched to the banks of the Danube and shot at the river by members of the *Nyilas*.

Kormos organized small groups of young Jewish men and supplied them with black *Nyilas* uniforms and forged *Nyilt Parancs* (Open Orders). Their objective was to rescue the wives and children of those hiding in the war plants and who were already deported from Budapest, but still within the borders of Hungary. As the result of these daring operations, several dozen women and children were brought back to Kormos' war plants.[25]

By the beginning of November, in addition to his rescue efforts, Kormos organized a resistance group, composed of three hundred fifty army deserters and Jewish escapees, who were bivouacked at the "*Warsdorf Pamutszövö Gyár*" (Warsdorf Cotton Mill), located in *Újpest* (New Pest). Kormos was known at that time in *Újpest* as Captain Lajos Tákos, the commanding officer of a regular army unit. The principal tasks of this resistance unit were to prevent the destruction of utility plants, which were located in Újpest,[26] and to manufacture forged documents. These documents provided cover for those Jews who were part of the rescue operation and also for some of the leaders of the underground Hungarian Communist Party.

Kormos was in close contact with Staff Captain Géza Boda, who worked at the Ministry of Defense. Kormos also had connections at Police Headquarters as well, including Dr. Gábor Kemény, Division Director of the Criminal Office, and Detective Lieutenant Colonel István Bozsik. These officers provided Kormos with vital information and help.

Life in the Csángó Street War Plant[27]

The war plant on Csángó Street was in a working-class neighborhood of factories and tenements. It consisted of two permanent buildings: the two story high factory and a single level office building. The ground level of the factory building housed some twenty large power looms. The second level consisted of five assembly rooms which contained hundreds of Hungarian army jackets, products of the war plant. The buildings were enclosed by a high wall, topped with barbed wire, a heavily reinforced double door and a smaller steel door used for entrance and exit, and surrounded on two sides by tenement buildings. In the back, a shorter wall capped by chain-link fence and barbed wire evoked the feelings of both imprisonment and safety. In addition to the permanent edifices, a wooden shed occupied part of the front yard, which contained a haystack. Buried under the haystack was a black Skoda passenger car. Only a few people knew of its existence. The casement windows of the factory building were boarded up for blackout purposes. László Gyetvay, a recent army deserter, guarded the entrance. Kormos knew Gyetvay from before the war and "appointed" him as the official "army guard." He often carried messages for the hidden Jewish men. By the middle of November, most of these messages consisted of urgent requests for their family members to join them at Csángó Street.

The "Commander" of the factory was "Chief Warrant Officer Rázsó," who wore a brand new army uniform covered with medals. His real name was Dr. Ranchburg, a Jew in hiding. It was Ranchburg´s partnership with Gyékis that brought him into contact with Kormos who gave him a new identity and the command of the Csángó Street war plant. "Rázsó" also had direct operational responsibility for the four young Jewish men who were involved in some of the rescue operations described earlier. The rescue team used the Skoda car when they went out on their forays.

Between the end of October and the end of November, when their family members joined the men, the number of people at Csángó Street increased to approximately one hundred seventy. Three of the assembly rooms were converted into living quarters with three level bunk beds. Since the heating system did not function and a corner of the factory building was missing as a result of bomb damage, the interior was very cold.

In late October, six members of Pauker's family joined him in Csángó Street. My family's story was typical of those who had been hiding there. My father (István Pick) had been inducted into a Jewish labor company (No.101/351) shortly after the German occupation of Hungary in March 1944. My mother, grandmother and I had been forced out of our apartment in the middle of June 1944 and moved into a Yellow-Star House with our maternal relatives. On October 25, 1944 my father's company commander, a decent person, gave his men a furlough and disclosed that, upon their return, they would be transported to German labor camps. Deciding to hide, my father sought the help of Gyékis, with whom he had had prior business relations. Gyékis sent my father to Csángó Street. Three weeks later, my father sent a message via Gyetvay to us, requesting that we join him immediately. We were reunited on November 15.

Most of the newcomers quickly integrated with those already there and friendships began to form. Natural affinities developed among some of the men and women whose spouses were already deported or missing. The pervasive sense of desperation and a strong need for human warmth and companionship often resulted in hastily blossoming romances that coalesced into relationships with uncertain futures.

Some people stayed in Csángó Street only for a short time. For example, a pharmacist and his wife remained only one night. They were afraid to stay more than one night in the same hiding place. Some people remained there for three or four weeks and then moved on.

On November 27, a crisis developed. A young man contracted high fever and became delirious. It was clear that he required immediate medical attention. Rázsó and the leaders were in a grave dilemma. On the one hand, a man's life was in imminent danger but, on the other hand, the lives of one hundred sixty-nine persons could be jeopardized. The leaders decided that they would allow a physician into the war plant to treat the man. A few days after the doctor's visit his condition improved.

On December 2, Kormos' life intersected with those hidden in Csángó Street. On the last day of November, Alföldy, the man who had been hiding Kormos and others for months, betrayed him to the agents of the Police Bureau for Political Security. Alföldy knew of the existence and addresses of three hiding places. He also knew of the existence, but not the location, of the fourth place in *Újpest*. He disclosed all this information. The motivation for his betrayal was not clear. There are two plausible explanations. The first is that Alföldy wanted to extract more money from Kormos, but he was penniless by then. The second is that somebody may have found out about Alföldy's duplicitous game and was blackmailing him. Alföldy did not know precisely where Kormos was staying because he often changed his location. On December 2, three teams, each composed of five armed detectives, were sent to each location. The team that was sent to the Csángó Street war plant found Kormos there. In mid-morning the detectives burst into the common room where most people congregated. Their leader shouted orders: "Men to the right! Line up against the wall! Women and children to the left and form a line! We know who you are! A bunch of stinking hiding Jews! We are detectives from the Police Bureau for Political Security!"

Most of us thought that our fate was sealed. Many prayed, many sobbed. About a half hour later, the leader of the detectives emerged from the office. He informed the desperate group that henceforth, we were under his personal protection. Then the detectives left taking only Kormos with them. We later discovered that, as usual, money spoke; the detectives had been bribed by our leaders.

Seconds before the men had burst in Pollák, one of our group, had jumped from a second story window onto the glass roof of the adjacent building. The glass shattered under his weight and he fell into a haystack where he hid. Two detectives probed the haystack with pitchforks, but they did not find him. The next night, Pollák rejoined us.

Between November 29 and December 2, 1944, most of the remaining Jewish population still alive in the Yellow-Star houses, a total of over 60,000 people, were transferred to the newly established Central Ghetto in a dilapidated section of the inner city.

On December 17, two policemen arrived at the Csángó Street war plant. They informed Rázsó that the tenants of the building across the street were growing suspicious of the activities at the war plant. The police officers told us that they were going to escort the group to the Central Ghetto. Of the approximately one hundred fifty people who started out, only sixty-three arrived in the Ghetto. The remainder escaped.

Upon arrival in the Central Ghetto the group was divided into three sub-groups. Twenty-two persons were housed at Klauzál Square No. 7; my family was part of this group. The two other groups were placed in nearby buildings.

The Central Ghetto was liberated on January 18, 1945 by units of the Soviet Army. All twenty-two persons at Klauzál Square No. 7 from the Csángó Street war plant survived.

Epilogue

Kormos was transported to the Headquarters of the Police Bureau for Political Security. There, they beat and tortured him for two days to force him to disclose the location of the fourth hiding place in *Újpest*. However, he refused to talk. Thanks to Kormos' silence members of the *Újpest* operation were able to escape and relocate to another suburb of Budapest (*Rákospalota*). However, their plans to save the utility plants of Budapest had to be abandoned.[28]

The fate of Jews in the other two hiding places set-up by Kormos and betrayed by Alföldy was not as fortunate as those in the Csángó Street war plant. Hundreds were deported to Germany, seventy-six were arrested, many of whom were shot beside the Danube River. The exact number of the victims cannot be established.[29]

Two sources provide information on Kormos' fate. They agree that he managed to escape, but disagree how he escaped.[30] After his escape, Kormos was hidden in Buda at Dr. László Szentgyörgyi's home. He was liberated in February 1945. Pauker and his relatives survived the war. Frisch survived also.

In 1946 the survivors of the Csángó Street war plant held a reunion and thirty persons came to this event. Many survivors did not know about this reunion, consequently they did not come.[31] To date, sixty-four persons among those who had found temporary refuge in the Csángó Street textile factory, have been positively identified as survivors. The total number of Jews in Budapest whose lives were saved by Kormos undoubtedly was in the hundreds.

After his recovery from the beatings and torture, which required several months, Kormos was appointed as president of one of the "People's Tribunals" in 1946. His tribunal tried and indicted a number of fascist criminals. In 1948 Kormos became director of a State owned company. However, his frequent criticisms of the highest levels of economic leadership led to his dismissal from his job and he was expelled from the Hungarian Communist Party in 1949. Shortly thereafter, Kormos was declared an "enemy" of the people. Years of police harassment, frequent searches at Kormos' apartment and repeated arrests followed. Finally, in 1960 Kormos left Hungary and settled in Vienna, Austria where once again he established a successful business enterprise. He died in Vienna in 1969 without his heroism having been appropriately acknowledged. This paper attempts to rectify this omission and to encourage others to continue, on a more detailed level, the research in this heretofore-unrecognized chapter of Jewish rescue and resistance activities in the final phases of the Holocaust in Hungary.

Perhaps it is appropriate to note that some modicum of justice was handed out; Alföldy was sentenced to five years in prison in 1946 for the betrayal of Imre Kormos.[32]

Acknowledgments

I would like to express my gratitude to all whose help and encouragement have been critical to this work: Mrs. Sándor Hámori (Zsuzsanna Kormos), Mrs. Pál Reich and Mrs. György Szántó for the recollections, documents and photographs that they provided me, and Ms. Sarah Ogilvie for her help and research in the U.S. Holocaust Memorial Museum. In addition, Professor Gabor Vermes and his wife Ann, Mr. Gabor Kalman and Mr. Aron Golberg contributed invaluable suggestions.

Endnotes

1. Mrs. Sándor Hámori (Zsuzsanna Kohn-Kormos), letter to author, 5 July 1995.

2. Péter Hanák, ed., *History of Hungary* (Budapest: Corvina Books, 1991), 163-74.

3. Ibid., 175.

4. Mrs. Sándor Hámori (Zsuzsanna Kohn-Kormos), interview by author, video tape recording, Budapest, Hungary, 25 May 1995.

5. Randolph L. Braham, *Politics of Genocide: The Holocaust in Hungary* (New York: Columbia University Press, 1981), 125.

6. Hámori, interview.

7. Braham, Politics of Genocide. 288.

8. Ibid., 296-97.

9. Ibid., 194.

10. Ibid., 301.

Imre Kormos:
Unknown Hero of the Hungarian Jewish Rescue and Resistance

11. Ibid., 308.

12. Mrs. György Szántó and Mrs. Pál Reich, interview by author, audio tape recording, Budapest, Hungary, 27 May, 1995.

13. As shown on István Pick's original work identification cards, dated October 25 and 27, 1944 Serial Nos. 302 and 233.

14. Lujza Farkas, "A Hős és Árulója." (The hero and his betrayer), Képes Figyelő, 15 May, 1946.

15. Braham, Politics of Genocide. 366-70.

16. Hámori, interview.

17. Braham, Politics of Genocide. 732-41.

18. Ibid., 752-63.

19. Hámori, interview.

20. Elek Karsai, A Budai Vártól a Gyepüig (From the Castle of Buda to the Borderland), (Budapest Táncsis, 1965), 587.

21. Braham, Politics of Genocide. 838.

22. Lujza Farkas, "A Hös és Árulója."

23. "Kilenc-Házi Történelem" (History of Nine Buildings), Angyalföld, Vol. 1, No. 1, May 1976.

24. Braham, Politics of Genocide, 840.

25. Ibid., 840.

26. Lujza Farkas, "A Hös és Árulója."

27. Andrew Handler and Susan V. Meschel, ed., *Young People Speak: Surviving the Holocaust in Hungary* (Chicago: Franklin Watts, 1993), 129-135. Additional details in George S. Pick, "Shadows of Memory."

28. Lujza Farkas, "A Hös és Árulója."

29. Lujza Farkas, "A Hös és Árulója."

30. Lujza Farkas, "A Hös és Árulója." and "1944 Nyara" (Summer 1944) Part III, Magyarország (April 3, 1964), 16.

31. The author and his parents were present at the reunion.

32. Lujza Farkas, "A Hös és Árulója."

CHAPTER 16

The German Resistance to Hitler and he Jews: The Case of Carl Goerdeler

Peter Hoffmann

The collective guilt thesis of the powers allied against National-Socialist Germany during the Second World War,[1] first abandoned by Secretary of State James Byrnes in his speech in Stuttgart on 6 September 1946, has experienced a number of revivals. Most recently, D. Goldhagen, T. Hamerow, H. Mommsen and H. Heer have been active in this regard.[2]

In fact, there was in Germany from 1933 to 1945 a good deal of dissent and resistance which developed in a dialectic relationship to the criminality of the regime. Special courts killed 12,000 Germans[3] during the years of Hitler's rule. "Regular" German justice killed 40,000 Germans. Courts martial killed 25,000 German soldiers (western Allied courts martial killed fewer than 300 during the Second World War). The total number of Germans killed for political offenses or as suspects through judicial processes alone was 77,000.[4] Most of them died on the guillotine or were hanged. These numbers reveal not only the potential for popular resistance in German society, but also what happened to it.

In face of the persecution of the Jews and other minorities one rightly expects some continuance and proliferation of opposition among those still alive and outside concentration camps and prisons. In fact, there are significant examples of that.

One of them (inexplicably libelled as "antisemitic" by his modern critics), is *Carl Goerdeler*, the Mayor of Leipzig (1930-1936) and

277

Reich Prices Commissioner (1931-1932, 1934-1935). Goerdeler became the civilian head of the conspiracy against Hitler. He was active in it from 1937 to 1944. Goerdeler was sentenced to death by the "People's Court" in Berlin on 8 September 1944 for his part in the plot against Hitler and executed only on 2 February 1945. An examination of his record will reveal the opposite of what his detractors say.[5]

While Goerdeler waited for his execution, he hoped against hope that Hitler or Himmler might seek his advice, and that he might be asked to help end the war through his connections abroad. In 1935, in an interview with Hitler, he had, it had seemed to him, won the dictator's support for his own view on economic policy against a powerful rival, Economics Minister Hjalmar Schacht. Since then Goerdeler had been under the illusion that, given the opportunity, he would be able to persuade Hitler to see reason.[6] In his retrospective notes which he wrote in prison, also for the eyes of his jailers and the Secret State Police (Gestapo), he stated that he had *initially* worked loyally with the National Socialist government and its functionaries.

But Goerdeler had not worked loyally with the National Socialist government in matters concerning Jews. He had in fact intervened, in April 1933, in full formal dress, and in the company of his Deputy Mayor Ewald Löser, against the National Socialists' storm troopers, the SA, when these harassed and attacked Jews and businesses belonging to Jews, and he had used the Leipzig police to liberate Jews who had been detained and beaten by the SA in the first weeks of Hitler's rule.[7]

Goerdeler's critics do not mention these actions but they say that Goerdeler signed a list of physicians who were excluded from practice because they were Jews, and, that this demonstrated his anti-Jewish attitude. The facts are these:

1. In July 1934, a national law required that a "race authority" be established within municipal health commissions. After Goerdeler had balked against the official and unofficial pressures for months, he was finally forced in January 1935 to accept this.[8]

2. A government decree of 1933 excluded from practice under public health insurance plans Communist physicians, and "non-Aryan" physicians, who were *not* World War veterans or sons or fathers of World War veterans.[9]
3. Another decree of 1934 excluded physicians from *approbation* if they were descended from one or more Jewish grandparents, or if they were married to a "non-Aryan." But Jewish physicians who had been previously admitted to practice under medical insurance plans did not lose their approbation.[10]

On 9 April 1935 Goerdeler received a complaint from the Landesverband Mitteldeutschland des Centralvereins deutscher Staatsbürger jüdischen Glaubens e.V. (Saxon Association of the Central Association of German Citizens of Jewish Faith). The complaint concerned the new deputy mayor, a National Socialist, Rudolf Haake, because Haake had warned civil servants against consulting any Jewish physicians. The Association asked Goerdeler to put a stop to the unlawful boycott of physicians who were by law allowed to practice.

In April 1935 Goerdeler signed an internal memorandum listing "non-Aryan" physicians who were permitted by law to treat patients under the terms of the public health-insurance authority. The memorandum also listed those who were by law not permitted to do so.[11] Goerdeler confirmed the legal position which the Association had invoked. He protected those who were still legally entitled to practice and protected them against the efforts of National Socialists to exclude *all* Jews from practice.

The files of the Leipzig City Archives contain correspondence and minutes concerning restrictions for Jews in the use of public baths. Almost all the documents on this issue which originated in the Leipzig city administration bear the signature of the National Socialist Deputy Mayor, Rudolf Haake. In a reply to a complaint, Haake wrote, using the pronoun "I," under the date of 19 August 1935 that he had accepted the justification of the decree prohibiting Jews from the use of public baths in which they would come into contact with non-Jewish patrons.[12]

Goerdeler has been accused of anti-Semitism for allegedly sanctioning restrictions on the use of public baths by Jews.[13] Goerdeler's ultimate responsibility as Mayor is clear, of course. But his personal involvement appears to have been limited to answering an inquiry from the Saxon section of the National Conference of Municipalities on 19 September 1936. He wrote, using the passive voice in the third person, that from the end of July 1935 Jews had been prohibited from using the Leipzig municipal summer baths and indoor pools and other communal baths.[14]

The matter of the Mendelssohn statue was an important part of the context. The statue had been erected before the Leipzig Gewandhaus concert hall in 1892, in honor of its former director, Felix Mendelssohn-Bartholdy. The National Socialists considered Mendelssohn-Bartholdy a Jew under the definitions of the Nuremberg Laws of 1935, although he had been a Christian. For years, and particularly in the spring of 1936, before the summer Olympiad in Berlin, local Party leaders, including the National-Socialist Deputy Mayor, pressed Goerdeler to permit the removal of the statue from its place in front of the Gewandhaus at Leipzig. Goerdeler said no to all demands to remove the statue. Finally, in July 1936, he agreed to discuss the question, but not until after the summer, and *sine die*.

In the autumn of 1936 Goerdeler accepted an invitation from the German Chamber of Commerce to travel to Finland. Before he left, he secured high-level support from Goebbels and Hitler for his decision to leave the monument in place, and he instructed Deputy Mayor Haake accordingly.[15] While Goerdeler was away, Haake had the statue removed. When Goerdeler returned and demanded an explanation, Haake accused him of not sharing the Party's views on the Jews. Goerdeler resigned as Mayor. Haake declared that the matter of the statue was "only the outward occasion of the conflict," and that "Dr. Goerdeler's attitude in the Jewish Question had been revealed particularly clearly in the matter of the Mendelssohn-Bartholdy statue."[16]

Some have argued that Goerdeler had objected only to Haake's insubordination. Again, it might be argued that Haake accused

Geordeler to justify his own incorrect action. But such an explanation becomes untenable in the light of Goerdeler's actions two years later, when he was out of office, without any official standing, and when it was much more dangerous for him to oppose National Socialist anti-Jewish policies.

At the request of the former Head of the British Foreign Office, Sir Robert Vansittart, the British industrialist A.P. Young who had business and personal links with Robert Bosch in Stuttgart, met with Goerdeler in August 1938 in Rauschen Dune (a village on the Baltic Sea, north of Königsberg), where Goerdeler spent his vacation. Through Young, Goerdeler urged the British government to refuse to discuss the vital issues that Germany was interested in resolving, if the practices against the Jews continued.[17]

Under existing German statute law, this was treason against the country (Landesverrat). In a further meeting with A.P. Young, this time in Switzerland, in November 1938, after German authorities had driven 10,000 Polish Jews across the German frontier with Poland, but before the 9 November 1938 pogrom, Goerdeler told Young he was "greatly perturbed that there was not yet in evidence any strong reaction throughout the democracies, in the Press, the Church, and in Parliament, against the barbaric, sadistic and cruel persecution of 10,000 Polish Jews in Germany."[18]

Meeting A.P. Young in Switzerland, on 4 December 1938, Goerdeler again deplored "the cruel and senseless persecution of the Jews," and "the way in which the Nazi leaders enriched themselves by stealing Jewish property." He added that, "as soon as the planned persecution of the Churches begins, or the new persecution of the Jews is started, it is absolutely essential to break diplomatic relations" with Germany. He warned that Hitler was determined to conquer the world, and that for this purpose he had "decided to destroy the Jews—Christianity—Capitalism." Goerdeler urged the British government to apply strong pressure against Hitler's government "to save the world from this terrible catastrophe."[19]

In his last meeting with A.P. Young, on 16 March 1939, one day after the occupation of Prague and the rest of Czechia by German troops, Goerdeler "was emphatic in his view that Hitler was now on the wrong path," which would lead to his destruction—if the democracies moved swiftly. Goerdeler listed "three milestones of great historical importance" which Hitler had already passed on this path; he named as the first such milestone "The Pogrom against the Jews on November 9 and 10."[20]

The persecution of the Jews led Goerdeler to draft, in 1941, proposals for a solution to the "Jewish Question." He has been accused of "anti-Semitism" because in this paper he used the term "race" for the Jewish people, and because he proposed that Jews be treated as foreign nationals and as citizens of a yet to be founded Jewish state, unless they had lived within the borders of the German Empire before 1 July 1871, or unless their ancestors had lived within the borders of the German Empire before 1871.

The suggestion seems incomprehensible that naturalized German Jews should be deprived of their citizenship, after years of injustices and cruelties committed against them by German authorities, at the time when the systematic program of mass murder had gotten underway.[21] In fact Goerdeler's motive was to secure the Jews' status permanently against persecution.[22] In view of Goerdeler's actions on behalf of both German and Polish Jews it is impossible to suggest that he intended to make their position worse than it was. Goerdeler was not erratic. The only explanation for his proposals is that he was desperately seeking to persuade the murderers to accept a relatively less harmful alternative. The purpose of his memorandum was to try to wrest the weapon from the murderers' hands.

The Secret State Police records of interrogations of the plotters survive incompletely. The most important reason why these records can be accepted as accurate is that they are confirmed by independent contemporary sources such as diaries (Hassell, Groscurth), letters (Moltke, Bonhoeffer), the proclamations prepared for the day of the coup against Hitler, and numerous other forms of testimony. Furthermore, the accused could not hope to help their cases by indicting the regime of murder. It would be difficult to argue that the Gestapo interrogation summaries ought not to be believed when they report that the conspirators against Hitler said they had tried to overthrow him because of the anti-Jewish policies. Indeed, the Gestapo officials themselves were surprised, and at first incredulous at the plotters' moral posture. The Gestapo records show that fifteen anti-Hitler conspirators stated that their main motive, or, that one of their main motives for their opposition to National Socialism, was the persecution of the Jews. Their names are: Klaus Bonhoeffer, Admiral Wilhelm Canaris, Hans von Dohnanyi, Carl Goerdeler, Franz Kempner, Hans Kloos, Professor Adolf Lampe, Heinrich Count Lehndorff-Steinort, Brigadier Hans Oster, Colonel Alexis Baron von Roenne, Rüdiger Schleicher, Franz Sperr, Professor Alexander Count Stauffenberg, Berthold Count Stauffenberg, Peter Count Yorck von Wartenburg (all except Kloos, Lampe and Alexander Stauffenberg were executed). Twenty-two other anti-Hitler plotters are also on record as having been equally motivated: General Ludwig Beck, Dietrich Bonhoeffer, Major Axel Baron von dem Bussche, Professor Constantin von Dietze, Colonel Eberhard Finckh, Brigadier Rudolf-Christoph Baron von Gersdorff, Eugen Gerstenmaier, Lieutenant-Colonel Helmuth Groscurth, Hans-Bernd von Haeften, Ulrich von Hassell, Julius Leber, Carlo Mierendorff, Helmuth James Count Moltke, Johannes Popitz, Adolf Reichwein, Ulrich Count Schwerin von Schwanenfeld, Colonel Wilhelm Staehle, Colonel Claus Count Stauffenberg, Lieutenant-Colonel Theodor Steltzer, Brigadier Helmuth Stieff, Brigadier Henning von Tresckow, Adam von Trott zu Solz, Josef Wirmer.[23] There were also a number of Catholic priests and Lutheran ministers, and twenty-eight members of the White Rose student group who made the same declaration.[24]

On the day after the failed 20 July 1944 insurrection, Hitler and his propaganda minister broadcasted the version that "a small clique of ambitious, unscrupulous and criminal, stupid officers" had plotted to eliminate the Führer and "to exterminate the staff of the German Armed Forces leadership."[25] The Secret State Police soon discovered, however, that the conspiracy was much more widespread, and that its motives were entirely different than those alleged by official propaganda.

After the first two weeks of investigations following the attempted insurrection, however, the head of the Secret State Police investigating commission, SS Lieutenant-Colonel Walter von Kielpinski, wrote in a preliminary report dated 7 August 1944, under the heading "Criticisms of National Socialism:"

> Besides the treatment of the churches and of Christianity in the National Socialist state, certain points of view recur consistently in the statements of almost all persons now under investigation. [...] A number of conspirators opposed to the National Socialist State approved of anti-Semitism in principle but rejected the methods of its enforcement. Partly they emphasize humanitarian motivations, such as that the enforcement procedures had not been sufficiently humane and had not corresponded to the German character, partly they question the political expediency of causing severe tensions with the rest of the world by the rapid and rigorous elimination of Jewry.[26]

Since several conspirators had already declared the persecution of the Jews their chief motive, this report, too, was a distortion of the available evidence.

After three months of intensive investigations, in October 1944, the Secret State Police Investigating Commission reported that the arrested conspirators

> either reject in principle fundamental parts of the [National Socialist] program, or they dilute them to such an extent that hardly anything remained of the fundamental point [*grundsätzlichen Forderung*, referring to the removal of the Jews].

The Gestapo did find a few who expressed support for restrictions upon Jews, but even these condemned the methods and practice, so that their theoretical support was meaningless.

Finally, the Gestapo concluded:

The entire inner alienation from the ideas of National Socialism which characterised the men of the reactionary conspirato[27]rial circle expresses itself above all in their position on the Jewish Question. [...] they stubbornly take the liberal position of granting to the Jews in principle the same status as to every German.[28]

Endnotes

1. P.R.O. CAB 120/300/XC/1207. The Joint Chiefs of Staff Directive 1067, approved by President H.S. Truman, treated Germany expressly not as a liberated nation, but a defeated enemy nation. Secretary of State James Byrnes' speech in Stuttgart on 6 September 1946 signaled a fundamental change; the German nation was to be assisted in its return to an honorable place among the free and peace loving nations.

2. Daniel Goldhagen, Hitler's Willing Executioners, New York 1996; Theodore S. Hamerow, On the Road to the Wolf's Lair. German Resistance to Hitler, Cambridge, Massachusetts, London, England, 1997; Hans Mommsen, "Die moralische Wiederherstellung der Nation. Der Widerstand gegen Hitler war von einer antisemitischen Grundhaltung getragen," Süddeutsche Zeitung 21 July 1999, p. 15; The German Army and Genocide. Crimes Against War Prisoners, Jews, and Other Civilians in the East, 1939-1944, ed. by The Hamburg Institute for Social Research, The New Press, New York, 1999; Vernichtungskrieg. Verbrechen der Wehrmacht 1941 bis 1944. Ausstellungskatalog, ed. Hamburger Institut für Sozialforschung, 3rd ed., Hamburger Edition, Hamburg, 1997; Hannes Heer, Klaus Naumann, eds., Vernichtungskrieg. Verbrechen der Wehrmacht 1941-1944, Hamburger Edition, Hamburg, 1995.

3. Franz W. Seidler, Die Militärgerichtsbarkeit der Deutschen Wehrmacht 1939-1945. Rechtsprechung und Strafvollzug, Munich, Berlin, Herbig, 1991, p. 44 states that 10,191 death sentences against soldiers and employees of the armed forces were handed down until and including November 1944; he bases this, according to a source reference, upon Rolf-Dieter Breitenstein and Philipp Joachim, Die imperialistische Militärgerichtsbarkeit von 1898 bis 1945, Jur. Diss. Humboldt-Universität, Berlin 1983, p. 233, and a file in Militärarchiv Potsdam W-10-1168.

4. Trial of the Major War Criminals before the International Military Tribunal. Nuremberg 14 November 1945-1 October 1946, vol. XXXVIII, Nuremberg, Secre-tariat of the Tribunal, 1949, pp. 362-365; Martin Broszat, "Nationalsozialistische Konzentrationslager 1933 bis 1945," in: Konzentrationslager, Kommissarbefehl, Judenverfolgung, ed. Martin Broszat, Hans-Adolf Jacobsen, Helmut

Krausnick, Olten-Freiburg i.Br., Walter-Verlag, 1965, pp. 158-159; We Survived. The Stories of Fourteen of the Hidden and the Hunted of Nazi Germany, ed. Eric H. Boehm, New Haven, Connecticut, Yale University Press, 1949, p. VIII based on secret state police records; also Gabriel A. Almond, "The German Resistance Movement," in: Current History 10 (1946), pp. 409-527; cf. Wolfgang Sofsky, Die Ordnung des Terrors: Das Konzentrationslager, Frankfurt am Main, S. Fischer, 1993, pp. 56-57; further Walter Wagner, Der Volksgerichtshof im nationalsozialistischen Staat, Stuttgart, Deutsche Verlags-Anstalt, 1974, p. 945; Manfred Messerschmidt, Fritz Wüllner, Die Wehrmachtjustiz im Dienste des Nationalsozialismus. Zerstörung einer Legende, Baden-Baden, Nomos Verlag, 1987, p. 49-50, 70, 73.

5. Christof Dipper, "Der Deutsche Widerstand und die Juden," Geschichte und Gesellschaft 9 (1983), pp. 349-380 fails to cite anything conclusive and relies on suggestion, supposition, innuendo, and suppression of evidence; Martin Broszat, "Plädoyer für eine Historisierung des Nationalsozialismus," Merkur 39 (1985), pp. 382-383 relies on Dipper. Klemens von Klemperer in conference discussion, "Christianity and Resistance. National Socialist Germany 1933-1945," University of Birmingham, Birmingham, England, 22 April 1995, maintained that Goerdeler had signed a "decree" in 1936 restricting the use of public baths in Leipzig by Jews; there is no evidence that Goerdeler ever signed such a decree. In response to the author's questions, Klemperer replied (letter 15 August 1996) that according to his notes Goerdeler's typed signature appeared under a decree dated 19 September 1936 restricting the use of public baths by Jews; but Klemperer cannot produce or identify the "decree."

6. [Carl Goerdeler], Unsere Idee, typescript, Berlin Nov. 1944, Bundesarchiv Koblenz, Nl Goerdeler 26, pp. 10-11; Ritter, pp. 77-78, 430-431, 434-440.

7. Marianne Meyer-Krahmer, Carl Goerdeler und sein Weg in den Widerstand. Eine Reise in die Welt meines Vaters, Herder Taschenbuch Verlag, Freiburg im Breisgau 1989, p. 73.

8. Verhandlungen der Stadtverordneten zu Leipzig 1935, Stadtarchiv Leipzig, Band I, 30 Jan. 1935, Gesetz zur Vereinheitlichung des Gesundheitswesens, 3 July 1934, RGBl. I 1934, pp. 531-532; Erste Durchführungsverordnung zum Gesetz über die Vereinheitlichung des Gesundheitswesens, 6 Feb. 1935, Reichsgesetzblatt Teil I 1935 (RGBl. I 1935), Berlin, 1935, pp. 177-180.

9. Verordnung über die Zulassung von Ärzten zur Tätigkeit bei den Krankenkassen. Vom 22. April 1933, RGBl. I 1933, p. 222.

10. Verordnung über die Zulassung von Ärzten zur Tätigkeit bei den Krankenkassen. Vom 17. Mai 1934, RGBl. I 1934, pp. 399-410. Veterans who had been severely wounded were exempt from certain conditions of approbation. Physicians (the decree did not distinguish here between "Aryan" and "non-Aryan" physicians) who

The German Resistance to Hitler and the Jews:
The Case of Carl Goerdeler

had practiced medicine from a date before 1 October 1921 were also exempt from certain preconditions for approbation to practice under medical insurance plans.

11. Stadtarchiv Leipzig, Kap. 1 Nr. 122.

12. Stadtarchiv Leipzig, Kap. 1 Nr. 122.

13. Klemens von Klemperer in conference discussion, "Christianity and Resistance. National Socialist Germany 1933-1945," University of Birmingham, Birmingham, England, 22 April 1995.

14. Stadtarchiv Leipzig, Kap. 1 Nr. 122.

15. Goerdeler to Reichsstatthalter Martin Mutschmann 23 Nov. 1937, Stadtarchiv Leipzig, Kap. 10 G Nr. 685 Bd. 2.

16. Acta, das Felix Mendelssohn-Bartholdy-Denkmal btr. Ergangen vor dem Rathe der Stadt Leipzig 1859-1947, Stadtarchiv Leipzig, Cap. 26A Nr. 39; Goerdeler personnel file Stadtarchiv Leipzig, Kap. 10 G Nr. 685 Bd. 1 and 2. Manfred Unger, "Die 'Endlösung' in Leipzig. Dokumente zur Geschichte der Judenverfolgung 1933-1945," Zeitschrift für Geschichtswissenschaft 11 (1963), p. 944 cites Goerdeler as saying only that the matter could be examined; Unger, who was at the time head of the Stadtarchiv and had full access to all the records, suppressed the accusations against Goerdeler of having opposed the National Socialist anti-Jewish policies. See also Goerdeler to Mutschmann 23 Nov. 1937, Stadtarchiv Leipzig, Kap. 10 G Nr. 685 Bd. 2.

17. A.P. Young, The "X" Documents, ed. Sidney Aster, Andre Deutsch, London 1974, pp. 45-49, 59.

18. Young, p. 139.

19. Young, pp. 154-162.

20. Young, p. 177.

21. Eberhard Bethge, Dietrich Bonhoeffer. Theologe, Christ, Zeitgenosse, Chr. Kaiser Verlag, Munich, 1970, pp. 796, 836-837.

22. Goerdeler was naive in his faith in what he saw as reasonable and conducive to peace. His views on a reasonable adjustment of German and British interests before the war, and on a territorial peace settlement for Germany after the war, which he put forward in 1938, and as late as May 1944, provide an analogy. In 1944, Goerdeler wanted plans for an Allied invasion of France to be abandoned; maintenance of a German defensive capability in the east; evacuation of German forces from all occupied territories in the north, south and west; German eastern borders as in 1914; Austria and the Sudetenland to remain in Germany; autonomy for Alsace and Lorraine; no occupation but self-government for Germany; see People's Court judgement of 17 Jan. 1945 against Captain (Res.) Hermann Kaiser, Bundesarchiv, Koblenz, EAP 105/30; Spiegelbild einer Verschwörung.

Die Kaltenbrunner-Berichte an Bormann und Hitler über das Attentat vom 20. Juli 1944. Geheime Dokumente aus dem ehemaligen Reichssicherheitshauptamt, Seewald Verlag, Stuttgart, 1961, pp. 126-127, 410-412; Goerdeler, Idee, pp. 33-40; cf. Peter Hoffmann, Widerstand, Staatsstreich, Attentat: Der Kampf der Opposition gegen Hitler, R.Piper & Co., Munich 1969, pp. 749-751, note 104; Peter Hoffmann, "The Question of Western Allied Co-operation with the German Anti-Nazi Conspiracy, 1938-1944," The Historical Journal 34 (1991), pp. 437-464.

23. Beck and Tresckow committed suicide; Bussche, Dietze, Gersdorff, Steltzer and Gerstenmaier survived; Groscurth died as a prisoner-of-war; Mierendorff was killed in an air raid; the others were executed.

24. The names of the White Rose group include Alexander Schmorell, Hans Scholl, Willi Graf, Christoph Propst, Professor Kurt Huber, Helmut Bauer, Heinrich Bollinger, Eugen Grimminger, Heinrich Guter, Falk Harnack, Hans Hirzel, Susanne Hirzel, Traute Lafrenz, Franz Josef Müller, Gisela Schertling, Katharina Schüddekopf, Harald Dohrn, Manfred Eickemeyer, Wilhelm Geyer, Josef Söhngen, Willi Bollinger, Lieselotte Dreyfeldt, Wolfgang Erlenbach, Valentin Freise, Marie-Luise Jahn, Hans Leipelt, Hedwig Schulz, Franz Treppesch, Jürgen Wittenstein. Cf. Willi Graf, Briefe und Aufzeichnungen, ed. Anneliese Knoop-Graf and Inge Jens, S. Fischer, Frankfurt am Main 1988. Spiegelbild, pp. 110, 199-202, 420, 431, 443, 450, 471-474, 501, 520; Veit Osas, Walküre. Die Wahrheit über den 20. Juli 1944 mit Dokumenten, Deutschland-Verlag Adolf Ernst Schulze & Co., Hamburg 1953, p. 98. On Dohnanyi also Eberhard Bethge, Dietrich Bonhoeffer. Theologian, Christian, Contemporary, Collins, London, 1970, pp. 640-643; Ulrich von Hassell was appalled by the Nuremberg Laws, as his daughter noted in her diary on 18 September 1935. He condemned the laws as signifying "for our country the end of its culture"; Fey von Hassell, Niemals sich beugen. Erinnerungen einer Sondergefangenen der SS, Piper, Munich, Zurich 21991, p. 32. Hassell recorded his outrage at the November 1938 Pogrom in his own diary under 25 November 1938:

> But my chief concern is not with the effects abroad, not with what kind of foreign political reaction we may expect—at least not for the moment. I am most deeply troubled about the effect on our national life, which is dominated ever more inexorably by a system capable of such things.

Ulrich von Hassell, The von Hassell Diaries 1938-1944, Hamish Hamilton, London 1948, p. 20. Hassell's published diary—thus far only the portions from September 1938 to July 1944 have been published—refers to the situation of the Jews forty-three times; Hassell, pp. 76, 140, 198, 219, 272; Ulrich von Hassell, Die Hassell-Tagebücher 1938-1944. Aufzeichnungen vom Andern Deutschland, Siedler Verlag, Berlin 1988, p. 281; Heinz Eduard Tödt, "Judenverfolgung und Kirchenzerstörung im Spiegel der Hassell-Tagebücher 1938-1944," Erhard Blum, Christian Macholz und Ekkehard W. Stegemann, Die Hebräische Bibel und ihre zweifache Nachgeschichte. Festschrift für Rolf Rendtorff zum 65. Geburtstag, Neukirchener Verlag, Neukirchen-Vluyn 1990, pp. 707-715. On Goerdeler see also Volksgerichtshof-Prozesse zum 20. Juli 1944: Transkripte von Tonbandfunden, Lautarchiv des Deutschen Rundfunks, Frankfurt am Main, 1961, p. 119; on Oster also Fabian von Schlabrendorff, Begegnungen in fünf Jahrzehnten, Rainer Wunderlich Verlag Hermann Leins, Tübingen, 1979, p. 183; Alexander Stahlberg, Die verdammte Pflicht, Ullstein, Berlin 1987, pp. 314-315, 377; on Yorck also Theodor Steltzer, Sechzig Jahre Zeitgenosse, List Verlag, Munich 1966, p. 147; Bethge, Bonhoeffer (Engl. edn), p. 613; Trial XXXIII, p. 424; Philipp Freiherr von Boeselager, Der Widerstand in der Heeresgruppe Mitte (Beiträge zum Widerstand 1933-1945 40), Gedenkstätte Deutscher Widerstand, Berlin 1990, p. 10; Dietrich Bonhoeffer, "Die Kirche vor der Judenfrage," in Dietrich Bonhoeffer, Gesammelte Schriften, Zweiter Band, Chr. Kaiser Verlag, Munich 1959, pp. 44-53, 115-117, 144; Dietrich Bonhoeffer, Werke, Sechster Band, Chr. Kaiser Verlag, Munich, 1992, pp. 93-95, 98-100, 113-115; Bethge, Bonhoeffer (German edn), index "Juden;" "Dietrich Bonhoeffer und die Juden" in Ernst Feil und Ilse Tödt, Konsequenzen. Dietrich Bonhoeffers Kirchenverständnis heute (Internationales Bonhoeffer-Forum, Nr. 3), Chr. Kaiser Verlag, Munich 1980, pp. 171-214; Peter Hoffmann, Widerstand, Staatsstreich, Attentat. Der Kampf der Opposition gegen Hitler, Piper, Munich, Zurich, 41985, pp. 334-335, 399; [Constantin von Dietze], "Vorschläge für eine Lösung der Judenfrage in Deutschland," in: In der Stunde Null. Die Denkschrift des Freiburger "Bonhoeffer-Kreises:" Politische Gemeinschaftsordnung. Ein Versuch zur Selbstbesinnung des christlichen Gewissens in den politischen Nöten unserer Zeit, introd. H. Thielicke, ed. Ph. von Bismarck, J.C.B. Mohr (Paul Siebeck), Tübingen, 1979, pp. 146-151; Gerhard Ritter, Carl Goerdeler und die deutsche Widerstandsbewegung, Deutsche Verlags-Anstalt, Stuttgart, 31956, pp. 523-524 note 71; Stahlberg, pp. 342-345; Ivar Anderson, diary 14 Dec. 1942, Kungliga Biblioteket, Stockholm, Ivar Andersons papper L 91; Fabian von Schlabrendorff, ed., Eugen Gerstenmaier im Dritten Reich. Eine Dokumentation, Evangelisches Verlagswerk, Stuttgart, 1965, pp. 42-43; Inge Scholl, Die weisse Rose, Verlag der Frankfurter Hefte, Frankfurt am Main, 1952, passim; The White Rose. The Resistance by Students Against Hitler. Munich 1942/43, The White Rose Foundation, Munich, 1991, p. 60; Hassell (1988), pp. 62-63, 67-68, 130, 330; Spiegelbild, p. 501; Dr. Theodor Haubauch in his People's Court trial on 17 Jan. 1945, Volksgerichtshof-Prozesse, p. 100; Benedicta Maria Kempner, Priester vor Hitlers Tribunalen, Bertelsmann, Reinhard Mohn, Gütersloh, n.d., pp. 231-233; Spiegelbild, p. 501; Michael Balfour and Julian Frisby, Helmuth von Moltke. A Leader against Hitler, Macmillan, London and Basingstoke, 1972, p. 218; Freya von Moltke, Michael Balfour, Julian Frisby, Helmuth James von Moltke 1907-1945. Anwalt der Zukunft, Deutsche Verlags-Anstalt, Stuttgart, [1975], p. 215; [Helmuth] James von Moltke, Briefe an Freya 1939-1945, ed. Beate Ruhm von Oppen, Verlag C.H.Beck, Munich 1988, pp. 317-319; Hassell (1988 German edn), pp. 70, 330; report on Popitz's trial, Princeton

University, A. W. Dulles Papers, IV g 10 b 57/44 gRs 4 Oct. 1944; Detlef Graf von Schwerin, "Dann sind's die besten Köpfe, die man henkt." Die junge Generation im deutschen Widerstand, Piper, Munich, Zürich, [1991], p. 426; Ger van Roon, Wilhelm Staehle. Ein Leben auf der Grenze, 1877-1945, Gotthold Müller Verlag, Munich, 1969, p. 88; Peter Hoffmann, Claus Schenk Graf von Stauffenberg und seine Brüder, Deutsche Verlags-Anstalt, Stuttgart, 1992, pp. 133, 151, 226 (see also Engl. ed., Stauffenberg. A Family History, 1905-1944, Cambridge University Press, Cambridge, New York, Melbourne, 1995, index "Jews" and Stauffenberg, Claus Schenk, Count von, "persecution of Jews"); Ivar Anderson, diary 14 Dec. 1942, Kungliga Biblioteket, Stockholm, Ivar Andersons papper L 91; [Helmuth Stieff], "Ausgewählte Briefe von Generalmajor Helmuth Stieff (hingerichtet am 8. August 1944)," ed. Hans Rothfels, Vierteljahrshefte für Zeitgeschichte 2 (1954), pp. 300, 303; Stahlberg, p. 380; Henry O. Malone, Adam von Trott zu Solz. Werdegang eines Verschwörers 1909-1938, Siedler-Verlag, Berlin, 1986, pp. 143, 160, 209; Diana Hopkinson, The Incense Tree. An Autobiography, Routledge & Kegan Paul, London, 1968, p. 163; Spiegelbild, pp. 199-202; Osas, p. 98; Gerhard Schäfer, Landesbischof D. Wurm und der nationalsozialistische Staat 1940-1945. Eine Dokumentation, Calwer Verlag, Stuttgart, 1968, pp. 159-160, 164-165.

25. Völkischer Beobachter, 21 July 1944, p. 1.

26. Spiegelbild, p. 168.

27. Spiegelbild, p. 471. Axel von dem Bussche, referring to the mass shooting of Jews he had witnessed at Dubno on 5 Oct. 1942, declared that "the 20th July in essence would not have happened without those things;" interview 19 July 1984.

REFLECTIONS

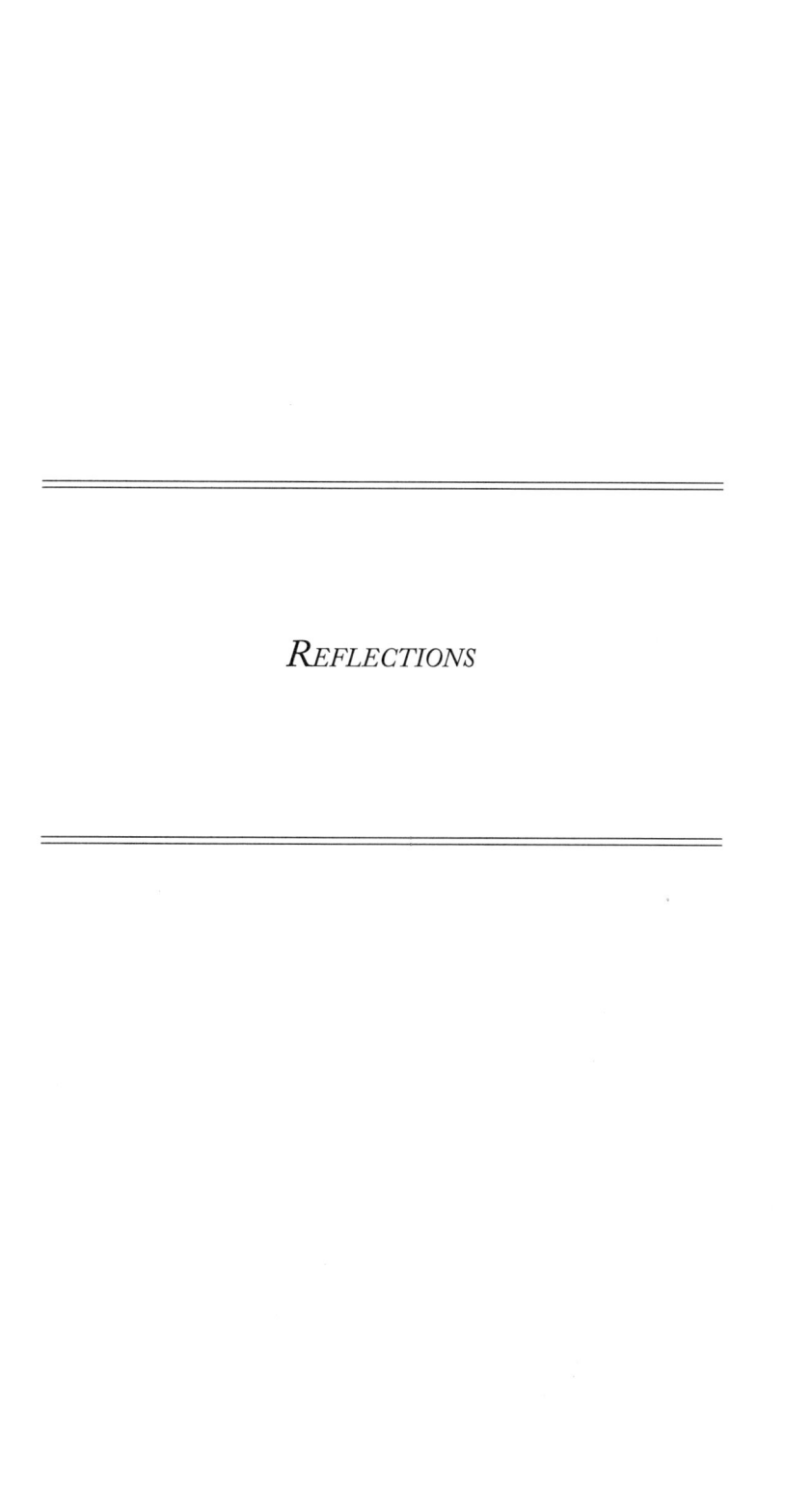

CHAPTER 17

Lessons of the Holocaust: The Early Warning System

Franklin H. Littell

Four days and sixty-nine years ago, a "terrorist" incident occurred that created the excuse that brought the last agonies of the German Weimar Republic to a visible end. Hitler, whom the old President, General von Hindenburg, referred to as "that Austrian corporal," had been named *Reichskanzler*. His *NSDAP*, although still well below fifty percent of the electorate, was the single strongest parliamentary bloc. Naïve apparatchiks in the conservative parties thought they could get him in harness and control him. That was January 30, 1933, and the republic had already had two and a half years of government by executive decree, under the *Notfallsklause*—the emergency paragraph in the constitution. During this interim of political expediency, made desperate by the suffering of millions thrown out of work in the Great Depression, the robust give and take of democratic government had withered and the violent climate of public terror had gained ascendence.

Less than a month later, February 27, came "the Reichstag fire." The story remains obscure to this day. Was the minor figure who was reported to have set such a fire a publicity-seeker? Was he a setup by the Nazis? The only point about which agreement congeals is the judgment that he was "not too bright," perhaps even mentally retarded. In any case, the following day the parliament rushed through an emergency ordinance to save the country from "Communist terrorism."

Three weeks later, with the Communists prevented from sitting in the session and only the Socialists voting against, the Reichstag shouted out the Enabling Act (*Ermächtigungsgesetz*). This suicidal act of March 23, 1933 was the concluding outward display of even the formalities of German self-government until after World War II. The substance of democratic self-government already had been eaten away by violence in the streets, by the assassination of key political leaders who opposed the Nazi machine, and by the soulless manipulations of political and clerical intriguants who had substituted secretive backroom deals in place of public policy based on open and informed debate.

The overwhelming conviction that emerges from review of this record of the decline of a people's self-respect into the disaster of dictatorship is this: *It didn't have to happen.* There were warning signs, which we can now itemize in an Early Warning System, as to when a free government is losing it, when violent men are bobbing to the top of the turmoil. Parallel to this perception is another aspect of Early Warning now susceptible to scientific analysis: the precise identification of a "5th column" that only puts on the mask of a legitimate political party, while in structure and program it undermines the self-governing of a free people.

Item: by 1923, the *NSDAP* was already a potentially genocidal movement. All it lacked was the hand on the throttle of power and, in ten years (by public violence and the quiet subversion of centers of authority e.g., the universities, the churches, the professions, etc.), the *NSDAP* had successfully infiltrated and gutted both the political and the non-governmental centers of power. Many general histories refer to the "Nazi victory" in the last elections, to the Nazi assumption of power "by parliamentary means," to the Nazi "take-over." That language is misleading: on the contrary, by external violence and Internal penetration during the previous decade the Nazis had already set up a parallel regime within the hollow shell of the formalities of the dying republic.

Lesson Number Two: it is not only important to act as responsible and self-respecting citizens when a free government is losing its way: it is also imperative to identify and suppress organizations that by their actions and structures show they are disloyal and potentially genocidal. There are those of our friends who say, from time to time, that the Nazi genocide of the Jews was a "dark hole" in the universe of understanding, that nothing can be generalized or learned from it. This is poetic language, and has the merit of warning us to tread softly on sacred ground. However, there are also as it were sacred lessons, lessons to be written on out hearts and brains in indelible ink.

On the Second Lesson, the importance of suppressing "5th columns" in time: bizarre opinions may in America receive First Amendment protection: aggressive and violent actions and structures are not so entitled, even if they are temporarily being held on a tight leash. If you will forgive the comment, it is a rampant bad habit of us teachers and preachers, not to mention those lawyers, to fail to distinguish between opinions and actions. This bad habit is as dangerous as the equally rampant failure to distinguish between unlimited individual freedom and responsible political and religious liberty. Or, to take another example of rampant failure to make essential distinctions: *The Christian Century*, a prominent "liberal" Protestant journal, indulges in what our colleague Deborah Lipstadt has identified as the fallacy of equivalence. In the 1930s, the *Century* even-handedly criticized both the British Empire and the new German Empire for exploitation of peoples; today the *Century* finds an equivalence in the Israeli strikes at PLA military centers, in which some civilians die, and the PLA's targeting school children and women shoppers in terrorist strikes. Both are violent.

There is a profound difference, although the ideologues and the space walkers deny it, between the clash of opinions in open forum and the mobilization of terrorist violence against non-military targets. We have in hand, after a century of genocide, the scientific analysis by which a potentially genocidal movement can be identified in time. (1933 is too late. 1938 is much too late. The time to act decisively was 1923, when the opinions that had been trumpeted freely in the 1920 Nazi Party Program were translated into concrete, violent and treasonous action against the Republic.) Faulty ideas can be preached against. Erroneous opinions can be refuted in public debate. But the deliberate mobilization of violent assaults on our liberties as democratic peoples, privileged to live in republics or constitutional monarchies, must be defeated by resolute, timely, prophylactic action at law.

Now, on a matter of clarity and definition: we hear and read a great deal these days about something called "terrorism." With the spectacular incidents of September 11th, which yanked our happy island back to the mainland of civil conflict and violence in public affairs, "terrorism" comes naturally to the lips. Billions of dollars are committed in Washington D.C. to set up bureaus to fight "terrorism." The American president condemns "terrorism" and "terrorist" regimes. In response, of course, the dictators in Baghdad and Damascus and Teheran condemn the USA for "terrorism." To go to what some—not of this company, of course—take to be the highest authority: the *Reader's Digest* last month dedicated a most unusual volume of print (February issue, pp. 73ff) to presentations on "terrorism." In point of fact, Brian Jenkins of the Rand Corporation published a splendid analysis of "terrorism" in September of 1982 in *The Annals of the American Academy* to which little has needed to be added in two decades.

For our purpose, the noun "terrorism," with its several derivatives, has little use in designing action to prevent evil. In fact, on closer inspection, the information on "terrorism" deals neither with infiltration and subversion nor with the shape and style of potentially genocidal movements. The topic is the nature of modern war. Civilians bear the brunt of the assault. As our colleague at the University of Hawaii, R.J. Rummel, has demonstrated (*Death by Government*, 1994), in modern war—was during the Age of Genocide—the losses in civilian lives are far greater than the losses in uniformed personnel. To be blunt, if you want to survive a modern war, get into uniform.

Here, in retrospect, the historical record does show a connection between something loosely called "terrorism" and the defined crime of Genocide: the heavy costs are paid by non-combatants, by innocent children, women, and the elderly. In their inherently violent structure and style, *on their way to power*, potentially genocidal movements ("5th columns") are destructive of healthy political development; *when they are in control*, they are genocidal toward *internal*, targeted unwanted minorities—counted among the "surplus populations" that Richard Rubenstein discusses in *The Age of Triage* (1983) and also aggressive toward *external* "enemies."

The implementation of an Early Warning System, for which I have been arguing since the 1960s, is overdue.[1] The structural "grid" that identifies a potentially genocidal movement, in time, is known. The template foe effective interception is available. To continue a political posture of moralizing generalities, without dedicated attention to the precise measures necessary to neuter the internal enemies, parallel to the reasonable measures to frustrate external enemies, is irresponsible bordering on the criminal.

Thinking only in the old categories, we are trapped in a dead-end street. While aggressive regimes are a constant military threat to their neighbors, the free peoples cannot be brought even to self-defense until all other escapes are closed. That is assuredly one of the "lessons" of World War II. The mounting of an Early Warning System on potentially genocidal movements, paralleled by the development and vigorous support of an international police agency, can provide the fresh moral and political initiatives the free world so urgently needs.

For more than three decades the participants in the Annual Scholars' Conference have dedicated themselves to remember the human cost of apostasy in Christendom and to learn how Jews and Christians, men and women of many nations and educational disciplines, can study and work together to affirm life.

We know the terrible loss of life that comes when the barriers fall and the flood waters cover the earth. The old rabbis taught mourning for the fall of the Temple—the sign to monotheism in the midst of a lascivious, brutal, corrupt, exploitative empire. It is my conviction, as a professing Christian, that when the Christians recognize the meaning of the fall of Christendom, they will teach mourning as the beginning of wisdom and renewal from the crimes that we name "the Holocaust."

In the name of the six million victims of intelligent, modern, calculated Evil, and not forgetting the guilt of the complicit bystanders as well as the cunning of the perpetrators, let us here and now renew our pledge to work from here on out: to affirm life—and not to serve death, to breather hope—and not to counsel despair, to block violence—and to bless compassion.

Endnotes

1. See attached Selective Bibliography and Autobiographical Note on how the present idea of Early Warning System was drawn from the concept of the "DEW Line" and then applied to defense against potentially genocidal movements.

Lessons of the Holocaust:
The Early Warning System

A Selection of Franklin Littell's Writings on his

"Early Warning System"

Wild Tongues (New York: Macmillan Co., 1969). The application of a "grid" or "template" to distinguish a terrorist movement from a legitimate participant in debate in the public forum and in the quest for power in the free society.

"Early Warning: An Essay," in *Holocaust and Genocide Studies III* (1988) 4:483-90.

"Early Warning: Identifying Potentially Genocidal Political Movements," *Jerusalem Letter/Viewpoints* (1 December 1989), pp. 1-6.

"Early Warning: Detecting Potentially Genocidal Movements," in Hays, Peter, ed., *Lessons and Legacies: The Meaning of the Holocaust in a Changing World* (Evanston: Northwestern University Press, 1991), pp. 305-15.

"Creating an Early Warning System," a lecture at a conference in New York City, 5 April 1995, discussing the 20th century confrontation with genocidal ("terrorist") movements and proposing an "Early Warning System" (privately printed in pamphlet form, eight pages).

"Creating an Early Warning System: the 20th Century Confrontation with Terrorist Movements," the Annual Ida E. King Lecture at the Richard Stockton College of New Jersey, 7 November 1996; privately published in bound form, twenty-four pages mimeographed.

"Early Warning System" in *Encyclopedia of Genocide*, edited by Israel W. Charny (Santa Barbara, CA: ABC_CLIO, 1999), I, 261-265, with a section by the Editor on "Franklin Littell's Writings on Early Warnings of Genocide," p. 262.

CHAPTER 18

Reflections on the Consideration of the Holocaust in American Life

Michael Berenbaum

Three books have appeared within the past year that examine—or perhaps attack is the more accurate term—the place of the Holocaust in contemporary culture. Peter Novick's well-researched work *The Holocaust in American Life* confines itself to the American experience; Tim Cole's *Selling the Holocaust: From Auschwitz to Schindler How History is Bought, Packaged and Sold* considers not only the American experience but also that of Israel, Poland and, but ironically only in a minor way, Germany, while Norman Finkelstein's *The Holocaust Industry: Reflections on the Exploitation of Jewish Suffering* builds on the foundation set by Novick but gives it a decidedly politically left interpretation, one freed from precisely the balance and thoughtfulness that give Novick's work a sense of authority.

This is not the occasion for a lengthy review of the three works which, while different in kind and in emphasis, share a critical approach to the state of Holocaust education and scholarship. However, some of what I presented at Lehigh University relates to the very subject of these works and engagement in dialogue is both timely and appropriate. First, permit me to address Tim Cole's work.

"*By the Waters of Babylon we sat and we wept as we remembered Zion,*" the Psalmist said appropriately. The place from which we remember the event shapes the content of that memory. This is perfectly acceptable in Jewish memory: indeed, it is normative. Certainly, the recollection of Zion immediately after the destruction

301

in Jeremiah's chapters of consolation is rather different than that within the Biblical book of Ezra or the anguished cries of Lamentations. There is a legend told in the Talmud of two rabbis passing by the Temple Mount:

> Once Rabban Yohanan ben Zakkai was walking with his disciple Rabbi Yehoshua near Jerusalem after the destruction of the Temple. Rabbi Yehoshua looked at the Temple ruins and said: "Alas for us! The place that atoned for the sins of the people Israel lies in ruins!" Then Rabbi Yohanan be Zakkai spoke to him these words of comfort: "Be not grieved my son. There is another equally meritorious way of gaining atonement even though the Temple is destroyed. We can still gain atonement through deeds of loving kindness." For it is written: "Lovingkindness I desire, not sacrifice" (*Hosea* 6:6).[1]

Rabban Yochanan ben Zakkai's reponse was directly related to the revolution that he was imposing on Jewish history, the movement from a land-centered, sanctuary centered, Jerusalem-centered religion to one that could survive in exile with remnants of that worship in the synagogue that could be constituted anywhere a quorum of Jews gathered and the Torah which was portable and could move with Jews from place to place and be transported in the hearts and minds of its people. Place, memory and agenda are related.

Stories are retold for a reason and they resonate for a reason. The dialogue between memory and place of its recollection, between an event and the transmission of an event is appropriate and it is little wonder that time and distance, as well as the agendas for the future shape the content of memory. I believe this is not only appropriate but also inevitable for a community as well as an individual. It is also very deeply Jewish. Midrash and Hasidic Tales as well as rabbinic commentary are in essence a retelling of ancient stories with new emphases that speak to the contemporary generation. This process is often masked because of the tradition's reluctance to claim innovation and reveal its essential creativity and it is denied by some who merely argue with a wink of the eye that it was there from the beginning, revealed to Moses at Sinai. So perhaps I am less scandalized than Cole regarding the transformation of memory in dialogue with contemporary needs and having been party to such a deliberate transformation I believe that the process can be done with integrity and is pure. I was disturbed not by what Cole was aiming to prove, but by his use of evidence. Four illustrations should suffice.

Cole, as Finkelstein, begins his work with an opening quote by Arnold Jacob Wolfe taken from a 1980 dialogue between Wolfe and myself that I reprinted in *After Tragedy and Triumph: Modern Jewish Thought and the American Experience*, which was published in 1990. According to Cole, Wolfe said:

> It is a simple fact that in New Haven, the Jewish community of 22,000 spends ten times as much money on the Holocaust memorial as it does on college students in New Haven. I think that is shocking.... The community is saying: "We have money for the Holocaust and that's all...." It seems to me that the Holocaust is being sold....[2]

The actual quote is more interesting and cannot be used because it is absurd. Wolfe said:

> The community is saying: "We have money for the Holocaust, and that's all." We have decreasing funds for almost everything else you can think of and certainly for Jewish studies in Midrash or Talmud or philosophy or even Bible, but we have $1 million if you are willing to teach the Holocaust.[3]

> Finkelstein begins his book with Wolfe's final line and adds the other half of the line "it is not being taught." However, it is not a simple fact. The statement regarding the comparative expenditures for the memorial and for college students may have been true for the year in which the Holocaust memorial was built in the late 1970s, but it was not true for the past two decades (if

it ever was true) and Cole's readers should know it. As director of the Hillel at Yale in 1980, Wolfe was in the business of raising funds for Jewish college students and his personal struggles with the leaders of the New Haven Jewish community were what they were. In the decades since his departure, the Hillel Foundation at Yale has moved to the center of the campus, housed in a building that is large and well-endowed, and the Judaic Studies program at Yale is flourishing, with distinguished faculty and excellent students, teaching the Bible, Talmud and Midrash. In fact, Harvard was forced to return a $3 million endowed chair in Holocaust Studies because some of its faculty believe that the "Holocaust was not a proud chapter in Jewish history." Since when are academic subjects decided upon because of their proudness or imagine for a moment the uproar that would have followed such a statement by a German professor speaking about German history.

What is the point? When the figure of $168 million for the construction of the Holocaust Memorial Museum is bandied about, I find it both intriguing and misleading. If I remember correctly the actual figure was in excess of $190 million but must be seen in the context in which the Jewish community spent more than $9 billion a year or some $90 billion in the decade of the nineties during which Holocaust Museums were opened in Washington D.C., Los Angeles, Houston and Tampa-St. Petersburg. So if the Holocaust is being sold, then it is fair to say that Jewish education is being sold, that synagogues are being sold, that universities are being sold, that hospitals are being sold. To build institutions in the United States and elsewhere, monies must be raised and there is nothing sinister or wrong about it. It is essential.

I was personally disturbed by Cole's repeated reference to a Holocaust cookbook and his objection to its kitsch. I doubt if he has read the book, but I have and wrote an introduction to it because it is a document that emerged from the Holocaust, no less a document than the children's drawings and poems from Theresienstadt or than the many diaries that have been published. Starving women sought to return in their imagination to their homes and their families and to reconstitute from memory the recipes that were an essential part of their lives. In the five years since its publication we have learned that this process of preserving recipes was not limited to Theresienstadt alone, but was found in other concentration camps as well. I was persuaded of the authenticity of the document and I am respectful of the responses of the women who shared their recipes to their own situation. In fact, I found it moving and whenever I spoke on the book, I asked that those who bought the book only cook from it for an event of joy, for a *simcha* and tell the story—so much for kitsch.

Cole misrepresents fact. He writes: "there is no place for Holocaust and Jewish heroism in Washington, D.C., but only Jewish victimization, and the telling of the story of the 'Holocaust' in all its gory horror."[4] He must have forgotten the exhibition that occupies about ten percent of the bottom floor of the permanent exhibition dealing with resistance or the exhibition on the Warsaw Ghetto Uprising that is situated just after the Wannssee Conference exhibit and the deportation exhibit. When resistance occurred, it often took place just on the eve of deportation. It was often a decision not how to live, but about how to die; it was a last stand, a statement that was made regarding all but certain death. The Holocaust Museum was built after Yad Vashem and consciously sought to avoid the equation between Holocaust and heroism. I think it achieves a historically appropriate balance, one that even the creation of the Miles Lerman Center for the Study of Jewish Resistance as part of the Center for Advanced Holocaust Studies will not be able to change.

As to the telling of the story of the "'Holocaust' in all its gory horror," elsewhere, Cole criticizes the decision not to use actual hair in the Museum's exhibition, a decision I vehemently opposed. Among the planners of the Museum and its lay leaders, the decision as to whether to use actual hair was both a generational and a gender decision. The older the lay leaders, the more they shied away from using actual hair and women tended to be more upset by its use than men. In the end, over the objection of many of his key staff, the late Jeshajahu Weinberg, then in his mid-seventies and recovering from a stroke, decided that the divisiveness such a display would engender was not worth the cost. I believed then as now that the issue was museological. The controversy surrounding the hair had demonstrated that it is a powerful artifact. The question was whether we could create a display that effectively conveyed the power of the artifact, without being so overwhelmingly powerful that the visiting public could not take it. Finkelstein and others have criticized the use of walls that conceal some particularly graphic material without understanding that walls permitted us to introduce graphic material at a time when no one was quite certain how the public would react to such materials. Now that the sense of "taste" and "proportionality" in the Holocaust Museum is widely respected, these privacy walls could be removed—and should be removed—and this material could be treated as all other material. Over time that will happen as will the introduction of hair into the exhibition.

Cole quotes noted Holocaust scholar Omar Bar Tov that the

> museum concludes with scenes of newly arrived survivors in Palestine. Zionism was, it seems an appropriate answer to Nazism. And since Nazism is gone and the State of Israel is alive and well, we no longer have any reason to worry.[5]

With all due respect for Bar Tov, that is not how the Museum concludes. From there the visitor can see interactive films relating to American knowledge of the Holocaust, can view a film entitled *Testimony*, see the fragments of tombstones that are a casting of the Remu Synagogue Wall in Cracow and exit with a quote that is the seal of the Museum, from the words of Elie Wiesel "For the dead and the living, we bear witness." Indeed if there was nothing to worry about why would we bear witness for the living?

As to the film, Cole is wrong when he writes: "With its use of the survivors the Washington, D.C. Holocaust is given a suitably upbeat ending."[6] Lay leaders, led by the most influential chairman of the Development Committee, pressed for a happy ending. The professional staff withstood that quest for an upbeat ending because the dialogue between past, present and future requires that we represent the past faithfully. Truth is orphaned when we try to mitigate the awesome evil of the Holocaust. The central theme of the story of the Holocaust is not regeneration and rebirth, goodness or resistance, liberation or justice, but death and destruction, dehumanization, devastation and, above all, loss.

Permit me to reiterate: I concur with Cole that in the representation of the Holocaust a process of nativization has taken place. I believe that we differ in our assessment of the legitimacy, integrity and inevitability of such a process. I concur with him that we have created a Holocaust myth, not as opposed to truth but rather as a story that has strong sentiments and is used to transmit and reinforce basic social values. As a historian of religion, I often believe that myth is the story we tell that underlies the most powerful beliefs we hold. It is not the antithesis of truth but its embodiment. I just do not believe that Cole has offered a sophisticated enough reading of the Museum to understand where it reinforces and where it undercuts the traditional American myth. In short, he has not read the text of the Museum accurately.

Norman Finkelstein's work, *The Holocaust Industry*, begins on a false note and concludes on a bizarre one. His opening page quotes Rabbi Arnold Jacob Wolfe: "It seems to me that the Holocaust is being sold—it is not being taught." While such a statement may have been half true in 1980 when it was first said, it is disingenuous today unless Finkelstein believes that the hundreds of university professors and thousands of high school teachers who teach the Holocaust throughout the world are selling the Holocaust and not teaching it. The statement is offered for its shock value even though it is manifestly false. As to his bizarre conclusion: convinced leftist that he is, Finkelstein is at once offering us a significant class and political analysis of the Holocaust industry and rising to defend German industry, Swiss Banks, and international insurance companies that are being victimized by the "Holocaust industry." He conspicuously avoids grappling with the most serious issue and perhaps the place where true scandal may arise, the distribution of these funds among the various claimants. His claim that there were one hundred thousand survivors of the Holocaust is without substance.

Finkelstein's research is derivative. He relies upon Peter Novick and he repeats his discovery and builds upon it for his conclusion. Thus we learn that there was little interest in the Holocaust until 1967. Because Novick did not follow theological controversies, there is no mention of the highly charged and controversial work of Richard Rubenstein whose *After Auschwitz: Radical Theology and the Future of Judaism* received significant attention before the Six Day War and forced Jewish theology to consider the twin revolutions of contemporary Jewish life: the Holocaust and the rise of Israel, well before the events of June 1967.

We learn derivatively from Finkelstein who relies on Novick, that Elie Wiesel only achieved prominence after the Six Day War. Yet a year earlier, Steven Schwarzschild, one of Israel's most severe critics, had called Wiesel "the de facto high priest of our generation," the "one man who speaks most tellingly of our time, of our hopes and fears, our tragedy and our protest."[7] On June 4, 1967 the day before the Six Day War broke, out the 38 year-old Wiesel was receiving an honorary doctorate from the Jewish Theological Seminary and giving its commencement address. I remember that well because I went from the Seminary graduation to the Six-Day-War. Obviously, Wiesel had emerged far before June 1967, at least among his peers of academics, scholars and rabbis ranging from Steven Schwarzchild to David Hartman, from Richard Rubenstein to Louis Finkelstein and Saul Lieberman. But I suspect that Norman Finkelstein may never have heard these names or know of their standing in the Jewish community.

Finkelstein does not share Novick's caution as a serious historian. Everything is black and white. Yet Novick maintains that, before the 1982 Lebanon war, there is little reason to believe that even without the Holocaust framework American Jews would have seen Israel's situation in other than black and white terms. And since then, while remaining on the whole supportive of Israel, increasingly larger numbers of American Jews no longer see Israel's situation in black and white terms. Novick asks: How plausible is it to think that

American policy toward Israel has been shaped by the memory of the Holocaust? Not very. When the Holocaust was most fresh in American minds, support for Israel was limited.

Novick correctly traces the shift of the Holocaust from the margins to the center of American Jewish consciousness at some point in the late 1960s and thereafter reflected and in turn promoted far reaching changes in the way American Jews came to understand themselves and their circumstances. Finkelstein writes with little subtlety. He takes liberty with facts. The Washington Post is described as Jewish-owned in 1961 when Philip Graham was its editor.[8] Even a cursory reading of Katherine Graham's impressive biography would lead one to say that the Washington Post—unlike The New York Times—was a Jewish owned newspaper only in the Nuremberg definition of Jewish, that is if we consider the religious identity of grandparents. Finkelstein presumes in a footnote to document his point that the Rosenberg Trial and the Arendt controversy were contemporaneous when they were a decade apart.[9] His reasoning is glib but not reasoned. Elie Wiesel and Israel Gutman supported Daniel Jonah Goldhagen. Elie Wiesel supported Jerzy Kosinski. Gutman and Goldhagen supported Wilkomirski (the author of Fragments who seems to have invented his background and imagined his childhood in the Holocaust). Connect the dots together and this is Holocaust literature. The reasoning is unworthy of comment. I may be a sentimentalist but I believe that Primo Levi and Nelly Sachs, Jean Amery and Paul Celan have written important and substantial works. Lawrence Langer is not alone as a brilliant literary student of the Holocaust. One would expect more substantial polemics. Finkelstein is out of date.

Peter Novick correctly notes that the rise of interest in the Holocaust coincided with the emerging importance of Israel for American Jews after the Six Day War and after the Yom Kippur War. He demonstrates the growing interest of American Jewish organizations, but does not consider whether the American Jewish establishment was merely playing "catch up" or actually leading the war. As one who worked on the inside, I think that a careful consideration of the evidence would indicate that the establishment was not leading but following its people. Certainly, it did not welcome the creation of the United States Holocaust Memorial Museum until the Museum proved successful. It was also certainly true that professors were following their students' interests in teaching the Holocaust.

Novick is careful not to suggest a coordinated program, a conspiracy. Finkelstein throws caution to the wind. He writes "The Holocaust became the weapon for deflecting criticism of Israel. Avowed concern for Holocaust memory was as contrived as the avowed concern for Israel." Yet in 1982 and during the period of the intifada, the Holocaust played a rather different role among Jews in Israel and elsewhere who dissented from Israel's policy in Lebanon and from the Israeli presence in Judea and Samaria. Some of the most prominent Holocaust scholars in Israel and the United States ranked in the forefront of such dissent.

He also seems quite unaware that many Jews today want to move away from both the perception of Israel as a victim state and the Jews as a victimized people. The attitude toward victimization is at best ambivalent. One source of opposition to the teaching of the Holocaust is Ismar Schorsch's mistaken fear of the lachrymose theory of Jewish identity. It portrays Jews as sufferers, as victims, not as independent actors. When we were building the Holocaust Museum, the criticism of its building reflected the fear that American visitors to the Museum would see the Jews as victims. The response of visitors to a Museum visit has alleviated such fears.

Finkelstein also seems unmindful that as the field has become more diverse, with many more voices joining the conversation; Elie Wiesel's make or break power in the field has diminished. Three examples may prove the point. His critique of the 1978 docudrama "The Holocaust," which has been vindicated over time, did not diminish its impact or its acclaim. The United States Holocaust Memorial Museum took form after Wiesel resigned as chairman in 1986. And while surely, I remained faithful to many of Wiesel's values including his insistence on the centrality of the Jewish experience and the unique voice of the survivor, we did not accept—and could not accept—his sense of the mystification of the event and its inexplicability, at least not as our starting point. We situated it in the world, in history and attempt to approach the inner chambers. Wiesel takes issue with this approach in his recent memoir. Surely he is not without influence, but he is not the end-all and be-all of Holocaust Studies nor could he be even if he ever aspired to that role. He is patently unfair and Elie Wiesel seems to be *the* particular target of his animus.

Kenneth Keniston once argued that there is no such thing as absolute objectivity. The most that we can hope for is for the writer to reveal his/her subjective perspective and let the reader compensate accordingly. Therefore, permit me a personal word. As a student in the sixties I was moved by Elie Wiesel's work. I read his early books with passion and understanding. I still do. They touched my soul. They still do. I found in him an authentic voice of the world of darkness. His work was central to my dissertation and to my first book. I taught the first seminar on his work and participated in the first international conference on his work. I worked with him in 1979-80 on the President's Commission on the Holocaust and in the end he dismissed me and I was left without a job having notified Wesleyan University that I was not returning for the next academic year. He has written an account of that firing that, to put it charitably, is less than accurate. I have not written of it, though the documentary material regarding it is available in the Museum's own archives. I returned to the Museum project only after he resigned. Perhaps it is time that an objective biography should be written of Wiesel; not a hagiography, a work that considers his writing and his celebrity, but Finkelstein is not its author. He dismisses Wiesel in footnotes by quoting Alfred Kazin and Irving Howe. The more clearly one reads their comments, the more inappropriate they seem. It is also time to assess Wiesel's role as celebrity, but surely any objective assessment must consider not only the honorarium he receives for speaking, but the fact that most of his speaking has little to do with the Holocaust directly. It is a shadow that looms large, yet increasingly less in what he says than in the way in which he is viewed. And I know how often he does without an honorarium and how frequently such funds are given directly to charity. I wonder in the name of full disclosure whether Finkelstein wrote his work without payment from his publishers, whether he will earn royalties on the work and receive an honorarium for speaking about it. Let he who is without sin, cast the first stone. Wiesel began his work when few were interested in listening, fewer willing to give heed. Like Raul Hilberg, Richard Rubenstein, Emil Fackenheim, Isaiah Trunk and many of that generation, they were working in isolation—and everyone who works with this material pays a price. One does not touch the fire without being burned.

I met Peter Novick as he was beginning research on *The Holocaust in American Life* in early 1991. I gave him complete access to my documents and also invited him to speak at the Museum's Research Institute several times even though I knew his words would be critical and his sentiments dissonant. We could and do disagree without being disagreeable. There is much to like in his work. He is serious and disciplined. He has done his homework and has spared little effort in reviewing documentary material. His field is history and he uses well the tools of his trade. The entire field of theology is unexamined and thus he misses some important and early considerations of the Holocaust and I believes misunderstands the role of Elie Wiesel and the timing of his emergence into prominence. His errors are magnified by Finkelstein's misplaced emphases.

Novick correctly observes the changed Jewish condition. Jews are winning acceptance on every level of American society. The absence of hostility toward Jews endangered survival or to put it in the language of Jean Paul Sartre if it takes an antisemite to make the Jew than the absence of antisemitism is dangerous to Jewish survival. Jews are an empowered people and Israel—far from being vulnerable to genocide—is objectively a regional military superpower and a well-developed country economically with all economic trends promising an ever more prosperous future.

We sometimes disagree because Novick is a scholar of the emergence of consciousness of the Holocaust and not a Holocaust scholar.

He covers the controversy surrounding Hannah Arendt's *Eichmann in Jerusalem: A Report on the Banality of Evil* and quotes Arendt's most succinct description of the banality of evil

> Banality of evil—phenomena of evil deeds committed on a gigantic scale which could not be traced to any particularity of wickedness, pathology or ideological conviction in the doer whose only personal distinction was a perhaps extraordinary shallowness.... However monstrous the deeds were, the doer was neither monstrous nor demonic.

And yet, he fails to consider that this is precisely the reason why her book was mistitled. Had she written *A Report on the Banality of the Evildoer* rather than on *the Banality of Evil*, her work might have been far better accepted. Yet the controversy ended when I was in graduate school, with the publication of Isaiah Trunk's *Judenrat*, which used the tools of scholarship to examine the role of Jewish Councils. Good scholarship often replaces less valuable literature. Why should someone read Bruno Bettelheim's *The Informed Heart* when one can read Terrence Des Pres' essay on Excremental Assault or Robert Jan Van Pelt's report on the construction of latrines at Auschwitz that give a far more complete picture of the dehumanization process? Finkelstein sees a political process. I tend to believe that good scholarship endures despite the controversies. Even Raul Hilberg's greatest critics regard his work as magisterial.

I suspect that Novick and I differ on three important points, one historical and two philosophical. My own reading of the evidence has convinced me that the turning point for American Jewry was the Six-Day War and that the Yom Kippur War only reinforced the perception of the threat of genocide and the vulnerability of Israel and of the Jewish community because of the oil boycott and the perception that the West was addicted to cheap supplies of energy and that power would reside in the control of natural resources. I also find it curious that Novick would omit the actual genocidal threat. Just prior to the Six-Day War Ahmud Shukeiry, Yasir Arafat's distinguished predecessor, threatened to drive the Jews into the sea. The very words he used triggered an association with the Holocaust as Jews subliminally recalled the U'*Netanah Tokef* prayer of the High Holidays: "On Rosh Hashanah it is written and on Yom Kippur it is sealed. Who shall live and who shall die? Who by Fire and who by water?" Many Jews were surprised by how much Israel had meant to them, by how deeply it touched them and there was an outpouring of support that transformed the American Jewish community, seemingly overnight.

He is correct that not the reality but the perception of the reality of Israel poised on the brink of destruction shaped the response of American Jews. I experienced the difference in the perception of reality as I boarded a plane for Israel just on the eve of the Six Day War. When I left for the airport those around me believed that I was en route to slaughter. When I boarded the plane the Israelis returning home understood that war was imminent, but they were prepared for battle and for victory not for defeat and slaughter.

For Israelis the change in Holocaust consciousness was far more related to the Yom Kippur War, wherein the Zionist dream of independence and an end to Jewish vulnerability was shaken by the dependence on the United States and the vulnerability of the attack. For Israeli Jews the turning point in Holocaust consciousness was the Yom Kippur War, which had come as a shock to Israelis who found themselves dependent upon the good will of gentile rulers for their very survival. In a moment of despair Moshe Dayan spoke of the destruction of the Third Commonwealth, perhaps even of the nuclear option. For seventy-two hours the fate of the Jewish state depended upon a decision to be made by three men. One was an antisemite who supported Israel, the other was a Jew by birth who had converted to Protestantism at Harvard, and the third was the first Jew to serve in his high office, who spoke of himself as "of Jewish origin." President Richard Nixon, and Secretaries of Defense and State James Schlesinger and Henry Kissinger came to the rescue with massive arms shipments and decisive American backing. Yet the Israelis came to identify for the first time with the traditional fate of exilic Jews—dependence. The Zionist dream of independence, that with an army and a flag, the nation state would put an end to Jewish vulnerability, was severely tested. And Israel, which had done so much to alleviate antisemitism and to give Jews a new sense of pride, suddenly became a source for antisemitism and not a defense against it.

Like many historians, Novick admits that he is doubtful that history has any lessons to teach. He writes:

> Hovering over all of this is the absurd maxim, *in extremis caritas*—believing that it is in imaging the most desperate circumstance that one gains insight into what Gentiles really think of Jews.

I suspect that Jews are not alone in this imagination. One of the reasons for the significant transformation of Christian doctrine regarding the Jews by Pope John XXIII and Pope John Paul II, Vatican Council II and the American Lutheran Church among others is because they believe that the extreme revealed something disquieting and that it is better to attack it at its roots so as to make it more difficult for such an extreme situation to arise again and for believing Christians to participate. One of the powers of Primo Levi's work is that he perceives precisely what is extreme about the camp and how that transforms the ordinary circumstances of ordinary men and what we can learn from it. The same is true for the work of Robert Proctor in Nazi Medicine, for Richard Rubenstein, who regards the Holocaust as a manifestation in the extreme of what is present in the mainstream and for numerous other scholars, writers, theologians, psychologists and sociologists.

Perhaps my most major disappointment in his work is that he does not seem to understand why the Holocaust is of interest to the American people. It is at those moments in the book that he resorts to opinion instead of looking for evidence, where evidence can be found. Perhaps it is the limits of the tools of his trade as a historian or of some other limitation but I think it is important to illustrate this tendency specifically. Our disagreement is evident in Novick's work.

I wrote:

> When America is at its best, the Holocaust is impossible in the United States. The Museum teaches fundamental American values of pluralism, democracy, restraint on the powers of government, the inalienable rights of individuals, the inability of the government to enter into freedom of the press, freedom of assembly, freedom of worship...

Novick comments, "If Americans need a demonstration of the way that these values were violated in the Holocaust we are in worse shape than I'd thought."[10] Perhaps we are or perhaps Novick should listen to the diverse groups that visit the Museum, whether they be inner city students or Naval Academy midshipmen, Roman Catholic parochial school children or African Americans whose churches have been bombed, to assess both the impact of a Museum visit and what they sense their needs to be. An objective assessment of the Museum must engage the objective information that exists regarding the impact of the Museum on its visitors. In the early days of the Museum's history, anecdotal information or the personal response of one critic or another may have sufficed, but after seven years and fourteen million visitors, other tools of assessment are available and though a historian may have to read in sociology or educational literature, one is not free to ignore such findings, at least not without offering a justification.

Similarly, Novick writes:

> The Washington Holocaust Museum has been overwhelmed by millions of non-Jewish visitors, "voting with their feet" for the encounter the Museum provides. Some unknown portion of that stream of visitors have been led to its doors by deeply felt interest and concern. For some equally unknown portion of visitors, the museum has become something that one has to "do" when one tours Washington, just as one has to "do" the Louvre in Paris.[11]

Frankly, I am touched by the comparison with the Louvre but disappointed with the sense of the unknown. One of the things that the Museum has done well is to survey its visitors and the reasons they came to visit. This material is available for the asking and the answers to Novick's "unknown portion of visitors" is probably available for the asking but surely available for the researching, if not with actual empirical research than certainly by reading the readers' comments book placed at the end of the Hall of Remembrance or speaking with visitors who might just fall into both categories. Perhaps more importantly, the question should not be what brought them in the door, but what did they learn within the Museum and what was the content of their visit?

I sense that Novick does not quite grasp why the Holocaust has taken hold within the United States though it was a European event, which occurred a continent away, more than half a century ago. He does provide the glimpse of one answer. The Holocaust has become the negative absolute. In a world of relativism, it has taken its place as the Absolute. We do not know what is good. We do not know what is bad. But we do know that the Holocaust is evil, absolute evil. It is for that reason why people use the word in the plural as they attempt to call attention to their suffering—the Black Holocaust, the Holocaust of the American Indians, the Holocaust in Kosovo, Rwanda, Bosnia. The Holocaust is the nuclear bomb of moral epithets. It is an event of such magnitude that the more we sense the relativism of values, the more we require the Holocaust as the Foundation for a negative absolute—absolute evil. I suspect this is the reason why the leaders of European nations have rediscovered the importance of the Holocaust for contemporary moral education. I also suspect this is the reason why it becomes the focal point for Papal visits to Israel, for German society and for American society. I also suspect that this is the reason why Holocaust deniers deny an event that all reasons, all standards of rationality demonstrate cannot be denied. It is in this function as negative absolute that the Holocaust may loom largest in the coming years.

And yet within the Jewish community, there is ample evidence of Holocaust fatigue, at least among prominent Jews religious and secular, conservative, liberal and progressive. What's the problem?

As the Holocaust enters into the larger domain it ceases to become the particular inheritance of the Jewish people. So Jews who want an increase in Jewish parochialism—and who correctly perceive that such parochialism is essential to Jewish survival—are angered that the particular experience of the Jews has been used in service of the universal. Their counterparts who believe in universalism are angered by the emphasis on the particular Jewish experience. They argue that we must tackle the larger issue of genocide and not the Holocaust, that we must consider slavery and what my feminist friends call man's inhumanity to people and not just genocide. Some are embarrassed by this particularism. Some fear that an emphasis on the uniqueness of the Holocaust is some sort of special pleading. They see it as a secret way of speaking of Jewish chosenness or an undisguised way of saying, as the book of Lamentations says, "there is no pain like my pain." Some continue to fear, despite overwhelming evidence to the contrary such as the popularity of the United States Holocaust Memorial Museum and *Schindler's List*, that the Jewish experience is parochial and will not be of interest to non-Jews, forgetting what we have seen again and again; the more deeply particular the human experience, the more universal it is, provided it is presented as a human story.

Some religious leaders object to the dissonant religious implications of the Holocaust. Ultra-Orthodox Yeshivot have difficulty studying the Holocaust. How does one speak of a benevolent, all powerful, God who is engaged in Jewish history after Auschwitz? How does one deal with Irving Greenberg's principle of authentic religious expression after the Holocaust: "no statement—theological or otherwise can be made, which can not be made in the presence of burning children?"

If Jews were afraid of genocide a quarter century ago, this fear is no longer prevalent and far less realistic. If a generation ago the enemies were external, today they are internal. Divisions between secular and religious in Israel threaten civil culture, the struggle between assimilation and parochialization in the United States threatens Jewish survival and Jewish participation in American culture. The absence of external pressure permits the Jews all sorts of options, including intermarriage, and forces Jewish identity to compete with other forms of identity available to participants in the global universe. Young American Jews are sent to Israel to find their Jewish identity. Their post-army Israeli counterparts become pilgrims to Nepal in search. For all those who have begun a journey of return to the Jewish people, there have been others who have ventured forth into uncharted territory.

Twenty-five years ago the story of Holocaust and Redemption resonated within the lives of many Jews. It rang true to their experience and it gave them the imperatives that were the content of Jewish life, solidarity, political activism, Jewish power. Today the story resonates less as an empowered Jewish people enjoys the fruits of its power and the freedoms of the global universe. Contemporary Jews have internalized these messages. They have less need of the Holocaust to reinforce these values.

Consciousness of the Holocaust has moved way beyond the Jewish community; we have transformed the bereaved memories of a parochial community into an act of conscience. *We have responded in the most deeply Jewish way of all: remembering suffering and transmitting that memory in order to fortify conscience, to plead for decency, to strengthen values and thus to intensify a commitment to human dignity.* That is how the Torah taught us to remember that we were slaves in Egypt.

Endnotes

1. Avot D'Rabbi Natan 4:5.

2. Tim Cole, *Selling the Holocaust: From Auschwitz to Schindler How History is Bought, Packaged and Sold* (New York: Routledge, 1999), p. 3.

3. Michael Berenbaum, *After Tragedy and Triumph: Modern Jewish Thought and the American Experience* (Cambridge and New York: Cambridge University Press, 1990), pp. 44-45.

4. Cole, p. 157.

5. Cole, p. 154.

6. Cole, p. 154.

7. Steven Schwarzschild, "Toward Jewish Unity," Judaism Vol. 1, No. 2 (Spring 1966), p. 157.

8. Norman Finkelstein, *The Holocaust Industry: Reflections on the Exploitation of Jewish Suffering* (London and New York, Verso, 2000), p. 19.

9. Finkelstein, p. 15.

10. Novick, p. 240.

11. Novick, p. 233.

Contributors

Michael Berenbaum is the director of the Sigi Ziering Institute, and professor of theology at the University of Judaism (Los Angeles). The former president and CEO of the Survivors of the Shoah Visual History Foundation and former director of the Research Institute of the United States Holocaust Memorial Museum, his most recent books include *A Promise to Remember* and *The Bombing of Auschwitz: Should the Allies have Attempted It?* (co-edited with Michael Neufeld).

Karin Doerr of Concordia University (Montreal), is an associate of the Montreal Institute for Genocide Studies and the Simone de Beauvoir Institute for Women Studies. She is co-author of *Nazi-Deutsch/Nazi-German: An English Lexicon of the Language of the Third Reich* (Greenwood Press, 2002).

Patrick Hayes teaches in the department of theology at Fordham University and in the department of religious studies at Iona College. He is completing a dissertation in ecclesiology in the School of Religious Studies at the Catholic University of America.

Peter Hoffmann is William Kingsford professor of history at McGill University (Montreal), and a fellow of the Royal Society of Canada. Among his major publications are *Stauffenberg: A Family History, 1905-1944*, 2nd ed. (2003); *German Resistance to Hitler* (1988); *Hitler's Personal Security*, rev. and expanded ed. (2000) and *The History of the German Resistance 1933-1945*, 3rd English ed. (1996).

Steven T. Katz is director of the Center for Judaic Studies at Boston University. Among his many publications is his multi-volume study *The Holocaust in Historical Context* (Vol. I, 1994). In 1999, he received the Lucas Prize from the University of Tübingen (Germany).

Dennis Klein is a co-editor of this volume. He teaches at Kean University (Union, NJ), where he directs its Jewish Studies Program. His writings include Hidden History of the Kovno Ghetto, a work published in

1997 by Little, Brown (Bulfinch) in collaboration with the U.S. Holocaust Memorial Museum.

Richard Libowitz co-editor of this volume, is visiting assistant professor of theology at Saint Joseph's University (Philadelphia) and is a vice president of the Annual Scholars' Conference. He is author/co-editor of many volumes on the Holocaust.

Marcia Sachs Littell is professor of Holocaust and Genocide Studies at the Richard Stockton College of New Jersey where she founded America's first Master of Arts Program in Holocaust and Genocide Studies. Since 1985 Dr. Littell has been the executive director of the Annual Scholars' Conference on the Holocaust and the Churches. She has written and edited numerous articles and books on the Holocaust. Her most recent publication is titled, *Women in the Holocaust: Responses, Insights and Perspectives.*

Franklin H. Littell is distinguished professor of Holocaust and Genocide Studies at the Richard Stockton College of New Jersey and emeritus professor of religion at Temple University. Known as "The Father of Holocaust Education in America," he is the author of more than two dozen scholarly books and over eight hundred major articles. Professor Littell is co-founder of the Annual Scholars' Conference on the Holocaust and the Churches.

Gary Mullen holds degrees from Penn State University and Southern Illinois University, where he wrote his doctoral dissertation on the theological themes in Theodor W. Adorno's critical social theory. He is currently an Adjunct Professor at Northern Virginia Community College and an editor for the Federal Election Commission in Washington, D.C.

Drew A. Parsons teaches history at the Evergreen Community School in Cresco, Pa. and is currently completing a Doctor of Letters degree at Drew University with a concentration in Holocaust and Genocide Studies. Reverend Parsons is the Pastor of the Wooddale United Methodist Church in the Pocono Mountains of Pennsylvania. He moderates county-wide Holocaust Education discussions for the Monroe County Library System and leads teacher training programs at East Stroudsburg University.

David Patterson holds the Bornblum chair in Judaic Studies at the University of Memphis (Tennessee) and is Director of the University's Bornblum Judaic Studies Program. He is co-editor of the *Encyclopedia of Holocaust Literature* (2002).

Susan Pentlin is a professor of modern languages at Central Missouri State University, where she teaches German and courses on the Holocaust. She has held two Fulbright grants to Germany, a grant from the National Endowment for the Humanities and one from the American Council of Learned Societies.

Rubina Peroomian is a Research Associate at UCLA. An authority on the Armenian Genocide and comparative genocide literature, her publications include *Literary Responses to Catastrophe: A Compari-son of the Armenian and the Jewish Experience* (1993). She has also written textbooks for use in Armenia.

George S. Pick was born in Budapest, where he survived the Holocaust. Prior to his retirement, he taught at Catholic University and worked for the Department of the Navy. He is the author of over fifty technical and Holocaust related publications.

Alan S. Rosenbaum is professor of philosophy at Cleveland State University (Ohio). He is author/editor of five books, including *Is the Holocaust Unique?* (2001) and *Prosecuting Nazi War Criminals* (1993).

Shimon Samuels is director for international liaison of the Simon Wiesenthal Centre, Paris. He is also honorary president of the Europe-Israel Forum, co-chair of ARARE (Academic Responses to Anitsemitism and Racism in Europe), and a board member of ENAR (European Network Against Racism).

Frederick Schweitzer is professor emeritus of European history at Manhattan College (Bronx, NY). He has engaged in Catholic-Jewish dialogue almost since Vatican II. With Marvin Perry, he is co-author of the forthcoming *Antisemitism: Myth and Hate from Antiquity to the Present* (St. Martin's Press). He is director of the Manhattan College Holocaust Resource Center.

Kevin Spicer is assistant professor of history at Stonehill College (Easton, Massachusetts). A member of the Church Relations Committee of the Center for Advanced Holocaust Studies, United States Holocaust Memorial Museum, he is currently writing a book on German Catholic priests who openly embraced national socialism.

Sharon Steeley a co-editor of this volume, received her M.B.A. from Saint Joseph's University. She is associate executive director of the Annual Scholars' Conference.

Paul Vincent teaches at Keene State College (Keene, NH), where he is director of the Cohen Center for Holocaust Studies. He is editor (with Harry Ritter) of *A Historical Dictionary of Germany's Weimar Republic, 1918-1933* (1997).

Renate Wind is professor at the University of Applied Sciences, Evangelische Fachhochschule, Heidelberg (Germany). Her writings include *Who Is Christ for Us?* by Dietrich Bonhoeffer, Renate Wind and Craig L. Nessen (2002).